COUNTDOWN

COUNTDOWN
A GUIDE FOR SURVIVING THE
URBAN APOCALYPSE

Justin Thyme
Illustration by David Ibarra

First Edition
Copyright © 2012 Justin Thyme
Published by Justin Thyme
Illustration by David Ibarra
ISBN-13: 978-0615621326
ISBN-10: 0615621325
All rights reserved.

Some of the information in this book may be considered illegal in certain jurisdictions. This information encompasses, but is not limited to, such topics as the use of lethal force with weapons and/or self-defense techniques. This book is offered for academic study only.

Neither the author nor the publisher assumes any responsibility for the use or misuse of information contained in this book.

To Mom and Dad and my mother and father in-law for all of your tireless help! You are my longsuffering baby sitters; this book would not exist without you! A special thanks to Richard for all of his insight, knowledge, and friendship. May our families survive whatever disasters may come our way! To my Uncle Chad, for listening to me say, "You're not going to believe this," several times a day, as well as helping me with the contents of this book.

Printed in the United States of America (Justin Thyme Press ©)

This book is dedicated to my lovely wife and our four incredible children. I love you guys!

Foreword

Americans are growing more and more anxious about their future. Guns, gold, and emergency food are flying off the shelves in record numbers, and TV shows about prepping are airing primetime. It seems that the prepper lifestyle is obtaining national attention, taking the right-wing-nut-job stereotype out of being self-reliant, as even Wyoming drafted a so called "Doomsday Bill" to prepare for a national crisis.

There are millions of Americans that are quietly preparing for their version of "the end." They are turning spare rooms into long-term food storage vaults, planting survival gardens, altering their homes to run on alternative sources of energy, taking self-defense courses, and stockpiling just about anything they feel will improve their chances.

The number of preppers has exploded in recent years. In fact, you might be living next door to one, if you're lucky. According to a recent *Daily Mail* article, there are approximately 3 million preppers in the United States today, but the numbers are probably significantly higher.

This movement will continue to spread like wildfire, especially in light of our doomed economy and the dread of an overstepping government. Prepping is not based on fear, but foresight, just like it would be poor timing to start considering taking swimming lessons while your boat is sinking.

At first it's pretty scary to find out what a facade our society really is, but once you get over the *Matrix*-like-blue-pill-red-pill choice, it's empowering to take charge of your own life and not rely on external means to dictate if you will live or die after a catastrophe.

This book is a culmination of research and lots of trial and error, with a focus on urban survival. I encourage you to stay and see how deep the American rabbit hole goes. The warm, comfy womb that we are accustomed to is about to give birth to a world that we will in no way recognize in due time. May the hard times ahead be softened by the knowledge contained within this book. God be with your family and mine.

~Justin Thyme

Contents

1 THE URBAN JUNGLE 11

2 ECONOMIC AND SOCIAL COLLAPSE 41

3 WHY PREPARE 49

4 PSYCHOLOGY OF SURVIVAL 57

5 FOOD PREPARATIONS 68

6 H2O 93

7 FIRST AID 112

8 VETERINARY DRUGS FOR HUMAN CONSUMPTION 140

9 EMERGENCY HEATING AND COOKING 151

10 EMERGENCY LIGHTING AND POWER 164

11 BOB INCH GHB REK EDC MPL 183

12 SECURITY AND DEFENSE 212

13 URBAN MOVEMENT, COVER, AND CONCEALMENT TECHNIQUES 243

14 COMBATIVES 263

15 TERRORIST HAZARDS 289

16 LIFE AFTER AN EMP ATTACK 318

17 THOSE WHO DON'T HAVE TO DIE 328

18 LESSONS LEARNED FROM HURRICANE KATRINA 339

19 ECONOMIC RIOTS AND CIVIL UNREST 368

20 DEFENSIVE DRIVING FOR ESCAPE AND EVASION 382

21 CARJACKING—DON'T BE A VICTIM 392

22 CASH WILL BE KING AND PRECIOUS METALS WILL BE QUEEN 399

23 BLACK-MARKET TRADING 410

24 COPING WITH DISASTER 424

25 CONCLUSION 432

1
THE URBAN JUNGLE

Cities Are Artificial
Every city is an artificial construct. Cities formed as people came together to conduct business, participate in social interaction, benefit from efficiencies in public services (such as schools, sewers, water, etc.), and a common defense. Yet cities cannot survive alone. They need resources from the country, most notably food, water, and electricity. While electricity and water can sometimes be created or found within city limits, the acreage requirements for food dictate that no city could possibly feed its own people.

In the world today, there are twenty cities with more than 10 million people:

Tokyo, Japan - 28 million
Mexico City, Mexico - 18 million
Mumbai, India - 18 million
São Paulo, Brazil - 18 million
New York City, USA - 17 million
Shanghai, China - 14 million
Lagos, Nigeria - 13 million
Los Angeles, USA - 13 million
Calcutta, India - 13 million
Buenos Aires, Argentina - 12 million
Seoul, South Korea - 12 million
Beijing, China - 12 million
Karachi, Pakistan - 12 million
Delhi, India - 11 million
Dhaka, Bangladesh - 11 million
Manila, Philippines - 11 million
Cairo, Egypt - 11 million
Osaka, Japan - 11 million
Rio de Janeiro, Brazil - 11 million

Tianjin, China - 10 million
Moscow, Russia - 10 million
Lahore, Pakistan - 10 million

Think upon these numbers alone. Consider where the resources came from in order to support people in the millions. Over 50 percent of the world's human population resides in urban areas, a proportion projected to grow substantially by 2050, concentrating pressures on the ecosystems supporting these urbanizing regions. The support mechanisms in place work beautifully when in harmony, but like a house of cards, when one falls, the rest are soon to follow.

Risks in the City
The city presents some serious risks during a crisis. The five most notable are:

- Collapse of social order.
- When the trucks stop, America stops.
- Failure of water treatment and delivery system.
- Depletion of food supplies.
- Failure of the power grid.

While not every situation will appear in every city, every situation will most certainly appear in some cities. Will that include yours? We'll tackle these one at a time.

Collapse of Social Order
Social order is a delicate thing, and it exists as a psychological barrier that could easily collapse under the right conditions. We all saw this during the L.A. Riots following the Rodney King trial verdict as citizens of L.A. set fire to their own town, yanked people from vehicles, then beat them to death, and even fired guns at firemen attempting to save their buildings! Imagine store owners lying prone on the roofs of their stores with AK-47s, firing at anyone who approached. This is exactly what happened in Los Angeles. Worse yet, imagine the lawless horde firing at the rescue copters trying to bring in supplies to the desperate masses. More recently we were all witness to the looting, violence, and total breakdown of society following Hurricane Katrina in New Orleans.

What allowed this to happen? Simple: The simultaneous melting away of the psychological barrier of *order*. Once people realized 911 couldn't handle the load, or was offline, that the local police were helpless or had simply abandoned their posts, law and order ceased to exist in their minds. They then conducted their lives in the way they always wanted to, but couldn't because of the rule of law. That is, they ran out to the local stores and just took whatever they wanted (looting). They took out their racial frustration on innocent victims who happened to be driving through the area, and they let loose on a path of destruction that only stopped when men with rifles (the National Guard) were called in to settle things down. In other words, only the threat of immediate death stopped the looting and violence. Rifles work wonders!

The National Guard eventually got things under control. This event was isolated, however, to one city. Picture hundreds of cities experiencing the same thing. Will the National Guard be able to handle the load? Not likely. What about local police? They aren't fools; if things look bad enough, they'll grab their families and head for the hills, just like they did in New Orleans. No pension is worth getting killed for. A few U. S. cities could be transformed into literal war zones overnight. It would require all-out martial law and military force to have any chance whatsoever of bringing order to those streets. The reality is that there are not enough military in the U.S. to secure all of the cities if this happens.

The collapse of social order is perhaps the greatest risk of staying in the city during a crisis. What exactly would cause the collapse of social order? Lack of three things: food, water, and money. When people run out of food, some will begin ransacking their neighborhood, searching for something to eat. Remember that in a city, a "neighbor" does not mean the same thing as a "neighbor" in the country. They are not necessarily your friends. It won't take long then for violence to take over in some cities.

While certain regions will certainly manage to keep things under control and people will form lines at the local (depleted) Red Cross shelter, other cities will see an explosion of violence. Envision the gang infested regions of L. A., Chicago, Detroit, New York, St. Louis, and New Orleans. Do you think those people are going to stand in line and wait? They already have guns, now they finally get to use them. Pent-up racial tensions and hostilities will simply serve as justification for shooting people of the same or other color in order to get their food.

Even if the food somehow gets into the cities, lack of money (due to the government not sending out social security, welfare, disability, and unemployment checks) could cause the same thing. Eventually, lack of money will result in looting and mass theft. As theft balloons, it also results in a collapse of social order. The same thing goes for water, but only faster.

The collapse of social order is also very dangerous because it doesn't require any *actual* collapse of the power grid, telecommunications, transportation, or banking. Social order is a psychological artifact. It is a frame of mind, and any global panic can quickly remove the mental barrier that currently keeps people lawful.

When Trucks Stop, America Stops

The truth is that our "just in time" inventory and delivery systems leave us incredibly vulnerable to a nationwide disaster.

You see, it is very expensive to hold and store inventory, so most manufacturers and retailers rely on a continual flow of deliveries that are scheduled to arrive "just in time", and this significantly reduces their operating expenses.

This is considered to be good business practice for manufacturers and retailers, but it also means that if there was a major nationwide transportation disruption that our economic system would grind to a halt almost immediately.

Once store shelves are picked clean, they would not be able to be replenished until trucks could get back on the road. In the event of a major nationwide disaster, that could be quite a while.

So what could potentially cause a nationwide transportation shutdown?

Well, it is easy to imagine a lot of potential scenarios - a volcanic eruption, a historic earthquake, an EMP attack, a solar megastorm, a war, a major terror attack, an asteroid strike, a killer pandemic, mass rioting in U.S. cities, or even martial law.

If something caused the trucks to stop running, life in America would immediately start changing.

The First 24 Hours

- Delivery of medical supplies to the affected area will cease.

- Hospitals will run out of basic supplies such as syringes and catheters within hours. Radiopharmaceuticals will deteriorate and become unusable.
- Service stations will begin to run out of fuel.
- Manufacturers using just-in-time manufacturing will develop component shortages.
- U.S. mail and other package delivery will cease.

Within 1 Day

- Food shortages will begin to develop.
- Automobile fuel availability and delivery will dwindle, leading to skyrocketing prices and long lines at the gas pumps.
- Without manufacturing components and trucks for product delivery, assembly lines will shut down, putting thousands out of work.

Within 2–3 Days

- Food shortages will escalate, especially in the face of hoarding and consumer panic.
- Supplies of essentials—such as bottled water, powdered milk, and canned meat—at major retailers will disappear.
- ATMs will run out of cash and banks will be unable to process transactions.
- Service stations will completely run out of fuel for autos and trucks.
- Garbage will start piling up in urban and suburban areas.
- Container ships will sit idle in ports and rail transport will be disrupted, eventually coming to a standstill.

Within 1 Week

- Automobile travel will cease due to the lack of fuel. Without autos and busses, many people will not be able to get to work, shop for groceries, or access medical care.
- Hospitals will begin to exhaust oxygen supplies.

Within 2 Weeks

- The nation's clean water supply will begin to run dry.

Within 4 Weeks

- The nation will totally exhaust its clean water supply. Lack of clean drinking water will lead to increased gastrointestinal and other illnesses, further taxing an already weakened healthcare system.

This timeline presents only the primary effects of a freeze on truck travel. Secondary effects must be considered as well, such as inability to maintain telecommunications service, reduced law enforcement, increased crime, increased illness and injury, higher death rates, and likely, civil unrest.

Failure of Water Treatment and Delivery Systems

Will the water treatment facilities fail during a crisis? Many will. Some won't. The problem lies in figuring out whether yours will. Certainly they depend on electricity, and testing conducted on some plants has already revealed weaknesses in the system.

In one such test the water treatment plant released a fatal dose of fluoride into the water system when tested. The computers thought they were 99 years behind in releasing minute doses of fluoride, so they made up the difference. If you happened to be downstream drinking that water you were dead. Fluoride, no matter what misinformed dentists tell you, is actually a fatal poison. A major crisis will likely demonstrate this fact in more than one city.

According to the American Water Works Association, Americans drink more than 1 billion glasses of tap water per day. For safety and security reasons, most water supply plants maintain a larger inventory of supplies than the typical business. However, the amount of chemical storage varies significantly and is site specific. According to the Chlorine Institute, most water treatment facilities receive chlorine in cylinders (150 pounds and one ton cylinders) that are delivered by motor carriers. On average, trucks deliver purification chemicals to water supply plants every 7–14 days. Without these chemicals, water cannot be purified and made safe for drinking. Without truck deliveries of purification chemicals, water supply plants will run out of drinkable water in 14–28 days.

The most important question here, though, is about what will happen when the water stops flowing, or if it is flowing, but not drinkable? As you are probably aware, while people can live without food for long periods of time (3 weeks), water is needed on a daily basis. You can go 3 days without it, at most, but beyond that, you'll quickly turn to dust.

That means people will do anything to get water, because not to have it means certain death. Guess where it's going to be the most difficult *to get*? You guessed it: in the cities. During the first day of the water crisis, many people still won't figure out what's going on. They'll assume it's a temporary breakage of a water main and the government will get it fixed within hours. As those hours stretch into the next day, these people will get very worried. By the second day, more and more people will realize the water isn't coming back. At that point, you could easily see a breakdown of social order, as described in the previous section. (These things can cause a domino effect.) People will begin their search for water, and the first place they're likely to go is where they always go for liquids, the grocery store, the local Wal-Mart, or the 7-11. The shelves will be cleaned out rather quickly.

Beyond that (because those fluids aren't going to last for long), you're going to see people engaged in a mass exodus from the cities. They'll take the gas that they have left in their tanks and they'll leave the city in search of water. Some will go to "Grandma's house" out in the country where they might at least find a pond or stream to drink from. Others will simply go on an expanded looting mission, stopping at any house they see and "asking" the residents (with a gun in their face, likely) if they have any water to "donate."

As a result of this, if water stops flowing, here are the events you can expect to see in some of the worst-off cities:

- Looting of all the grocery, convenience, and supermarket stores by the second or third day (Remember New Orleans?)
- Minor outbreaks of violence during the looting (Shop owners may attempt to defend their shops with firearms, aka L. A. Riots.)
- Mass exodus of residents from the city in search of water.
- Ransacking of any houses or farms within a gas-tank radius of the city, presumably by desperate people with guns.
- Massive traffic jams on the outbound highways as people run out of gas and abandon their vehicles (if bad enough, this could actually block the highways and trap people in the cities: Remember Hurricane Rita?)
- Large-scale outbreak of water-borne diseases as people use streams and rivers as both a water fountain and a bathroom. People crapping upstream are going to infect the people drinking downstream. Very few have any kind of water filtration device. This last point is extremely critical. Once the water flow stops, disease is going to strike.

Depletion of Food Supplies

Food supplies will likely dwindle quickly as we approach a possible crisis due to people stocking up for a just-in-case scenario. Once the crisis actually hits, expect to see breakdowns in the transportation sector that will result in major delays in food delivery. This means food may arrive in sporadic fashion in some cities (if at all).

Once this happens, food suddenly becomes very valuable to people (even though they take it for granted today). And that means any small shipment of food that arrives will be quickly grabbed and eaten, or stored. It only takes one week without food to remind people how much they actually need it, so expect the atmosphere to be that of a near panic if food is delayed by as little as three days. The level of alarm will vary from city to city. Some cities or towns may experience very little difficulty receiving food. Others may face near starvation.

Remember, the cities depend entirely on food shipped in from the farms and food processing companies. Also, note that if a mass exodus begins, the highways may be jammed up at critical locations, causing gridlock for the trucking industry. If we're lucky, some trucks will continue to roll. If we're not, assume that nothing gets through.

A shortage of food ultimately results in the same behavior as a shortage of water. First, people eat what's in the pantry, then they loot the grocery stores. After that, with all local supplies depleted and no hope on the horizon, they leave the city and start ransacking nearby homes.
Some will hunt in local forests, but most city dwellers don't know how to hunt. In any case, anyone with the means to leave the city will likely do so soon after their food shortage begins.

Failure of the Power Grid

Electrical power is like the air you breathe. You don't really think about it until it's gone and you are gasping for it. The power grid is a dependable friend that is constantly meeting your every need. The grid is like having 200 servants relentlessly doing tasks for you that go unnoticed, from heating, cooling, refrigerating, lighting, entertaining, and traveling: the list is almost endless. But when the grid goes down and your hired servants don't show up for work anymore, that's when things change very quickly in the city. Everything turns upside down, because generally people who live in the city are rather accustomed to literally driving up to a window and speaking a taco into existence and paying for it with a debit card. It doesn't matter how much your net worth is, if there is no power to draw it out from. The guy with three bucks to his name will be wealthier than you are. The power grid and money are the life blood of the city.

On the first day people will be confident that the power outage is temporary and will be restored and life will continue as normal; but as time goes on, anxiety will quickly grow into terror, and people will begin to chase for what they feel is missing in their grid-dependent lifestyle. Without power, Costco, Wal-Mart, grocery stores, and banks will all most likely be closed, and if you're lucky enough to find a place open, then they will only deal in cash. By the third day, small, privately-owned businesses will deal in pawn-shop style commerce, bartering, or even letting well known customers keep a running tab, hoping things will come back online soon.

High-crime areas will be impacted by grid failure almost immediately, starting out with small outbreaks of violence, looting of grocery stores, and stealing expensive items that cannot run without power. These areas are very poorly prepared for such an event, and they depend on the prepared to fulfill their needs.

Other Side of the Tracks
The key to urban survival is to know what your *advantages* are and what your *disadvantages* are. How well do you truly know your surroundings? Social order is a very fragile psychological barrier that can easily implode. You've heard

the term the "other side of the tracks." This is of great importance during a disaster and possibly life-and-death knowledge. That line you cross over from well-manicured lawns and white-picket fences to looking like the movie set of *Boyz-n-the-Hood*, with "ghetto birds" flying around shining their million-watt spotlight, is a clear indicator. It only takes minutes for a violent mob to form during the right conditions. Generally, it starts out with someone trying to be funny, act on a dare, or show off to the opposite sex: all of which becomes a recipe for the unexpected. You just might be the spark that ignites their fire, just by being in the wrong place, at the wrong time, during a disaster. Some people feel they have a green light not to recognize authority if law enforcement is involved with a disaster or lack the numbers to enforce the law. It's not like these people all of a sudden turn evil. They already possess the malcontent for such acts; it's just suppressed by the law that would normally have the power to police them.

Gang Members
A vast army of heavily-armed criminals has embedded itself in every major city in the United States. In fact, nearly every community in America is now affected by these thugs. Drugs,

theft, and brutal violence are all part of the everyday lifestyle of the members of this army. Once civil unrest erupts in America, they will go on a crime spree that will be unprecedented, as they burn large areas of some U.S. cities to the ground.

The FBI tells us that there are now 1.5 million gang members involved in the 35,000 different gangs that are active inside the United States.

When you have lots of teens and young adults sitting around with nothing but time on their hands, bad things are prone to happen. As the family unit continues to decline in America, young people are looking for a sense of belonging. For many youths, a gang becomes a new "family" for them. But unfortunately, these new "families" do not exactly teach "family values". Instead, they teach our young people about how to be brutal and violent.

These gangs are becoming very organized and very heavily armed. The FBI says that rifles, machine guns, grenades, and even artillery rounds are being found in the possession of gangs more frequently than ever.

Down in Miami, thieves have become so bold that they have actually been breaking into parked police cruisers and stealing guns and ammo out of them. When people are stealing guns directly from the police, this is a sign that it is very late in the game.

Meeting Location

You may not be able to phone your family or friends during a disaster, or send a quick email for a meeting location, due to the amount of wireless traffic, but texting is often a likely option. The best *plan* is to have a *plan* and a designated location for everyone to meet. If you work near your children's school but live 15 miles from there, then the obvious meeting location would be their school. Have alternate routes of getting to your designated location and an ample time frame for waiting for each other.

Avoid trying to find your loved ones outside of where you plan to meet, otherwise you may miss each other and make a big, confusing mess out of the original, simple plan. If a significant amount of time passes, leave a message for them by means of a note or message with someone who can pass it on, with specific details explaining that you are OK and waiting for them, along with where you are going to look and when you will return to the original meeting location. Use previously planned code words for your meeting locations to avoid being followed.

Pity Parties
Don't open you door unless you know and trust the person on the other side. During any type of crisis expect acquaintances and strangers to start knocking at your door with sad stories of desperation that will be told in a life or death tone. If you pay close attention, you will often find holes in their stories, and after listening to the facts, you will discover they are abusing the crisis for monetary gain. If you give any food or water, give very little and say in a firm manner, "That is all I can give." If you want to donate charitable supplies, give them to a church or a trusted organization so you will not attract unnecessary attention. Otherwise, this could put your home and your loved ones in a compromised situation, where a mob could show up armed and overrun you violently, and at the very least, steal your supplies. Don't be afraid to use the word "NO" regularly when TSHTF.

Chemical Plants and Hazardous Materials
Chemical plants and refineries are often located in cities; these are obvious places to avoid in a disaster, especially during an earthquake, flood, or fire-type disaster. Don't wait to be told to evacuate, just leave before you get trapped by road blocks or under-qualified authorities that would rather take orders than ensure your safety.

Fuel

Your vehicle is your only means of traveling with ample supplies, so a good rule of thumb is to never let your fuel gauge get below half a tank, preferably keeping it full whenever possible.

At the first sign of a disaster, or immediately thereafter, top-off your vehicle with fuel and fill extra fuel-safe containers to have as a reserve. Fuel is the only item that you can't store much of in the city, legally or safely. Don't forget that your driving range is determined by your fuel, and without power, gas pumps will not work. If you plan on bugging out to meet up at a pre-determined survival location, don't plan on being able to purchase fuel along the way, unless the event is just isolated to your area.

The unprepared will only have a day, or less, of fuel and create a parking lot of dead cars. Fuel will be an extremely sought after commodity, just like potable water. If you decide to bug out as a last resort, stay off the main roads and look far ahead for roadblocks. Keep items like fuel, water, and food out of site. As you use the fuel in your vehicle, fill it with the reserve fuel so you're constantly full. Do not let your vehicle get under a quarter of a tank before refueling. Always have someone "riding shotgun" in the literal sense, to be another set of eyes and defense for the driver. If you don't have to leave your retreat right away, I would suggest waiting for at least two weeks for the marauders to pass through like locusts, looting ahead of you for a safer passage.

Quarantine, Marshal Law, and Sealed-Off Cities

A lurking threat that may manifest itself, such as in the aftermath of Hurricane Katrina, is the possibility that the government will quarantine or seal off the exits of a city to keep all of the residents contained within its boundaries, so as not to allow them to flee or leave. This could be done for purely noble reasons, like controlling an outbreak of disease/plague from spreading to nearby communities, or for more diabolical reasons, like exerting control over population centers by stopping the free movement of people.

If you lived in New Orleans during the evacuation advisory, the only time you could leave was before Hurricane Katrina hit. Afterward, you were trapped and could only leave when and where you were permitted. Countless people tried to walk out of the city and were turned back at gunpoint by the National Guard, only to be sent back into the hell-hole until they could be processed and evacuated. Regardless of why, the issue is should you choose to remain in the city, you may not have the option of leaving once the disaster response begins.

For years the alternative media has warned about the US military possibly being used against the American people in a time of economic collapse or any sort of martial law scenario. Detention drills such as Vigilant Guard 2010 Riot Control have brought widespread attention to the fact that portions of our own military are training to take on crowds of American citizens demanding food and Constitutional rights in a time of crisis.

Black Helicopters in Covert Urban Warfare Drills
In January of 2012, video was captured at night of five
military helicopters buzzing over downtown LA conducting
what the LAPD has described as special-ops, urban-warfare
drills. Joint military-training exercises involving helicopters
have been conducted in downtown LA and throughout the
U.S., including New Orleans, Denver, Miami, Tampa,
Boston, and Chicago.

The Blackhawk helicopters, staged at Dodger Stadium
throughout the exercise, were later spotted flying very low
over the Staples Center as the LA Lakers played inside. David
Duran, a former U.S. Army aviator, told CBS affiliate KCAL9
News, that the training is likely a dry run for a future
mission.

The training has been ongoing in LA since January and
involves "the use of military helicopters flying after dark
throughout the city," according to an Associated Press
report.

Residents were warned "not to panic" if they witnessed the training and were assured that the activities had "been carefully planned and are safe".

However, initial reports before the exercises began claimed that the training would only involve police, when in fact 150 U.S. troops from the U.S. Special Operations Command are also involved as part of urban warfare training.

"They do a lot of mockup training," said Duran. "But it's always best to get the closest terrain layout to what the objective is."

"If it's a mountainous terrain, they go to the mountains; if it's a desert terrain, they use the desert; if they're in a coastal terrain, they use the coast," said Duran. "If it's an urban terrain, you know, whatever's needed."

The exercise is yet another in a spate of recent military drills to hit heavily populated areas throughout the country.

Rob Richardson of Off Grid Survival notes:

> Maybe it's just the prepper in me, but when I heard the U.S. Military will be conducting a massive training exercise in the streets of Los Angeles, I must say it made me feel a little uneasy. And how could it not? With the passage of the National Defense Authorization Act, which gives the President the power to arrest and detain American Citizens, it makes one wonder why the military is conducting drills in Urban America. While it could be, as LAPD insists, just a training exercise, the timing sure does make you wonder what's going on."

Is this the latest example of Americans being incrementally conditioned to accept a state of de facto martial law?

Armed Drones

First, we were bombarded with the news that 30,000 drones would be spying on us domestically, and within weeks the agenda moved to arming the drones with non-lethal weapons. CBS DC reports that the Montgomery County Sheriff's Office in Texas "is considering using rubber bullets and tear gas on its drone."

This is a frightening new advance and a shocking indication of how dangerous the very near future will be. Unmanned aerial and land vehicles, deployed and designed to make autonomous decisions with deadly repercussions, may soon occupy the heartland of America.

Solutions in the City

OK, so you're stuck in the city. You've made the decision to stay. You've read the scenarios above, you believe they make sense, and you're intelligently frightened. What now? You really only have two strategies: stay and defend your home and/or bug out.

Important: This is not an either/or situation. You can begin by staying in your house and assessing the situation. You'll want to have a bug-out vehicle stocked and ready, even if you may never actually choose to bug out in the end. You'll have to be the ultimate judge of this. Just remember that when you bug out, you face major risks and disadvantages. Among these:

- You're severely restricted in how much you can carry.
- You have limited range due to finite fuel supplies.
- You expose yourself to social chaos, roadblocks, random violence, etc.
- Your house will certainly be looted while you're gone.
- You run the risk of mechanical breakdowns of your vehicle.

In general, unless you have a pre-planned safe house as your final destination, I don't advise bugging out. Just "heading for the hills" is a very poor plan. You might not make it. But heading for "Grandma's house" or some pre-designated area could be a very good plan indeed, depending on whether Grandma is ready, willing, and able to accept you!

For these reasons (and more), staying and defending your house is sometimes the only reasonable course of action, even if it seems dangerous. For the most part, looters and people looking for food are going to have plenty of easy victims, so if you show a little force by defending your property, you are more likely to send people on to the next house.

That is, until the next house is already empty and yours is *the only* house on the block with any food and water left. If you're in a bad enough area, your neighbors may "gang up" on you and demand your supplies or your life. This definitely is a worst-case scenario, and unless you have a house full of battle-ready rifles and people trained to use them (and the willingness to shoot at the neighbors), you're sunk. This is why the best situation by far is to keep your neighbors informed and help them get prepared. Then you can act as a group, defending your neighborhood and sharing the supplies you have with anyone willing to help defend you. (Don't think for a second that your neighbors won't remember all that food stored in your garage!)

In this kind of situation your neighbors realize you are their lifeline. You supply them with food and water, and they will help support you because they are, in effect, supporting their own lives. The best situation is when your neighbors have their own food and water provisions; that way, they aren't depleting yours. Then they have a strong incentive for teaming up with you on defending their own neighborhood.

Storing and Hiding Your Food
Storing food is just as important in the city as in the country, but hiding it is far more important. If you're dumb enough to put everything you own in obvious places, you might as well not buy it in the first place. Pillagers will undoubtedly find it. To count on having any amount of food left over after the raiders break in, you'll need to hide it or move it to a secure location.

The best way to hide your food is to bury it. You'll need airtight containers, long-term food that won't rot, and to plan ahead. Bury your food at night so nobody will notice, and make sure you don't leave the map on the refrigerator door! (It's better to memorize it!) Try to get the ground to look normal after you're all finished. You'll want to bury your food as early as possible, because it gives the grass time to regrow over the spot. If you're in an area that snows, you'll have a great concealment blanket! Most food marauders won't go to the trouble to dig up food, especially if you insist you don't have any.

An alternative to burying (that would be faster and easier) would be to simply build a false wall in your garage and seal up your food on the other side. Sure, you might lose a few feet of useable space in your garage, but the trade-off is the confidence that everything is safe and sound.

Another plan is to have some smaller amounts of food stashed around the house, letting them find something. Better to give them something and send them on their way. The art of hiding your food is an ancient one. You need to become creative. Use the walls, the floors, and the structure of the house. If hiding your food is simply not an available alternative, then try not to advertise it. Keep it put away in your house or garage in as discreet a manner as possible. Don't make a point of telling people that you have a year's supply (or more). Word gets around fast that Mr. Jones has a ton of food in his garage. Boxes of food fit nicely under beds, behind furniture, in the attic, etc. Be creative!

To sum up proper food storage, you really have four strategies:

- Store it all in your house, and plan on defending it by force.
- Bury it in your yard in case you get overrun by looters.
- Store part of it in your house, and hide the bulk of it.
- Relocate all of it as soon as you recognize a major disaster is in progress.

Storing Extra Water
Water can be stored in exactly the same way, although you might want to bury the barrel before you actually fill it. Make sure you treat your storage water, rotate it, or have filters on hand when you get ready to use it. If you don't have a yard,

or it's impractical to bury your water, you'll have to store water inside your house. This can get very tricky because water takes up a lot of space and it's very difficult to conceal. It's best to get containers made for long-term storage, but in a pinch, use whatever you can find, just make sure it's clean and of food-grade material. Unfortunately, many of these receptacles will deteriorate quickly or break easily. Consider what will happen if your water freezes. Will your vessels endure? Be sure to leave enough air space to handle the expansion.

In order to prepare yourself for the water shortage, assuming you're going to stay in the city, stock up for at least six months of water at a minimum of two gallons of water per person, per day. That's nearly 400 gallons of water if you have two people. Of course, even with the best in-house preparations, you still may find yourself depleted of water supplies. In this situation, one of your best defenses is to have a tried-and-true water filter (the best is the Katadyn brand) that can remove parasites and bacteria from the water. You can also treat your water in other ways (iodine, distillation, silver solution, bleach, and so on). Armed with these items, you can safely use stream or river water (or even stagnant water) for drinking.

Lighting
To light your home when there's no electricity, try the following:

- Use LED flashlights and rechargeable solar-charged batteries.
- Use propane-powered lanterns. You can find these in the camping section of your local Wal-Mart. Be sure to purchase extra mantles and store lots of propane.
- Purchase quality oil lamps and stock up on oil. You can also purchase cheap kerosene lamps from Wal-Mart, then simply purchase and store extra kerosene. You can be an anti-Wal-Mart activist after you get your supplies.
- Buy extra candles.

- Purchase lots of olive oil. Not only can you cook with it (and besides, it's a lot healthier than corn or vegetable oil), but it also burns as a clean candle fuel. You can float a wick in a jar half-full of olive oil and light the wick. Voila, a home-made candle. Olive oil is a fantastic item for your storage anyway, because even if you purchase all the grains in the world, you'll still need cooking oil, and you obviously can't buy powdered cooking oil. Well-stored olive oil can last for thousands of years.

Giant Logs

Did you know that people won't steal giant logs? Although they may effortlessly rip-off chopped wood, most people won't have any way of hauling away logs. They're too heavy and the vehicles won't have any gas left anyway. For this reason, your best bet in regard to stocking fuel for your house is to stock up on UNCUT wood logs. It takes a lot of extra research to find out how to get them, but you can find a source if you look hard enough. You can usually get a permit to go out and cut your own too. The effort is worth it because it will give you a ready to go to source of heat and fuel that cannot be easily stolen. The catch, of course, is that you'll need equipment to cut and chop the wood. A chain saw is nice in this way, but it requires fuel. Fortunately, chain saws don't use much fuel, so if you have a way to store as little as 50 gallons or so, you've got enough to power your chainsaw for a few years (at least)! You'll need fuel stabilizers, too, which you can buy at your local Wal-Mart. (Be sure to buy extra chains for your chain saw, too.)

You'll need splitting hardware as well. You can buy log splitters or just buy an axe, a wedge, and a sledgehammer. Better yet, buy all four so you have a choice of what to use. Don't forget, wood splits much better when it's frozen, so you might just wait until the cold hits in wintertime to start splitting your wood. Only split a little at a time, because you don't want to end up with a big pile of nicely-split wood sitting out in your yard just *asking* to be taken.

If you already have trees on your property, you're all set. Cut down about five cords right now, so they can start drying out, then chop them as needed.

Relations with Neighbors
I've already mentioned the importance of getting along with your neighbors, helping them become aware of these issues, and encouraging them to prep just as you are. It's indeed crucial to your city-based survival plan. Every neighbor that becomes self-reliant is one less neighbor you'll have to support.

The range of neighbor situations, from best to worst, is as follows:

- Best case: Your neighbor is prepared for any type of disaster and has his own supplies.
- Good case: Your neighbor is aware of a potential crisis, and even though he doesn't have his own supplies, he's willing to help defend yours as long as you share.
- Bad case: Your neighbor is an extreme liberal that has no interest in preparing for a disaster, figuring he will just depend on the government or simply come to you if things get bad enough. He is aware of *your* supplies, but doesn't have any of his own.
- Worst case: Your neighbor isn't aware of anything and is a violent, angry neighbor that has been in and out of prison. He is going to be caught off-guard by the ensuing events and will likely attempt to use violence to get what he needs or wants, even if he has to use lethal force.

Your decision on whether to stay in the city may depend greatly on the quality and quantity of your neighbors. If you live in a bad enough neighborhood, do what you can to move. If you live in a good neighborhood, do the best you can to educate and inform your neighbors.

Gun Control

No matter how you felt or thought about gun control in the past, it's time to face disaster-induced reality. The gun-control politicians (and the people who support them) have placed Americans in a position where not only the police can't protect us in a timely manner, but we can't legally defend ourselves either. Criminals unlawfully have firearms; citizens lawfully don't. Intentionally or otherwise, gun-control supporters have created a condition where an unfortunate number of innocent men, women, and children are going to be in danger during a crisis simply because they couldn't obtain the proper self-defense weapons.

It also happens that the cities are where the rioting will likely be the worst and where firearms are most likely to be banned from legitimate ownership (and where criminals may wield near-absolute power for a while). We're all going to need as many law-abiding, gun-toting citizens as possible in order to fend off the criminals and establish some degree of order. If society recovers from it, we can review the fallacy in the cause and effect logic that keeps people voting for gun-control laws, but in the meantime, millions of people are going to have to resort to breaking the law in order to protect their families. When there is no law, you become the law.

One More Reason to Move Out

If you can, your best bet may be to move to a city or state where people are a lot more accepting of firearms. You'd be surprised at what a difference the locale makes. Check the gun laws in any state you're considering moving to. Obviously, "cowboy" states like Arizona, Texas, and Wyoming will have fewer restrictions on guns (and, interestingly, they have less of a problem with gun violence). States where the population is denser (like California & New York) tend to have much greater restrictions on private ownership of firearms.

Bugging Out

Suppose a disaster has transpired, and you've changed your mind about this city thing. You're smack-dab in the middle of one of the worst-hit cities in the country. The plundering is getting worse, the power has been out for weeks, and your water supplies are running low. You still have enough gas in your tank to make it out of town, if you can get past the gangs, that is. You've decided to bug out!

Don't try to bug out in a Chevy Geo. Choose to have a vehicle that's not necessarily a daily commuter. A hybrid, compact car may get great gas mileage, but has many drawbacks during a SHTF scenario. A compact car severely limits what you can haul with you and where you can go. You will likely need a big, heavy 4x4 truck in order to go off-road, around stalled vehicles, or drive over debris. Get something that can carry at least 1000 pounds of supplies. True, it requires more fuel, but you can carry the fuel as cargo. A roof rack is a great way to double your space and mount extra fuel, just cover with a tarp to keep prying eyes at bay. Don't bug out unless you can have someone "riding shotgun." You will need an armed passenger in case you run into not-so-nice people.

If you have a designated place of refuge, head straight for it. If not, you're basically driving anywhere you can go for survival, so try to head for a forested area (not next to the side of the road, of course) and near a creek or river, where you can obtain continual reserves of fresh, running water.

Where is this forest? Where is the running water? Is it easy to get to? Have you made dry runs already? As the old adage goes, "practice makes perfect."

Did you have fleeing to your local ski resorts in mind? The mountains have their own set of dangers. Are you used to driving on winding, narrow, vertigo-inducing roads, especially in a large vehicle, possibly followed by a fully-loaded trailer? Even if you are an experienced driver, what about people who aren't? Mountain roads are typically one to two lanes, so if there are accidents or roadblocks, it isn't as if you can simply drive off the mountain to get to your final destination. You must consider inclement weather. When it rains, especially during the winter, black ice will form, and you know what that means, your vehicle will be slipping and sliding all over the place. How about a landslide? Hopefully you will not be in its path. What if it is freezing? Will you freeze too? Let's say disaster strikes in spring, well the weather may be nice, but that's when all of God's hungry creatures will be hunting for berries and humans too. Summer may seem better, but because utilities will be out, visitors and even locals will have camp fires. What if there is a wild fire? How are you to escape? Although you will have coverage, food will not be readily available, unless you are a naturalist and know the difference between poisonous and edible native plants, as there aren't many mountain farms, nor much livestock. Vacation chalets will be quickly overrun by desperate folk with the same idea as you.

Don't be discouraged; just think before you act. Educate yourself so that when you have to bug out, you know where to go, what to do, and how to live with what you have.

Conclusion
Choosing to remain in the city is a rational choice for many people in many situations. However, as you have seen from the dangers described, the further away you can get from the population centers in general, the better your chances for survival.

Most people, perhaps yourself included, have a difficult time actually accepting that a major disaster is going to be as bad as described. After all, what if you leave the city, sell all of your earthly possessions, quit your job, move to the country, and then nothing bad happens? You will have disrupted your whole life, and you may find yourself jobless, broke, and homeless. You *could* assume it will be a mild event, which I suppose is also a credible possibility. In that case, surviving in the city will be quite feasible, especially if you have neighbors that can support your efforts, and you don't live in a dangerous area with high racial tensions. However, the very nature of a *major* disaster means that if only one or two *major* infrastructure components go down, the ripple effect will quickly create a much-worse scenario. It seems there is very little room for "mild" effects unless they are miniscule. The most likely predictions point to massive disruptions, severe shortages in food and water, loss of power, and a breakdown of social order in certain areas where the population density is high.

You can survive anything with good planning, an open mind, and plenty of practice. Why not start now?

2
ECONOMIC AND SOCIAL COLLAPSE

Collapses have happened to every empire in human history. It seems to be a natural law that empires can grow to a certain level and then they implode. The Roman Empire was the most powerful civilization on earth 2,000 years ago. Their similarities to America today are striking. Just like America, Rome's armies were spread too thin in too many foreign countries. Barbarian invasions, just like our terrorist attacks, cross border intrusions, as we experience in Mexico's drug wars, were constant. The government was corrupt and the only way to get anything done was through bribery or by raising taxes. This is no different than the choke hold banks and corporations have on our government today. America, like ancient Rome, has a blind fate that it's our destiny to never fall.

Most Americans have absolutely no idea what is going on in the dark corners of America, and when people find out the truth it can come as quite a shock. Many of you will not believe some of the things Americans are doing just to survive. Some families are living in sewers and drain tunnels, some families are living in tents, some families are living in their cars, some families will make ketchup soup for dinner tonight, and some families are even eating rats. Some homeless shelters in America are so overloaded that they are actually sending people out to live in the woods. As you read this, there are close to 50 million Americans that are living below the poverty line, and that number rises a little bit more every single day.

America was once known as the greatest nation on earth, but now there is decay and economic despair almost everywhere you look. Yes, money certainly cannot buy happiness, but the lack of it sure can bring a lot of pain.

As the economy continues to decline, the suffering that we see all around us is going to get a lot worse, and that is a very frightening thing to think about.

Those of us that still live comfortably are often completely unaware of what life is like out on the streets of America at this point. There are millions upon millions of Americans that have lost all hope and that are living on the very edge of life and death. There are millions upon millions of Americans that are barely hanging on and there are no jobs for them. The suffering that those families are going through is very real. When you are making 8 bucks an hour it can be incredibly tough to make it from month to month.

Just look at how much it costs to buy the basic things that we need. Without gasoline, most of us would not even be able to get to our jobs. The price of gasoline has increased 83 percent since Barack Obama first took office, and it is poised to soar even higher. There are hundreds of communities all over the country where third-world conditions are setting in.

The following is how one internet blogger from www.*theeconomiccollapseblog.com* describes what life is like in a decaying suburb of Phoenix called Maryvale:

> Crime and gangs are widespread. Most houses have either fallen into disrepair or been remade with outside walls sporting spikes and ironwork. Many of the front lawns are now just dirt (or worse, gravel), the pools green and lethal.

Now we stand on the precipice of another major global financial crisis. Economic conditions in America are going to become significantly worse. The politicians in Washington D.C. may make sure that the boys and girls on Wall Street are always taken care of, but there will be no bailouts for the large number of Americans that are about to lose their jobs and their homes.

If you want an idea of what is coming, just look at what is happening in Greece. Unemployment and poverty are rampant—25 percent of the businesses have shut down and one-third of all money has been pulled out of Greek bank accounts.

For years, a lot of prominent voices out there were screaming and yelling about the dangers posed by our soaring trade deficits and our soaring budget deficits. The American people did not WANT to listen. They just kept sending the same politicians back to Washington D.C. over and over.

As a result, those same Americans will find themselves doing things that they never dreamt of before just in order to survive.

Things We Can Learn About the Future of America from the Death of Detroit

Do you want to know what the future of America is going to look like? Just check out what is happening in Detroit. The city of Detroit was once one of the greatest industrial cities in the history of the world, but today it is a rotting, decaying, vicious, post-apocalyptic hellhole. Nearly half the men are unemployed, nearly half the population is functionally illiterate, more than half of the children are living in poverty, and the city government is drowning in debt. As economic conditions have worsened, crime has exploded. Every single night in Detroit there are frightening confrontations between desperate criminals and exasperated homeowners. Unfortunately, the police force in Detroit has been dramatically reduced in size. When the police in Detroit are called, they often show up very late if they even show up at all. Detroit has become lawless, where violence is the currency of the streets. If you want to survive in Detroit, you better be ready to fight, because there are hordes of desperate criminals that are quite eager to take everything that you have. Don't look down on Detroit too much, because what is happening in Detroit will soon be happening all over America.

The following are things we can learn about the future of America from the death of Detroit:

- When the economy falls apart, desperate people will do desperate things and many homeowners will fight back. Justifiable homicide in Detroit rose by a staggering 79 percent during 2011.
- In major cities where people are scrambling just to survive, any confrontation can quickly escalate into a life or death affair. The rate of self-defense killings in Detroit is currently 2200 percent above the national average.
- The essential social services that you are enjoying today will not always be there in the future. Officials in Detroit recently announced that due to budget constraints, all police stations will be closed to the public for 16 hours a day.
- More Americans than ever are realizing the benefits of self-defense. The following is an excerpt that was recently published by the *Daily*:

  > The last time [Julia] Brown, 73, called the Detroit police, they didn't show up until the next day. So she applied for a permit to carry a handgun and says she's prepared to use it against the young thugs who have taken over her neighborhood, burglarizing entire blocks, opening fire at will, and terrorizing the elderly with impunity.

- When crime gets so bad that the police are powerless to stop it, vigilante groups begin to form. In fact, crime is so bad and the citizens are so frustrated by the lack of police assistance that they have resorted to forming their own organizations to fight back. One group, known as "Detroit 300," was formed after a

90-year-old woman on Detroit's northwest side was brutally raped in August of 2011.

- When criminals become desperate, they will steal literally anything that is not bolted down. In Detroit today, thieves have stripped so much copper wiring out of the street lights that half of all the lights in some neighborhoods no longer work.
- As things fall apart, eventually a time comes when it is not even safe to drive down the road in the middle of the day. In Detroit recently, 100 bus drivers refused to drive their routes out of fear of being attacked on the streets. The head of the bus drivers' union, Henry Gaffney, had this to say:

> Our drivers are scared; they're scared for their lives. This has been an ongoing situation about security. I think yesterday kind of just topped it off, when one of my drivers was beat up by some teenagers down in the middle of Rosa Parks and it took the police almost 30 minutes to get there, in downtown Detroit.

- One of the clearest signs of decline in America is the state of our education system. Only 25 percent of all students in Detroit end up graduating from high school. Many other major cities will soon have graduation rates similar to Detroit.
- A growing percentage of Americans cannot even read or write. This is a very frightening indication of what the future of America could look like. According to one stunning report, 47 percent of all people living in the city of Detroit are functionally illiterate.
- When a major city becomes post-apocalyptic, home prices fall like a rock. The median price of a home in Detroit is now just $6,000.
- When crime and looting become commonplace, homes in an area can become totally worthless. Some homes in Detroit have been sold for a single dollar.

- Just because we have a high standard of living today does not mean that will always be the case. Detroit is just a rotting shell of what it once was, and what is happening to Detroit will happen to much of the rest of America very soon. The following is what one British reporter found during his visit to Detroit:

> Much of Detroit is horribly dangerous for its own residents, who in many cases only stay because they have nowhere else to go. Property crime is double the American average, violent crime triple. The isolated, peeling homes, the flooded roads, the clunky, rusted old cars and the neglected front yards amid trees and groin-high grassland make you think you are in rural Alabama, not in one of the greatest industrial cities that ever existed.

Detroit is not alone. One in six Americans is now below the poverty line and one in five families are on food stamps. Those numbers are increasing rapidly. More than 43 million are unemployed, the average American household is carrying $75,600 in debt, and the poorest 50% of all Americans now own just 2.5% of all the wealth in the United States.

So what is causing all of this? Where in the world did all of the good jobs go?

Well, the truth is that millions of them have been shipped overseas. Our politicians promised us that merging our economy with the economies of other nations where it is legal to pay slave-labor wages to workers would not create more unemployment inside America. They were dead wrong. Now we are being told that we just need to accept a lower standard of living. An increasing number of unemployed Americans have become so desperate that they have started to look for work overseas. For example, the number of Americans that are submitting applications for temporary work visas in Canada has approximately doubled since 2008. Other Americans are willing to learn foreign languages and travel to the other side of the world if that is what it takes to land a decent job. Do you now understand how much trouble we are in? The long-term trends that are destroying us only continue to get worse.

We were handed the keys to the greatest economic machine in the history of the world and we have wrecked it. So prepare for really, really hard times ahead. The era of endless prosperity is ending. Next comes the pain.

3
WHY PREPARE

Besides the financial scares of 2011, it was also the worst year for natural disasters in U.S. history! The National Oceanic and Atmospheric Administration (NOAA) reported that 12 separate weather/climate disasters occurred in the United States, each of which caused at least $1 billion in aggregate damage in 2011. The previous record, set in 2008, was nine, according to the NOAA, with an aggregate damage total of approximately $52 billion, according to the Insurance Information Institute. (This number reflects both insured and uninsured losses). On average, there are usually only about three major disasters per year. At this point, disasters are happening inside the United States so frequently that there seems to be no gap between them. We just seem to go from one major disaster to the next. 2011 has only been worse. Hopefully, after everything that has happened, it has become abundantly clear to all of us why we need to prepare for emergencies. The world is becoming an increasingly unstable place, and you never know what is going to happen next.

Thankfully, the U.S. has not experienced a disaster on the level of Hurricane Katrina again, but what makes 2011 different is that we have never seen so many major disasters happen so rapidly. Since the beginning of 2011, we have had to deal with record-setting winter storms, nightmarish tornadoes, "once in a century" earthquakes, historic flooding all over the country, severe drought, and some of the worst wildfires the U.S. has ever experienced.

Is there a reason why the United States is being hit by one major disaster after another, or is all of this just a really unfortunate coincidence?

The following are just a few of the large-scale natural disasters that the United States has had to deal with in 2011.

Texas Wildfires

The state of Texas had been on fire for nearly 300 consecutive days before finally being extinguished. That was the worst wildfire season that Texas had ever experienced. At least 3.6 million acres burned. Vast stretches of Texas have been transformed into desolate wastelands. Over one week alone, the Texas Forest Service responded to more than 180 new fires. The incredibly dry weather and the scorching temperatures combined to turn the state of Texas into a tinderbox. Bastrop County Complex fire, near Austin, Texas, destroyed 1,691 homes, making it the most destructive single wildfire in Texas history.

Historic Drought

In 2011, approximately 81 percent of the state of Texas experienced "exceptional drought" conditions. Not only did this create an ideal environment for wildfires, it is absolutely crippled ranchers and farmers. Farmers in Texas lost over half of their cotton crops. Ranchers were forced to slaughter huge numbers of cattle, because the drought had made it impossible to feed them. At that time, the number of U.S.

cattle was down to its lowest level since 1963. In the months' following, the price of beef jumped significantly. It is hard to describe just how bad things were in Texas. Overall, it is estimated that the drought caused more than $5 billion in damage to the agricultural industry.

Flooding in the Northeast
Hurricane Irene stormed up the Northeast coast in the late summer of 2011, bringing record-breaking rain and floods to inland areas and washing away covered bridges that had stood in place for more than a hundred years. As a result of Hurricane Irene, millions of people lost power and dozens of people lost their lives. Hurricane Irene caused the worst flooding that Vermont had experienced since 1927, and the total economic damage from Irene reached 18.7 billion dollars.

Disturbing Earthquakes
The number of major earthquakes around the globe is significantly increasing. Back in 2001, the world had 1,361 earthquakes of magnitude 5.0 or greater. In 2011, we had over 2,800, which would be the highest number this decade by far.

The U.S. experienced two of the weirdest earthquakes that it has seen in ages. The earthquake in Virginia that made headlines all over the nation is being called a "once a century" earthquake. The east coast very rarely sees anything like this happen. The earthquake in Virginia was felt all the way down in Georgia and it was felt all the way up in Ottawa, Canada. It was felt as far west as Cleveland, Ohio. In Washington D.C., the earthquake caused quite a bit of panic. Congressional buildings were evacuated and so was the Pentagon. The earthquake actually cracked the Washington Monument and it also caused significant damage to the U.S. Treasury building. That exact same day, there was another very "unusual" earthquake in another area of the United States. A magnitude 5.3 earthquake shook the area along the Colorado/ New Mexico border. That was the largest earthquake that region had experienced in more than 40 years. Sadly, it's not just the U.S. that was hit by noteworthy earthquakes in 2011.

A ferocious tsunami spawned by one of the largest earthquakes ever recorded slammed Japan's eastern coast, killing hundreds of people as it swept away boats, cars, and homes while widespread fires burned out of control.

Hours later, the tsunami hit Hawaii and warnings blanketed the Pacific, putting areas on alert as far away as South America, Canada, Alaska, and the entire U.S. West Coast. In Japan, the area around Fukushima, a nuclear power plant in the northeast, was evacuated after the reactor's cooling system failed. Senator Ron Wyden recently warned that the Fukushima fuel pool is a national security issue for AMERICA.

Nuclear expert Arnie Gundersen recently said:

> There's more cesium in that [Unit 4] fuel pool than in all 800 nuclear bombs exploded above ground... But of course it would happen all at once. It would certainly destroy Japan as a functioning country... Move south of the equator if that ever happened, I think that's probably the lesson there.

Earthquakes can't be thought of in the same way as before. We are realizing that the scope and magnitude of possible destruction is so far-reaching, as to affect the entire globe. It's not just your local bridge that may collapse, but a catastrophic nuclear-reactor meltdown that could spread radioactive waste thousands of miles away.

Tornadoes
With all of the other natural disasters that we have had recently, it is easy to forget that we just went through one of the worst tornado seasons of all time.

The United States experienced a truly bizarre tornado season in 2011. In April, there were approximately 600 tornadoes all across America. That is the most tornadoes that have ever been recorded in a single month inside the United States. Usually, we only have about 1,200 tornadoes for the entire year. The massive tornado outbreak in the southeast at the end of April is being called the worst natural disaster since Hurricane Katrina. One F5 tornado that ripped through the Tuscaloosa, Alabama region was reportedly a mile wide and some scientists estimated that it had winds that exceeded 260 miles an hour.

By the time it passed, Tuscaloosa resembled a war zone. The tornado that ripped through Joplin, Missouri is being called the deadliest single tornado in more than 60 years. It ripped a path of destruction more than a mile wide and more than 6 miles long directly through the city.

Sadly, there were a lot of other major disasters in 2011 that we just don't have the time to discuss. So why is all of this happening? Is there a reason for all of this chaos, or has it just been one of those years?

Whatever your opinion is, what we should all be able to learn is the imperativeness of preparedness. Natural disasters can strike at any time. Whether it is a hurricane, tornado, flood, earthquake, volcano, or wildfire, if you wait until the disaster strikes to prepare, you are going to suffer the consequences.

Most natural disasters are only temporary. Even more frightening is what an economic collapse, a war, a deadly plague, a nuclear disaster, an EMP strike, or a weapon of mass destruction could mean.

As we have seen during so many disasters in the past, when something really bad happens, food and supplies vanish from store shelves almost immediately. If transportation is cut off, you could be on your own for an extended period of time. Our world is becoming a highly unstable place. If someone had told you all of the crazy things that were going to happen in 2011, would you have believed them? It seems like with each passing year things are getting crazier and crazier. Yes, we can all hope that things will return to "normal", but we would be foolish if we didn't also take precautions.

Disasters can be divided into two broad categories: disasters resulting from human activities and natural disasters.

Disasters Resulting from Human Activities

- Electrical blackouts
- Acts of terrorism
- Political wars
- Civil disturbances, rioting, and looting
- Radiation leaks
- EMP strikes
- Oil spills
- Geoengineering (weather modification)
- Water fluoridation
- Genetically-modified foods
- Human-animal hybrids and transgenic clones
- Secret germ laboratories
- Industrial chemical releases
- Economic collapse or severe economic blows such as a great depression or hyperinflation

Natural Disasters

- Epidemics
- Tsunamis
- Hurricanes/cyclones
- Tornados
- Earthquakes
- Floods
- Avalanches
- Landslides
- Wildfires
- Droughts
- Famines
- Winter freezes
- Heat waves
- Crop failures
- Volcanic eruptions
- Asteroid strikes
- Comets
- Meteorites
- Pestilence
- Solar storms

Local disasters are limited to your property and/or local community. Examples would include tornados, which could level or otherwise severely damage your home and the homes of your neighbors. Another example would be the derailment of a freight train resulting in the release of toxic gases from a tanker car into your neighborhood and surrounding area.

Regional disasters affect a larger area but are limited to one region of the country. Hurricane Katrina was an example of a regional disaster. Other examples would include earthquakes, droughts, and crop failures.

National disasters, as the name implies, would affect the entire nation. A war would be an example. Other examples would include an economic depression, a severe stock market crash, or collapse of the currency.

Global disasters affect the entire planet. In today's global economy it would be easy for a national disaster to quickly escalate to a global one. An economic depression in the US, for example, would affect our trading partners as well. With the US dollar acting as the major reserve currency for most of the world, a collapse of the currency would be disastrous for nearly every nation, including those as far off as China and Japan. In fact, never before in history has the potential for a human-caused disaster of global proportions been more possible. In our highly-mobile society it is also very possible for a natural disaster, such as an epidemic, to quickly spread around the globe becoming a pandemic. As we will see, the amount of provisions that you will want to store will depend on how long you anticipate an emergency could last, which in turn will depend on the magnitude or scope of the disasters that you consider possible for your area. If a hurricane hits your community, a one-week supply of food and water will probably be sufficient, for certainly help will arrive within a week. But a collapse of the currency, resulting in a global disaster, might require that you store enough supplies to last for several months.

4
PSYCHOLOGY OF SURVIVAL

S—Size up the situation, surroundings, physical condition, and equipment.
U—Use all your senses.
R—Remember where you are.
V—Vanquish fear and panic.
I—Improvise and improve.
V—Value living.
A—Act like the natives.
L—Live by your wits.

In any true survival situation, everyone is a potential victim, but not everyone is a potential survivor. Your will power can be that defining factor, not your gear that saves you. A determination to survive, whatever the cost, will often compensate for a limited knowledge of survival skills. Avoiding panic and controlling your **FEAR** is paramount: **f**alse **e**vidence **a**ppearing **r**eal.

The way you think affects the way you act. If you know your job, you will probably act quickly and effectively. If you are uncertain or doubtful of your ability to do your job, you may hesitate and make wrong decisions. Positive thinking is a necessity. You must enter survival situations with absolute confidence in your ability.

Fear is a basic human emotion. It is mental and physical. In itself, fear is not shameful if controlled. It can even help you, by making you more alert and more able to complete your task. For example, a fear-induced adrenaline rush might help you respond and defend yourself or your loved ones quickly during an unpredicted event or combat situation. Therefore, fear can help you, so use it to your advantage.

Worry undermines the body, dulls the mind, and slows thinking and learning. It adds to confusion, magnifies troubles, and causes you to imagine things that really do not exist. If you are worried about something, talk about it with someone you trust. That person may be able to help solve the problem.

Be prepared and accept that you and your family could be thrown into a survival situation. Train with your family. Turn your power off, practice with your gear, find out what your body can endure, and most of all, recognize and study what your reaction to fear will be. Focus on the here and now because your mind will want to wander into fantasy and play out different "what if" scenarios that will tax your mind and body. Conserving energy is the key to survival, but staying constructively busy will keep your mind off situations that encourage fear. Staying busy will give you a sense that you are in control of your future.

Anger and frustration will most likely become an issue. You will have to complete tasks with minimal resources, and this reality will most likely become frustrating. It is inevitable that something, if not everything, will go wrong, but remember, this is beyond your control. With your life, or that of someone else's, being at stake, every mistake feels magnified. A few moments of frustration can easily turn into anger. The solution is to quickly cope with your frustrations and your new reality, then the higher your chances of survival will be. Frustration and anger can encourage impulsive reactions, irrational behavior, and poor decision making, which can lead you to the "I quit" mentality.

Use your emotional intensity to act in a productive manner! Transfer that energy into doing something. Just think about when you have had a cold, if you sat around doing nothing, all you thought about is how terrible you felt. By getting up and doing something, anything, your actions distract you from how you are feeling.

Depression is very normal when faced with the reality of subsistence. An unsatisfied person becomes angrier as he fails to reach his goals. If the anger does not help you to succeed, then the frustration level goes even higher, leading to depression. When a person reaches this point, he starts to give up! The focus goes from a proactive "What can I do" to "There is nothing I can do" mentality. Depression is a feeling of hopelessness. The solution is to allow yourself to be sad momentarily, but not to let it consume you to the point where you give-up. Think of your family, or anything that can raise your spirits, because such thoughts can give you the desire to try harder and live one more day!

You may be overcome with guilt. The circumstances leading to your survival situation are sometimes very dramatic! You were the only survivor and are questioning why you are the only one still alive? It is common for survivors to feel guilty about being alive while others are dead. Acknowledge these feeling, but don't allow them to hinder you in surviving. When used in a positive way, guilt can encourage you to work harder to survive! You are alive for some greater purpose. Whatever reason you give yourself, please do not allow any of these dark feelings to prevent you from staying alive!

Pay close attention to signs of fear in other survivors in your group. Deal with their fear immediately; otherwise fear will spread like wildfire and jeopardize the ability of the rest of the group to have clear mental faculties and physical toughness. Don't let your group fall prey to demoralization.

Survivors will go through a grieving process before they can accept the loss of their former life. The sooner a survivor moves forward and readjusts to their new, current life the better their chances of survival become. There are countless stories of individuals perishing even though they had ample food, water, and shelter; they succumbed to fear, helplessness, and an overall feeling that they had no control over their survival outcome.

While the will to live is a basic instinct, it is becoming weaker as we become more civilized and reliant on technology. Lots of young people would rather play computer games rather than venture outside. If they ever found themselves in a disaster, they would find it very difficult indeed.

The most important factor in survival is to vanquish fear and have a "stop at nothing" will to live attitude. Survival psychology is something you can learn and always carry with you. Never quit, it's always darkest before the dawn.

Trapped Chilean Miners

One of my favorite stories of survival is the one where 33 Chilean miners were trapped underground for 69 days, at 2,300 feet underground. For 17 long days, no one knew the miners' fates. Rescuers drilled frantically here and there, sending down probes in hopes of finding the mine's emergency shelter.

One probe came back with a note tied to the end: "Estamos bien en el refugio, los 33,"—"We are OK in the refuge, the 33." Joy, however, was tempered. Government officials estimated that it could take up to four months to dig a tunnel wide enough to bring up the miners. The bore hole that had reached them was widened enough to send food, water, medicine, clothes, and a mini camera to enable video messages to their families. A telephone line was threaded down, plus a fiber-optic cable for videoconferencing. They were able to watch live TV and movies on a small projector. Psychologists, health experts, and nutritionists were consulted about how the miners could stay sane and healthy in their 600-square-foot chamber until their rescue. To survive, they must endure constant 90% humidity, avoid starvation, battle thirst, guard against germs/infection, and stay sane enough to safely do the work necessary to aid in their own rescue. Yet even if they accomplished all of that, they faced another danger: the constant darkness.

Decades of research have shown that the human body is built to function on the rhythm of the rising and setting sun. If sunlight doesn't tell our brains when we should be asleep, and if we don't eat, exercise, and sleep on a fairly regular daily schedule, humans can develop all sorts of health problems over time, from irregular metabolism, to heart disease, to deficiencies of key vitamins. Disruptions to our body's 24-hour clock can impair motor skills. (Doctors who toil over long shifts are far more likely to get in car accidents.) They can make us irritable or depressed. To feel the effects of those disruptions each day would be like trying to live life in a constant state of jet lag.

Even though the miners could roam the intact tunnels, they soon showed signs of cabin fever. There were reports of joyriding on mine vehicles; the miners rejected a delivery of peaches; and they grew more aggressive in demanding wine and cigarettes. But there were also bright spots, like the birth of one miner's daughter, which he was able to watch via video link. The parents had originally planned to name her Carolina, but down in the mine, the father changed his mind. "Call her Esperanza, or Hope," he said. Chilean Independence Day brought a special treat of empanadas, a traditional Chilean pastry filled with meat, onions, olives, and raisins.

Chile's president, Sebastian Pinera, announced that the rescue would take place well ahead of schedule. Journalists descended on the site as the hour grew near, and more than 3,000 people gathered to watch the rescue on giant TV monitors in the nearby provincial capital, Copiapo, hometown to most of the miners.

Millions more watched worldwide on TV or online. Experts warned that the miners might be suffering from ailments brought on from captivity or from their trip up in a tiny capsule. Remarkably, when they emerged, one by one, they looked perfectly healthy and wore sunglasses donated by Oakley to protect their eyes from the glare. One miner, a former soccer celebrity, bounced a soccer ball on his foot. All were reunited with their families, who had kept vigil above ground.

The miners didn't have to worry about employment, either. Companies lined up to offer them jobs that fit their experience, like bulldozer driver, mechanic, electrician, and risk-reduction specialist. Plus, they're hoping for a book deal. But while one or two of the miners enjoyed the media limelight, the rest were ready to go back to their own lives, and some were even ready to return to the mines.

Self-Amputation While Trapped

Jonathan Metz, 31, a Connecticut man who attempted to amputate his own arm after it was trapped in a furnace credits "human spirit" for his survival. "Trust me, whether it's cutting your arm off or finding some other way, I think all people would be astounded by what they're capable of."

Metz explained how he was reaching for a fallen vacuum cleaner piece when his arm became stuck in the vents of the furnace. "The next five to 10 minutes was sheer panic," Metz said. "It became apparent to me that I had a major problem. I spent the next 12 hours screaming for help, but no sound was escaping the basement." He said he became desperate when he started to smell rotting flesh and knew he had to take extreme measures if he was going to survive. "I thought there must be some other way, so I kind of started looking around my surroundings again. Maybe there was something I missed. You know, what would MacGyver do if he were here? It took me about six hours to psych myself up to the point where I thought I was capable of actually doing what I thought needed to be done." His fantasy, he said, was that he could cut off the arm, run upstairs, put it in his freezer, call 911, then go to the hospital and get it reattached.

Metz said he first used a hacksaw blade and then a larger blade, which he hoped would make the operation go smoother, just below the shoulder on his left arm, leaving only some fat. He nearly succeeded but couldn't make it through a bundle of nerves.

"I don't know how many strokes it took," he said, "but it was quite a few. So yes, every one, I was re-evaluating in some way, was it too late to stop? Or what was the point where there was no going back?"

Metz started and stopped a couple of times, once when the blood flow became too much. He said he had to use a telephone cord to fashion a second tourniquet, replacing the one he had made with his shirt. He said he used his mouth and neck to pull the cord tight around the arm as he cut. When he realized he couldn't get the arm off, he leaned against a wood pile, tightened the tourniquet again and resumed calling for help. Every five minutes, he said, his microwave would beep, reminding him that the leftovers he had been reheating for a late-night snack were ready. He said the chirps tortured him at first, but they later became a source of strength, telling him he had made it through another five minutes.

He made one final thrust at the boiler and was able to open its release valve, sending brackish, rust-colored water onto the floor. He scooped it into his mouth with a flip-flop he had been wearing. "It was just enough to at least mentally make me feel like, here's a way out of this." He said thoughts of his fiancée, family, friends, and his little beagle, Portia, also kept him going.

Friends and coworkers at The Travelers, where Metz works in financial services, grew worried when he did not show up for work and missed a softball game. When he did not answer the doorbell at his home, a friend called police, who found Metz in the basement. Firefighters ripped apart the furnace with heavy tools, including a spreader normally used to take the door off a car. Once they did, the arm just gave way. His doctors say Metz is doing well. They have since fitted him with a prosthetic arm. Metz says he is not feeling sorry for himself.

There will be no more procrastinating either. He has even gone on to marry the girl that inspired his heroism. "In the short term, it's going to be difficult," he said, "but in the long term, boy if you need a kick in the pants to get you to tackle, take on those dreams or whatever your aspirations are, this was it."

Dr. David Shapiro, a trauma specialist, who operated on Metz, said he could not have lived much longer. "I've never experienced somebody who had the ability to go through something like this," Dr Ellner, Metz's other surgeon, said. "He provides a lot of inspiration for myself, not just as a physician but as a human being."

Survival stories have always been popular. Entire television series now feature teams of people pitted against one another to overcome some test or challenge. Disaster movies were popular back in the '70s, when the *Towering Inferno*, *Airport*, and the *Poseidon Adventure* let us watch people get picked off one by one. Why do we love this stuff? Maybe it's because these stories reflect humanity's greatest strength: the power of adaptation. Whether we're talking about natural disasters, accidents, the exploration of the Colonial American wilderness or long-term science expeditions to Antarctica, the psychology of survival is fascinating because we like the idea that one's mental attitude can make the difference between life or death.

Sure they had times of doubt, incredible odds of not surviving, but they made a decision to survive; they had the will to live. Without that will, even daily living can seem like an impossible task. "IT IS suffering to live." That is what Ryunosuke Akutagawa, a popular writer in early 20th-century Japan, wrote shortly before committing suicide.

However, he prefaced that statement with the words: "Of course, I do not want to die, but . . ." Like Akutagawa, many of those who take their life do not want to die as much as they want to end whatever is going on. The wording so commonly found in suicide notes suggest as much. Such phrases as "I couldn't take it any longer" or "Why go on living?" show a deep desire to escape life's harsh realities. Committing suicide is like treating a cold with a nuclear bomb. People seem to be able to bear or tolerate depression as long as there is the belief that things will improve.

Reasons Why We Give Up

- We forget how important our cause is.
- We have not conditioned our hearts to face difficult challenges.
- We do not attempt to succeed with all our might.
- We focus too much on our failures or shortcomings.
- We do not learn from our own mistakes or the mistakes of others.
- We do not receive any encouragement, but instead ridicule.
- We do not focus on the rewards of our efforts.
- We have not noticed that others with fewer advantages have succeeded.
- Children of God forget the words of Jesus, "But with God all things are possible."
- We spend too much time trying to analyze a problem, rather than doing something about it.
- We try too early in our labors to assess how well we are doing.
- We open our ears repetitively to those who advise us to quit.
- We blame others and make excuses for not doing what we should.
- We do not realize that others are watching us and are influenced by our examples.

So what's the take-home message: DON'T GIVE UP! When your hope ends, despair, and even death, are sure to follow!

5
FOOD

Food Prices Are Rising Fast

If you do much grocery shopping, you have probably noticed that the cost of food has been rising at a very sharp pace over the past year. When you go to the grocery store these days you will notice that many of the new "sale prices" are the old, regular prices, plus an extra few cents. Other items have had their packages reduced in size in order to hide the price increases. With millions of American families just barely scraping by as it is, what is going to happen if food prices keep rising this quickly? The food prices are especially painful if you are trying to eat healthfully. Most of the low price items in the grocery stores are garbage. Eating the "typical American diet" is a highway to cancer, heart disease, and diabetes. But if you try to stick to food that is "nutritious" or "organic" you can eat up hundreds of dollars in a heartbeat. In fact, the reality is that tens of millions of American families have now essentially been priced out of a healthy diet. If this trend continues, there will be millions more that will not even be able to afford an unhealthy diet.

Sadly, this isn't a phenomenon that is just happening in the United States. The truth is that the entire planet is rapidly approaching a horrific global food crisis. In 2011, the global price of food rose by 37 percent and this has pushed approximately 44 million more people around the world into poverty. When food prices rise in the U.S. it may be agonizing, but around the world a rise in food prices can mean the difference between starving and not starving. That is why it has become so alarming that the global price of wheat has roughly doubled over the past year. Even before this recent spike in food prices the world was struggling to get enough food to everybody.

It has been estimated that somewhere in the world someone starves to death every 3.6 seconds, and 75 percent of those are children under the age of five.

So what is going to happen if food prices keep on rising at the current pace? That is a very good question. We really are starting to move into unprecedented territory. Nobody is quite sure what is going to happen next. So what is the cause? Well, a lot of people are blaming the Federal Reserve. All of the "quantitative easing" that the Fed has done has flooded the financial markets with money. All of that money had to go somewhere. Much of it has pumped up the prices of hard assets such as oil, gold, and agricultural commodities. But it is not just the Fed that is to blame. The truth is that central banks all over the world have been recklessly printing money. When the amount of money in an economy goes up, the purchasing value of all existing money goes down. In the United States, that means that your dollars will not go as far as they did before. Essentially, you're being robbed without even knowing it. It's not just monetary policy that is affecting food prices, though. In 2010 and 2011 we have seen an unparalleled wave of natural disasters and crazy weather. This has caused problems with crops all over the globe. In addition, U.S. economic policies are also playing a role. At this point, almost a third of all corn grown in the U.S. is used for fuel. This is putting a lot of stress on the price of corn. Also, there are some long-term trends that are not in our favor. For example, the systematic depletion of the Ogallala Aquifer could eventually turn "America's Breadbasket" back into the "Dust Bowl". If you have not heard of this problem, please do some research on it.

Things are going to get much worse, but already America is having a hard time feeding itself. According to *Feeding America's* 2010 hunger study, more than 37 million Americans are now being served by food pantries and soup kitchens. Is that number unusual? Yes, it sure is. The number of Americans that are going to food pantries and soup kitchens has increased by 46% since 2006. That is a shocking development.

So what is going to happen if the economy gets even worse? What is going to happen if there is a major food crisis in this country someday? Food prices have been going up for decades and they are going to continue to go up. The frightening thing, though, is how fast they are increasing now. As the U.S. middle class continues to be destroyed, the number of Americans that can't afford to buy enough food is going to continue to rise. Food prices are rising much faster than wages are, and that is not likely to change any time soon. Food is rapidly becoming one of the most important global economic issues of this decade. The farther one looks down the road, the bleaker things look for the global food situation. Hopefully you are prepared for that.

Our Food Supply is Fragile
Grocery stores don't stock weeks of food anymore. Most keep only 72 hours of food on the shelves. They re-stock based on

just-in-time delivery of food supplies. If the trucks stop rolling in your part of the country during a crisis, the store shelves will be emptied almost immediately. In fact, expect a shortage of mainstay items like milk and bread to occur similar to what happens before an approaching hurricane hits. Those who are aware of the problem but who haven't already made preparations will engage in a last-minute rush to buy a few extra supplies.

Transportation is Key

Without transportation, farmers can't get their crops to the wholesalers or food processing facilities. Food is heavy, generally speaking, and it requires trucks and trains to move it around—a literal ARMY of trucks and trains, weaving their way from city to city, optimized and prioritized by computers. If the computers freeze, the whole transportation infrastructure will shut down. Transportation also depends heavily on fuel, which means the oil-producing countries in the Middle East have to be able to produce the oil that gets refined into diesel fuel here in America. So, in other words, your food supply depends on Saudi Arabia being alive and well. Do you trust the people in charge in Saudi Arabia, Iraq, Iran, and Kuwait with your life? If you don't make preparations now, you trust them by default.

Cities Depend on Rural Land

Did you know cities would be ghost towns without the supporting imports of food from the country? We should all thank the farmers a little more, because they literally keep us all alive. Cities are like concrete islands. You might think a city is self-sustaining until you really think about it, but underneath it all that city is only days before becoming a ghost town, without the people in the country supporting it. You may already know that city people and country people have very different views on politics and life in general. Country people tend to be more religious and more conservative. City people tend to be more liberal. So there's more than a little animosity between country people and city people. When a crisis hits and the country people find they are without electricity and fuel, they will still survive, for the most part, because they're used to surviving. Any food that's harvested from the fields will be kept and stored by the farmers themselves. They will NOT be shipping this stuff to the cities unless they have excess goods and can find a transportation method that still works (and has fuel). Unfortunately, if some *national emergency powers* acts are signed into place by the President, the Federal Emergency Management Association, or FEMA, will have the legal power to actually confiscate and redistribute food.

This makes it all the more likely that farmers will harvest, then hide it, in order to keep it. That means even less food making it to the cities. What's the bottom line? Cities where food can't be delivered will eventually be gutted, looted, evacuated, and likely burned to the ground.

Start Stocking Food
You can do a lot if you start early. Regrettably, *early* might have been yesterday. Now we're way past *early*, and you need a reasonable plan to get food supplies that will store well and don't cost too much. You've probably already realized that buying up extra cans of soup at the grocery store is a really ill-advised way to spend your preparedness money. You need a better plan. Every $10 you spend at the store might feed a person for a few days. You need more leverage, where you can spend $10 and feed a person for a few weeks.

Buy Extra, Use FIFO
Go ahead and buy more food than normal when you're out shopping, and set it aside. Use the "first in, first out" rule to eat your older supplies first. Keep rotating your supplies so you never abandon food stored in the back of your shelves.

Buy Ingredients, Not Prepared Foods
Ingredients such as salt, honey, oatmeal, and wheat will last a lot longer than prepared foods like TV dinners, cereals, and food mixes. Naturally, as you purchase food ingredients, you'll want to practice actually using them! Remember

the basics. For example, if you purchase a bag of wheat, how exactly do you plan to make flour out of it? One survival book described throwing some wheat in a coffee can and pounding it into flour with a blunt stick. You can make a few cups of flour after ten or fifteen minutes of noisemaking.

The Seven Major Mistakes in Food Storage

1. **VARIETY**: Most people don't have enough variety in their storage. Many people only store the four basic items: wheat, milk, honey, and salt. Statistics show most of us won't survive on such a diet for several reasons. Many people are allergic to wheat and may not be aware of it until they are eating it meal after meal. Wheat is too harsh for young children. They can tolerate it in small amounts but not as their main staple. We get tired of eating the same foods over and over and many times prefer not to eat than to sample that particular food again and again. This is called "appetite fatigue." Young children and older people are particularly susceptible to it.

   Store less wheat than is generally suggested and put the difference into a variety of other grains, particularly ones your family likes to eat. Also store a variety of beans. This will add a variety of color, texture, and flavor. Variety is the key to a successful storage program. It is essential that you store flavorings such as tomato, bouillon, cheese, and onion. Also, include a good supply of the herbs and spices you like to cook with.

   These seasonings allow you to do many creative things with your grains and beans. Without them you are severely limited. One of the best suggestions I can give you is to buy a good food storage cookbook. Go through it and see what your family would really eat. Notice the ingredients as you do this, as it will help you more than anything else to know what items to store.

2. **EXTENDED STAPLES**: Few people get beyond storing the four basic items, but it is extremely important that you do so. Never put all your eggs in one basket (pun intended). Store dehydrated and/or freeze-dried foods, as well as home-canned and store-bought canned goods. Make sure you add cooking oil, shortening, baking powder, soda, yeast, and powdered eggs. You can't cook even the most basic recipes without these items. Because of limited space, I won't list all the items that should be included in a well-balanced storage program. They are all included in the cookbook *The All New Cookin' With Home Storage* by Peggy Layton and Vicki Tate, as well as information on how much to store, and where to purchase it.

3. **VITAMINS AND MINERALS**: These are important, especially if you have children, since children do not store body reserves of nutrients as adults do. A good quality multi-vitamin and vitamin C are the most vital. Others may be added as your budget permits.

4. **QUICK AND EASY COMFORT FOODS**: Quick and easy foods help you through times when you are psychologically or physically unable to prepare a complicated meal. Freeze-dried foods are wonderful since they require little preparation. MRE's (**m**eals **r**eady to **e**at), such as many preparedness outlets carry, are also very good. Comfort foods are the goodies such as Jell-O, pudding, candy, etc. These may sound frivolous, but people who have lived entirely on their storage for extended periods of time say these were the most helpful items to normalize their situations and make it more bearable, especially if you have children.

5. **BALANCE:** Time and time again, families buy all of one item, then all of another item, and so forth. Don't do that! It's important to keep well-balanced as you build-up your storage. Buy several things, rather than a large quantity of one. If something happens and you have to live on your present storage, you'll fare much better having a one month supply of a variety of substances than a year's supply of only two to three.

6. **CONTAINERS:** Always store your bulk foods in food storage containers. Tons of food gets thrown away by survivalists because it was left in sacks, where it became highly susceptible to moisture, insects, and rodents.

    If you are using plastic buckets make sure they are lined with a food grade plastic liner available from companies that carry packaging supplies. Never use trash can liners, as these are treated with pesticides.

    Don't stack them too high. In an earthquake they may topple, the lids pop open, or they may crack. A better container is the #10 tin can which most preparedness companies use when they package their foods.

7. **USE YOUR STORAGE:** One of the biggest problems with storing food is not knowing what to do with it. It's vital that you and your family become familiar with the things you are storing. You need to know how to prepare these foods. This is not something you want to learn under stress. Your family needs to be used to eating these foods. A stressful period is not a good time to totally change your diet. Get a food storage cookbook and learn to use these foods! It's easy to solve these food storage problems once you know what they are.

Urban Meat Trapping

The idea of urban meat trapping may seem farfetched, but in a 14+ day disaster, food is going to be nonexistent for non-preppers; even in our current time the homeless are known to eat dogs, cats, and rats.

If eating what is considered a pet offends you, remember that the meat protein in your diet once lived; it's just packaged so neatly that you forget that it was killed for your consumption. You should only practice urban meat trapping in a survival situation when no other food option is available, otherwise it is illegal, not to mention unclean. I would suggest practicing the technique, but allow an unharmed way of escape for the animal. Remember: "IF YOU KILL IT, YOU HAVE TO EAT IT!" Try not to waste any part of the animal: use the bones for improvised tools and the non-edible organs for bait. Urban meat may not go over well with some of your loved ones, but making a stew with lots of spices and anything else you can concoct will be more palatable and nutritious at the same time.

"The only rule is that you must not kill your own kind to live —that is murder and violates all the laws of the universe. Cannibalism after death, for life, is not!"
—Mykel Hawke (Captain, US Army Special Forces/Survival Instructor)

Donner Party

A common, but rarely talked about, subject in survival is the act of cannibalism, and all throughout history man has partaken in the practice as a means to survive. The Donner Party (sometimes called the Donner-Reed Party) was a group of American pioneers who set out for California in a wagon train. Delayed by a series of mishaps, they spent the winter of 1846–47 snowbound in the Sierra Nevada. Some of the emigrants resorted to cannibalism to survive, eating those who had succumbed to starvation and sickness. The journey west usually took between four and six months, but the Donner Party was slowed by following a new route called the Hastings Cutoff, which crossed Utah's Wasatch Mountains and Great Salt Lake Desert.

The rugged terrain and difficulties later encountered while traveling along the Humboldt River, in present-day Nevada, resulted in the loss of many cattle and wagons and contributed to divisions within the group.

By the beginning of November, 1846, the group had reached the Sierra Nevada where they became trapped by an early, heavy snowfall near Truckee (now Donner) Lake, high in the mountains. Their food supplies ran low, and in mid-December some of the group set out on foot to obtain help. Rescuers from Sacramento, California, attempted to reach the emigrants, but the first relief party did not arrive until the middle of February 1847, almost 4 months after the wagon train became trapped. Only 48 of the 87 members of the party survived to reach Sacramento.

Historians have described the episode as one of the most spectacular tragedies in Californian history and in the record of western migration.

Flight 571

Occasionally cannibalism still transpires in modern times. A famous example is the crash of Uruguayan Air Force Flight 571, after which some survivors ate the bodies of dead passengers.

On October 13, 1972, the team was on its way from Montevideo, Uruguay to play a match in Santiago, Chile. Fierce wind and snow hounded the flight as the plane trekked through the Andes Mountains. Due to poor weather and pilot error, the plane crashed atop of an unnamed mountain on the border of Chile and Argentina. Search parties from three countries searched for 11 days in vain to find the downed flight of 45 people, but were unsuccessful and all passengers were presumed dead. What followed next is one of the greatest examples of human survival ever recorded. Despite no food or heat, 16 members of the team stayed on top of the mountain for over two months through the brutal winter, while being forced to eat the remains of their fallen teammates before finally being rescued.

Food as Fuel
The body is a machine that needs fuel to operate. Food is this fuel. We store energy from the food we eat in the form of fat, carbohydrates, and proteins. When you go without food for any length of time, your body will start to burn this stored food energy. Carbs are the first to go, followed by fat. Having excess fat on your body may actually help you survive longer without food. After you burn up your fat, then protein steps up to the plate. If starvation sets in and you're using up proteins—basically the body itself—then you're in trouble.

Signs and Tips
Early signs of starvation include weakness, confusion, chronic diarrhea, irritability, and immune deficiency. After this point, your internal organs will shut down one at a time. The final stages of starvation will include hallucinations, convulsions, muscle spasms, and an irregular heartbeat. In a worst-case scenario, plants and insects can provide protein and food energy.

A good rule for each is to refrain from eating any that are brightly colored, spiny, or gives off a pungent odor. If you know you'll be hiking someplace remote, buy a book on edible plant species in the region and chow down.

Pros and Cons of Freeze-Dried, Dehydrated, MRE, Food Bars, and Basic Commodities.

Freeze-Dried

Very low moisture
Very lightweight
Long shelf life
Reconstitutes quickly
Retains original shape,
texture, color

Most expensive
Requires water
Bulkier than dehydrated

Dehydrated

Low moisture
Lightweight
Long shelf life
No waste
Not easily spoiled

Requires water
Long time to reconstitute
Looses taste after reconstitution
Process can affect nutritional value
Poor visual appeal

MRE (Meal Ready to Eat)

Eaten right from pouch
No water to prepare
Heated by many methods
Convenient to use

Poor taste by some
Artificial additives added
Expensive for amount of food
Poor nutritional value

Emergency Food Bars

Compact, convenient
Low cost
Five-year shelf life
Takes high heat well

Limited nutritional value
No substitute for a hot meal
Not adequate for prolonged use

Grains, Beans, and Basic Commodities

Very familiar	Not for short-term emergencies
Low cost	Very heavy weight
Long storage life	Large quantities of water/fuel
Good nutritional value	Time consuming to prepare

Flour, Whole Grains, and Rice

Properly-stored, bulk whole grains will last for years and even decades, making them a perfect choice for home food storage. They are also one of the cheapest items on a per pound basis to buy; you can get great discounts for buying in bulk. These are the suggested amounts for an adult's one year supply:

- Whole grain wheat berries (350 pounds).

- Other whole grains—barley, corn, oats, popcorn, and rye (100 pounds).

- Rice—white enriched, brown, and wild (45 pounds).

- Pastas—lasagna, egg noodles, spaghetti, wheat, and veggie (35 pounds).

Whole grains are packed with nutrients, protein and even oils. Do not substitute empty calories (white flour, white rice, and white pastas) for these recommended whole grains.

Cereal

While commercially prepared cereals, such as Cheerios and Raisin Bran, have shorter shelf lives and need to be rotated on a monthly or quarterly basis (use the oldest items and replace with new purchases), whole rolled oats, grits, quinoa, and similar dry grains processed for making gruel, or hot cereal, will last much longer. Choose a variety of several types of cereal, 75 pounds per adult, for a well-rounded one year's supply of stored food.

Beans

As with all categories, it's important to store foods that you know how to prepare tastefully and that your family actually eats. In the beans/legumes section of your home food storage, the recommended one-year amount is 75 pounds for each adult. Consider a combination of black beans, kidney beans, garbanzo beans (great for making hummus), lentils, pinto beans, navy beans, split peas, and other varieties as per your taste and favorite recipes.

Meat

Buying a side of beef and storing it in the deep freeze is one way to ensure a source of protein as long as the power stays on. Aim for about 75 pounds of canned or frozen beef, chicken, and fish per adult if you go that route. Dried beef, typically in the form of jerky, doesn't require power to remain preserved. It still has a relatively short shelf life, however. Unopened containers of freeze-dried meats can last for decades, making them the most stable and reliable way to store beef for long-term survival.

Dairy Products

Find and store powdered milk, buttermilk powder, dried yogurt culture for making yogurt, dehydrated or freeze-dried butter and cheeses. The goal is to have about 150 pounds of these items per adult, as well as about 25 dozen powdered eggs, and two dozen cans of evaporated and condensed milks.

If you have a milk cow and egg-laying chickens, this will obviously eliminate the need to store these hard-to-preserve items.

Vegetables and Fruits

Frozen, canned, jarred, dried, and freeze-dried vegetables and fruits, such as peaches in #10 cans, are another important component for your food pantry. Consider how much fruit and vegetables you like to eat in a week and multiply by 52 to build a year's supply.

Sweeteners
In addition to sweetening foods, tea, coffee, and other little luxuries, sweeteners (honey, maple syrup, sugar, Stevia) are a baking catalyst, necessary for making breads and rolls with yeast as leavening. About 50–75 pounds per adult, depending on your usage, will be more than enough for a year.

Oils and Other Fats
Good fats are necessary for your body's survival under any circumstances. Plan to acquire and store at least 60 pounds of oils and fats (including olive oil, coconut oil, safflower oil, etc.) for each adult benefiting from your food storage for long-term survival.

Leavening
Yeast, baking powder, baking soda, and/or sourdough starter are critical for baking, about 2 pounds leavening per person is typically sufficient for the year.

Salt
Plan to have 5 pounds of salt on hand for each adult.

Treats
At your discretion and according to your taste, store up coffee beans, tea, unshelled nuts, dried fruit, chocolate, and other treat items. Too much sugar has a taxing role on the body, so store candy in moderation. A little now and then may be a great morale booster, however.

Growing and Using Sprouts

Sprouts are great for everyday living and especially so in an emergency situation. Typical storage foods are traditionally low or nonexistent in vitamin C and many of the B vitamins. Yet it is exciting to note that the seeds from those same storage foods can be sprouted to give a rich source of these important nutrients. Sprouts are an excellent source of vitamin C and also contain many B vitamins.

You probably won't find a less expensive way to get these vitamins than from low calorie sprouts. Green leafy sprouts are a good source of vitamin A as well. Sprouts are high in fiber, protein, and contain enzymes that aid digestion. In addition, sprouting destroys the seed's natural preservative enzymes that inhibit digestion.

Different kinds of seeds you can sprout: The list below gives popularly sprouted seeds and is not all-inclusive, as you can sprout almost any kind of seed.

Alfalfa, radish, mung bean, sunflower, clover, and cabbage sprouts are generally eaten raw.

Kidney, pinto, and other miscellaneous beans are generally cooked.

Lentils, soy beans, green peas, and wheat are eaten raw or cooked. (In addition, all the sprouts that are generally eaten raw can be easily cooked.)

Alfalfa, one of the most popular sprouts, is a good source of vitamins A, B, C, D, E, F, K, and is rich in many minerals, as well as many enzymes needed for digestion.

Radish sprouts are high in vitamin C and potassium and have a rich flavor.

Sprouted wheat is high in Vitamins B, C, E, and has three times the vitamin E of dry wheat. Sprouted wheat also has many minerals.

Mung beans are an excellent source of protein and vitamins A, C, and E, along with many minerals.

Green-pea sprouts are rich in many of the B vitamins and vitamin C. Green pea sprouts make a rich addition to any green salad.

Soybean sprouts are an extremely rich source of protein and vitamins A, B, C and E. Soybeans are rich in minerals and lecithin.

Kidney beans, pinto beans, and miscellaneous beans are a good source of vitamin C, many of the B vitamins, and many minerals. Sprouting these beans also changes their indigestible carbohydrates to digestible carbohydrates, thereby greatly reducing the intestinal gas they otherwise cause.

Lentil sprouts are rich in protein, vitamin C, and the B vitamins. They have a mild, ground-pepper flavor.

Buckwheat sprouts make a great salad green. They are high in vitamins A, B, C, and D.

Sprouted sunflowers are a wealth of vitamins B, D, E, many minerals, and linoleic acid, the w6 EFA.

DO NOT eat tomato, pepper, or potato sprouts, as they are poisonous.

Growing Sprouts

Sprouts are easy to produce and require no special equipment or knowledge. All that is required to produce sprouts are seeds, moisture, warmth, darkness, and maybe ten minutes of your time each day.

Methods vary from high-tech production to something as simple as a quart jar or a cloth covered pan. Perhaps the simplest method is to take your seeds, place them in a quart jar, and cover them with water to start the process.

How to Grow Sprouts

It's often best to start small and continue to grow sprouts. They quickly grow and you don't want to have too many when you first start eating them.

Begin by placing 2–3 tablespoons of seeds into the glass jar.

Prepare the top of the jar by covering it with the woven fabric, screen, or pantyhose. Keep the cover secure with a rubber band, string, or lid ring.

Cover the seeds with water. Fill the jar with water to a height of 1–2 inches above the seeds.

Set the jar on the counter and allow the seeds to soak overnight.

After the seeds have soaked overnight, remove the water by simply turning the jar over and allowing the water to drain through the cloth. Ensure that all the water is out or it may cause the seeds to rot. Do not remove the seeds from the container.

Roll the container around to distribute the seeds all around the outside and let it remain on its side.

The sprouts will grow best in slightly warmer temperatures, but do not need sunlight at this point.

Rinse the seeds and jar everyday with cool water, twice a day if the temperatures are warmer. This step is important in order to remove any disease organisms or toxins that may accumulate in the jar while it sets. If a funky smell develops in the jar, you need to rinse it more often.

Continue rinsing for 4–5 days, until the sprouts are ready to harvest. Typically the sprouts will be between 1–2 inches in length when they are ready to be harvested.

Simply give them a good rinse and shake away any excess water.

After 4–5 Days

Spread the sprouts out on a tray or plate and place them in the sun for a short while, only 15 minutes or so. This allows the leaves to turn greener and important enzymes to become activated.

They're ready to use immediately on salads, sandwiches, soups, and dips—whatever you please!

Additional Tips and Advice

Not all water is fit to drink, much less grow sprouts. Ensure that you use quality water to keep your sprouts as healthy and nutritional as possible.

Use organic seeds! If you are growing your own anything, make it as healthy as possible!

If you want to remove the brown seed coats, simply place the sprouts in a bowl of water and swish them around a little. The seed coats will float to the top, where you can easily remove them.

To keep your sprouts fresh, store them in the refrigerator.

For sprouts you are going to cook, let the sprout grow only as long as the seed. For sprouts you will eat raw (except wheat), let them grow up to 2–3 inches. Expose mature alfalfa, wheatgrass, buckwheat, or sunflower sprouts to indirect sunlight for 4–5 hours. As they turn dark green, their vitamin A content dramatically increases. (This is an important step, for if you miss it, your sprouts will only have about 1 percent of this vitamin's RDA. Don't expose bean sprouts to sunlight as this will give them an unpleasant, bitter taste.) When your sprouts have grown to the desired length, rinse them again, and then put them in a sealed container, with something to absorb the water on the bottom, and store them in the refrigerator.

Sprouting Mung Beans under Pressure
Place soaked beans in a small colander inside another container. Place several layers of burlap over the top of the seeds, and then place a 3–5 pound bag of marbles or small stones on top of this. Water every 2 or 3 hours to ensure adequate moisture (this prevents the root systems from over developing in their search for water). Keep them in the dark at all times or they will turn bitter as they begin to green. When they are 2–3 inches long, remove them from the colander and refrigerate.

Using Sprouts

After sprouts reach their peak, they immediately begin to lose their vitamin C. Because of this, don't attempt to store sprouts longer than a week. Only grow small quantities of sprouts that can be used in a short period of time. If you plan on getting many of your vitamins from sprouts, it would be a good idea to have one or two small batches of sprouts growing at all times.

Cook sprouted beans using the same recipes you normally use. Sprouted beans cook in 2/3rds the time of unsprouted beans.

Heat destroys a percentage of the vitamins and enzymes gained by sprouting, so simmer or steam slowly, depending on your recipe, and don't cook longer than necessary.

You can sprout a mixture of seeds to make great green salads all by themselves. You can also use raw sprouts in just about anything:

Blended in drinks
Added to bean or lettuce salads
Mixed with already cooked breakfast cereals
Wrapped in tortilla or taco shells and smothered in your favorite sauce
Added to soups and stews just before eating
Sprout-filled won tons
Sandwiches laced with sprouts

Raw sprouts are so versatile that they can also be thrown into just about anything, then cooked:

Breads and biscuits
Soups
Pancakes
Eggs and omelets
Oatmeal or cracked wheat
Sauces
Mexican or Chinese foods
Potato patties
Casseroles
Dips
Stir fried all by themselves

When cooking sprouts it is better to steam or stir fry them, rather than boil them and discard the water. You only lose 20-30 percent of the vitamin C compared to 60 percent.

How Much to Store and Purchasing Tips
It is suggested that if you plan to get all of your vitamins from sprouts alone, that you store up to 125 lbs. of a variety

of seeds per person, per year, in a cool dark location.

If you have other sources for your vitamins, it is suggested that you have 30 pounds of seeds set aside for sprouts to be eaten raw, and 30 pounds of sprouts intended for cooking per person, per year.

Many specialty companies exist that deal exclusively in sprout seed. Usually these seeds cost several times more than other seeds of the same type. One study shows that mung beans sold exclusively for sprouting cost 4.5 times more than regular mung beans. Yet 99 percent of the time the cheaper seed will sprout and grow as quickly as the more expensive seed. It may be a waste of money to buy "sprouting seed" over regular seed. Before purchasing large amounts of storage seed intended for sprouting, purchase a small amount and test it to see if it sprouts well.

Do not attempt to store your sprouting seed for more than five years, unless it is stored in a cool (at least 60–65 degrees Fahrenheit), dry place. If you are storing large seed, it may be packed in the absence of oxygen. Seed may last up to 15 years stored in this way. As your seeds get old, they will take longer to sprout, and you will progressively get more seeds that won't sprout. The key again is to rotate, rotate, rotate.

Use several different kinds of sprouts to find out what you like before purchasing a large quantity of seed. Do not purchase seeds intended for anything except human consumption. Many seeds processed by farmers and gardeners for planting have been treated with fungicide and/or insecticide agents and are very **POISONOUS**. These seeds are usually, but not always, dyed red. If in doubt, make sure to ask.

MRE–TEOTWAWKI Battle Food

MRE stands for meal ready-to-eat and is currently the main individual operational ration for the U.S. military. The full MRE is a package about 1 foot long, 6 inches wide, and 2 inches thick. Wrapped in brown plastic and sealed at the ends, it looks like a giant candy bar. Inside the initial bag are several flat cardboard packages containing more brown pouches and, well, more brown pouches. Sorting this out is usually easy in broad daylight or in otherwise good lighting. Each brown package has black lettering on it indicating the contents. This is to keep you from boiling the package of crackers or opening the stew in your lap. MREs are meant to be completely self-contained meals that attempt to provide all the nutrition to sustain your on-the-go needs. Typical contents include entree, side dish, crackers, peanut butter/cheese spread, dessert, instant coffee/tea, matches, toilet paper, spoon, and a heater to heat the main entree. While everything in an MRE can be eaten cold, it usually tastes better warm. The packaging of an MRE is designed to withstand rough conditions and exposure to the elements. Each MRE provides an average of 1,250 calories (13% protein, 36% fat, and 51% carbohydrates) and 1/3 of the Military Recommended Daily Allowance of vitamins and minerals. A full day's worth of meals would consist of three MREs. MREs are made by contractors, following government specs, so contents can vary slightly, but quality has to stay high. You may see variations in origin and recipes, but the meals will be familiar from menu to menu.

Surprisingly, the food is generally palatable and fresh tasting. In some cases they are good, and in other cases, better than some hospital food, although not quite up to airline food. Tabasco sauce is fiendishly included in some of the meals, in a cute little bottle. There is just enough for flavor, but not enough to hurt yourself with.

This is not health food. It will keep you alive and keep you going under heavy exertion. A full day's ration should give you 4000 calories, well over the diet of most adults not running around in a battle zone. There's a lot of salt and fat in some meals—again, not a problem if you're active, but if you're using these as rations, look for supplements and go easy on the spreads and desserts.

The meals include almost no vegetables. There are tomato sauces and some small pieces of veggies, but you won't find broccoli or a salad. Fruits are also at a minimum. Most calories are from protein, starches, and fats, and generally in that order. Sauces may have extra dextrose for flavor, as well as for energy. This makes them very useful for survival (as a compact source of energy), but you will have to supplement your diet over the long run.

Officially speaking, the life of an MRE is dependent on how long, and at what temperatures, it is stored. At a minimum, MREs should last one month when stored at 120 degrees Fahrenheit (49 degrees Celsius) or five years at 50 degrees Fahrenheit (10 degrees Celsius).

 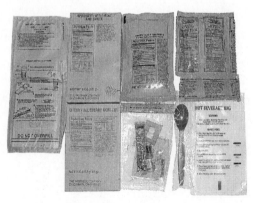

Practically speaking, they last a long, long, time. As long as the individual MRE components aren't damaged, punctured, or SWELLING, they should still be edible. If you want to really be safe, don't base your nutritional health on 10-year-old MREs. For occasional eating, they serve their purpose.

6
H2O

Contamination

Water is the most essential element to life on Earth. Without it, life wouldn't exist, including yours (three days tops). It is CRUCIAL that each person in your group has enough drinking water. In times of disaster assume any water not purchased or stored is contaminated. Even crystal clear streams can be tainted. We should value clean water as being more precious than gold. We are under the mistaken impression that our technology has permanently taken care of our water needs.

Every year 19.5 million Americans get bacterial, viral, and parasitic infections from polluted drinking water. This is frightening in the 21st century, because it's one of the oldest problems civilizations have had to deal with: keeping human waste separate from the water that we drink.

One of the most alarming discoveries of the last decade is that sewage treatment plants can't remove all contaminants from the waters of America. We're starting to see caffeine in fish. The coffee flows through us, flushes down our toilets, then goes to the sewage treatment plants, which are not equipped to remove caffeine. The caffeine flows out of the sewage plants into the nearby rivers. Maybe caffeine doesn't turn out to be a problem, but maybe something else will.

Treatment plants weren't designed to remove exotic chemicals, pharmaceuticals, or undetected viruses. None of this is surprising if you consider that unused and expired drugs can't be legally returned to the pharmacies where they were purchased. Many people just flush them down the toilet because the drug labels actually encourage patients to dispose of them this way (and they probably don't know what else to do with them).

It is also a regular protocol for hospitals to flush millions of pounds of unused medications every year, a practice that contributes significantly to water contamination. Let's not forget the drug companies that dump large amounts of their own pharmaceuticals into water supplies. Investigations have found that more than 270 million pounds of pharmaceutical compound residue is dumped every year into waterways nationwide, many of which serve as drinking water for millions of people. A 2008 Associated Press investigation found at least 46 million Americans are supplied with drinking water that has tested positive for traces of pharmaceuticals.

Since it has already been revealed that drug companies are failing to properly treat their wastewater before dumping it into rivers (even though they claim to be treating it), U.S. regulatory agencies need to step up and correct the problem. Regular monitoring of wastewater contaminant levels is the only way to halt the chemical contamination of waterways.

If U.S. companies are polluting water supplies in other countries, they should still be held accountable for their actions. There's no excuse for U.S. companies to pollute anywhere in the world just because they're operating outside of domestic borders.

A Horrific Global Water Crisis Is Coming
Rivers, lakes, and major underground aquifers all over the globe are drying up, and many of the fresh water sources that we still have available are so polluted that we simply cannot use them any longer. We are seeing drought conditions spread. We are starting to see massive "dust storms" in areas where we have never seem them before.

Every single year, most of the major deserts around the world are getting bigger, and the amount of usable agricultural land is becoming smaller. Whether you are aware of this or not, the truth is that we are rapidly approaching a breaking point. If dramatic changes are not made soon, water shortages are going to force large groups of people to move to new areas. As the global water crisis intensifies, there will be political conflicts and even wars over water. We like to think of ourselves as being so "advanced," but the reality is that we have not figured out how to live without water. When the water dries up in an area, most of the people are going to have to leave.

For instance, once Lake Mead dries up it will become impossible for so many people to live in and around Las Vegas. Right now most of us take for granted an unlimited access to clean water. When you take a hard look at the data, it quickly becomes apparent that everything is about to radically change.

Signs of an Impending Global Water Crisis

- Today, the United States uses approximately 148 trillion gallons of fresh water a year.
- According to the U.S. government, 36 U.S. states are already facing water shortages or will be facing water shortages within the next few years.
- According to the U.S. National Academy of Sciences, the U.S. Interior West is now the driest that it has been in 500 years.
- It is estimated that California only has a 20 year supply of fresh water left.
- It is estimated that New Mexico only has a 10 year supply of fresh water left.
- Things have become so dry in Arizona that now giant "dust storms" have been blowing through the city of Phoenix.
- Approximately 40 percent of all U.S. rivers and 46 percent of all U.S. lakes have become so polluted that they are now considered to be too dangerous to fish in, swim in, or get drinking water from.

- Eight states in the Great Lakes region have signed a pact banning the export of water to outsiders—even to other U.S. states.
- Worldwide demand for fresh water tripled during the last century and is now doubling every 21 years.
- It is estimated that 75 percent of the surface water in India is now contaminated by human and agricultural waste.
- If you can believe it, according to a UN study on sanitation, far more people in India have access to a cell phone than to a toilet.
- In the developing world, 90 percent of all wastewater is discharged completely untreated into local rivers, streams, or lakes.
- Every eight seconds, somewhere in the world a child dies from drinking dirty water.
- Due to a lack of water, Saudi Arabia is no longer trying to grow wheat and will be 100 percent dependent on wheat imports by the year 2016.
- Incredibly, a new desert the size of Rhode Island is created in China every single year because of drought and over pumping.
- In China, 80 percent of all major rivers have become so horribly polluted that they no longer support any aquatic life at all.
- Collectively, the women of South Africa walk the equivalent distance to the moon and back 16 times a day just to collect water.

More than a billion people around the globe do not have access to safe drinking water. That number is going to keep increasing. Without enough fresh water, people cannot grow enough food. Global food prices are already starting to skyrocket, and the coming global water crisis is only going to make matters worse. A massive, massive disaster is on the horizon. The era of endless amounts of cheap food and "unlimited" amounts of clean water is over. A horrific global water crisis is coming. You better get ready.

Water Storage Quantity

A water ration of as little as one pint per day has allowed life-raft survivors to live for weeks, but a more realistic figure is 1 gallon per person, per day for survival. Having 5 gallons per person, per day will allow personal hygiene, washing of dishes, counter tops, etc. Storing 6–12 gallons per person, per day would be needed for a conventional toilet, or ½ –2 gallons for a pour-flush latrine. For short-term emergencies, it will probably be more practical to store paper plates and utensils, and minimize food preparation, than to attempt to store more water.

In addition to stored water, there is quite a bit of water trapped in the piping of the average home. If the municipal water system was not contaminated before you shut the water off to your house, this water is still fit for consumption without treatment. To collect this water, open the lowest faucet in the system, and allow air into it from a second faucet. Depending on the diameter of the piping, you may want to open every other faucet to make sure all of the water is drained. This procedure will usually only drain the cold-water side, as the hot-water side will have to be drained from the water heater. Again, open all of the faucets to let air into the system, and be prepared to collect any water that comes out when the first faucet is opened. Toilet tanks (not the bowls) represent another source of water if a toilet bowl cleaner is not used in the tank.

Water Treatment

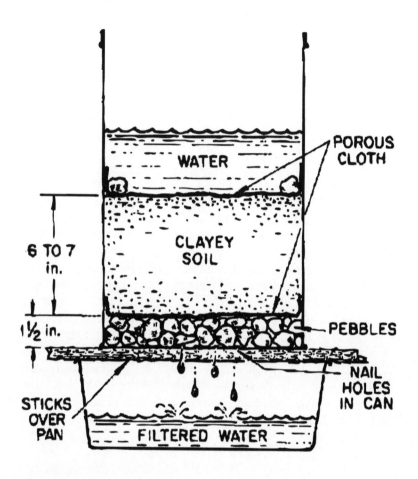

Expedient Water Filter

To make the simple, effective filter shown in the illustration, the only materials needed are those found in and around the home. This expedient filter can be built easily by proceeding as follows:

1. Perforate the bottom of a 5-gallon bucket, or similar container, with a dozen nail holes evenly spread over a 4-inch-diameter circle in the center of the container.

2. Place a 1.5 inch layer of small stones or pebbles in the bottom of the can. If pebbles aren't available, marbles, clean bottle caps, twisted coat hangers, or clean twigs can be used.

3. Cover the pebbles with one thickness of terrycloth towel, burlap sackcloth, or other porous cloth. Curl the cloth into a roughly-circular shape about 3 inches larger than the diameter of the can.

4. Take soil containing some clay (pure clay isn't porous enough and pure sand is too porous) from at least 4 inches below the surface of the ground (nearly all fallout particles remain near the surface except after disposition on sand or gravel.)

5. Pulverize the soil, and then gently press it in layers over the cloth that covers the pebbles, so that the cloth is held snugly against the walls of the can. The soil should be 6–7 inches thick.

6. Completely cover the surface of the soil layer with one thickness of fabric as porous as a bath towel. This is to keep the soil from being eroded as water is being poured into the filter. A dozen small stones placed on the cloth near its edges will secure it adequately.

7. Support the filter on rocks or sticks placed across the top of a container that is larger than the filter can (such as a dishpan). The contaminated water should be poured into the filter can, preferably after allowing it to settle as described below. The filtered water should be disinfected by some method.

If the 6–7 inches of filtering soil is a sandy-clay loam, the filter will initially deliver about 6 quarts/hour. If the filter is any faster than this, then the fabric layer needs to be removed and the soil compressed more. The filtering rate will drop over time as the filter begins to clog up. When this happens the top ½ inch of soil can be removed to increase the filtering rate. After 50 or so quarts, the filter will need to be rebuilt with fresh soil.

As with any filter, optimum performance will be achieved if sediment in the water will be allowed to settle out before passing the water through the filter. If the water is contaminated with fallout, clay can be added to help the fallout particles to settle out. The procedure is as follows:

1. Fill a bucket or other deep container 3/4 full with contaminated water.

2. Dig pulverized clay or clayey soil from a depth of 4 inches or more below ground surface and stir it into the water.

3. Use about 1 inch of dry clay or clayey soil for every 4 inches depth of water. Stir until practically all of the clay particles are suspended in the water.

4. Let the clay settle for at LEAST 6 hours. This will carry the fallout particles to the bottom and cover them.

5. Carefully dip out or siphon the clear water and disinfect it.

Boiling

This process is recognized as the safest treatment method. Bring water to a rolling boil for a minimum of 10 minutes. Cover the pot to shorten the time it takes to boil. For every 1000 feet (305 meters) above sea level, add one more minute to the boiling time.

Boiling water removes all chlorine, as well as the bacteria. If you don't plan on drinking the water right away, add bleach.

While the boiled water cools, keep it covered with a lid, as airborne bacteria can contaminate it. Anything that is not sterile (like a water storage container) may have bacteria in it. Boiling water only kills the germs in the water, so make sure that the water container used has also been decontaminated.

Bleach

In an emergency, think of one gallon of Clorox Regular-Bleach as 3,800 gallons of drinking water. When the tap water stops flowing, bleach isn't just a laundry aid, it's a lifesaver. It's the same in any natural disaster. As the shock wears off and the days wear on, the biggest demand is for drinking water. Time after time, relief crews hand out free Clorox with simple instructions: use it to kill bacteria in your water, and you'll have purified water to drink.

Here are the general guidelines. First, let water stand until particles settle. Filter the particles if necessary with layers of cloth, coffee filters, or fine paper towels. Pour the clear water into an uncontaminated container and add bleach per the ratio indicated below. Mix well. Wait 30 minutes. Water should have a slight odor of bleach. If not, repeat dose. Wait 15 minutes. Sniff again. Keep an eyedropper taped to your emergency bottle of Clorox, since purifying small amounts of water requires only a few drops. Bleach must be fresh for best use and results. A Clorox bleach representative had this to say:

> We recommend storing our bleach at room temperatures. It can be stored for about 6 months at temperatures between 50 and 70 degrees Fahrenheit. After this time, bleach will begin to degrade at a rate of 20% each year until totally degraded to salt and water. Storing at temperatures much higher than 70 degrees Fahrenheit could cause the bleach to lose its effectiveness and degrade more rapidly. However, if you require 6% sodium hypochlorite, you should change your supply every 3 months.

Don't pour purified water into contaminated containers. Sanitize water jugs first. Without water and electricity, even everyday tasks are tough. In lieu of steaming hot water, sanitize dishes, pots and utensils with a little bleach. Just follow the directions listed to keep dishes clean.

Whether you use bleach in an emergency or for everyday chores, it's always an environmentally sound choice. After its work is done, bleach breaks down to little more than salt and water, which is acceptable anytime.

Ratio of Bleach to Water for Purification

2 drops of Clorox Regular-Bleach per quart of water

8 drops of Clorox Regular-Bleach per gallon of water

1/2 teaspoon Clorox Regular-Bleach per 5 gallons of water

If water is cloudy, double the recommended dosages of bleach. Use ONLY Clorox Regular-Bleach, without scents, dyes, or additives. To insure that bleach is at its full strength, rotate or replace your storage bottles—at minimum every three months.

Clorox Bleach Sanitizing Solution
To sanitize containers and utensils, mix one tablespoon Clorox Regular-Bleach with 1 gallon of water. Always wash and rinse items first, and then let each item soak in the Clorox-bleach sanitizing solution for 2 minutes. Drain and air dry.

Dry Chlorine
Calcium hypochlorite has the added benefit of extended shelf life over household bleach, providing it's kept dry, cool, and in an airtight container. Dry chlorine may be stored up to 10 years with minimal degradation. If you want to keep chlorine in larger quantities, this is the item to store. It's available at swimming pool supply stores and many hardware and grocery stores. It also requires less storage space than its liquid counterpart. When purchasing calcium hypochlorite, make sure there are no other active ingredients in it. Calcium hypochlorite is the solid form with 65%–70% strength and sodium hypochlorite is the liquid form. BE CAREFUL, but don't be overly frightened. Just remember to keep it dry,

don't breathe the fumes, and add to water wearing gloves. Using simple precautions make it an excellent choice.

Iodine

Iodine emerged as a water purifier after WW2, when the US military looked for a replacement for Halazone tablets. Iodine was found to be in many ways superior to chlorine in treating small batches of water. Iodine is less sensitive to pH and organic content of water and is effective in lower doses.

Iodine is normally used in doses of 8ppm to treat clear water for a 10 minute contact time. The effectiveness of this dose has been shown in numerous studies. Cloudy water needs twice as much iodine or twice as much contact time. In cold water (below 41 degrees Fahrenheit or 5 degrees Celsius), you must double the dose or time. In any case, doubling the treatment time allows you to use half as much iodine.

If no instructions are provided on the container, use 12 drops per gallon of water. If the water is in question, double the amount of iodine. Mix well and allow the water to stand for 30 minutes before using. Iodine is light sensitive, must be stored in a dark bottle, and works best in water over 68 degrees Fahrenheit (21 degrees Celsius).

Make Rainwater Safe to Drink

Rainwater must be kept free of contamination to be safe to drink. To make sure the water you collect will be safe:

- Clean the tank, entrance pipe, roof, and roof gutters before the rainy season.
- Never collect water in containers that have been used for oil, pesticides, or other toxic chemicals.
- Allow the first rains of each year to run through the tank to clean it.
- Cover the tank and place a filter or screen over the inlets to keep out insects, leaves, and dirt. This will also help prevent mosquitoes from breeding.

- Take out water through taps, if possible. If water is removed with buckets or other containers, make sure they are clean.
- For added safety, add chlorine to the tank or connect a water filter to the tank.
- Do not stir or move the water. Any dirt or germs in the tank will settle and stay at the bottom that way.
- Sweeping the roof from time to time will also help keep collected rainwater clean.

Disinfect Water with Sunlight

Solar disinfection is an effective way to disinfect water using only sunlight and a bottle. Filtering or settling the water first will make it clearer so it will disinfect more quickly.

1. Clean a clear plastic/glass bottle or a plastic bag. Bottles made of PET plastic work best.

2. Fill the bottle half-full and then shake it for 20 seconds. This will add air bubbles to the water.

3. Then fill the bottle or bag to the top. The air bubbles will help to disinfect the water faster.

4. Place the bottle where there's no shade and where people and animals will not disturb it, such as the roof of a house. Leave the bottle for at least six hours in full sun or for two days if the weather is cloudy.

5. Drink directly from the bottle. This will prevent contamination from hands or other vessels.

Finding and Storing Urban Water

Besides storing at least 1 gallon of drinking water per person per day, there are several other ways you can quickly find and store water in a disaster scenario.

- Fill your bathtubs, sinks, pots, and any other large containers that can store water.

- Immediately turn off your water main to stop any contamination that will enter your water-heater tank.
- Water bed
- Back of toilet
- Ice cubes
- Rainwater
- Melting snow and ice
- Drained from canned food
- Parks
- City water fountains
- Aquariums
- Zoos
- Drainage ditches

Water from all open sources must be treated before consuming. First, a pre-filtering that removes large matter is accomplished by pouring the water through:

- A bandanna
- T-shirt
- Cheese cloth
- Bath towel
- Socks
- Pant legs

Staying Hydrated
You can never rely on your thirst as a proper way to gauge adequate hydration. You can judge how hydrated you are by the clearness and frequency of your urination, along with the amount produced. Most people will not drink enough water to stay properly hydrated on their own and will need to be reminded.

Signs of Mild to Moderate Dehydration

- Headache
- Dizziness
- Nausea

- Dry mouth
- Fatigue
- Dark urine

Signs of Severe Dehydration

- Extreme thirst
- Lack of sweating
- Convulsions
- Rapid breathing
- Low blood pressure
- Unconsciousness

People with a Greater Risk of Dehydration

- Infants and children
- Elderly
- Sick/chronically ill
- High altitudes
- Exercise
- Extremes in weather: hot/dry/cold/humidity
- Burn injuries
- Pregnant and nursing mothers

Remember: water is not just used for drinking, but also for hygiene and sanitation. Don't forget to calculate this into your survival planning. Drinking and hygiene needs must be met by potable water, but sanitation can be handled by non-potable water.

Water Storage Guidelines

- Food-grade containers (BPA free)
- Sturdy and leak proof
- Store out of light
- Keep away from chemicals and fuel
- Store where it won't freeze
- Treat water first if collected from an open source

- Factor in weight for storage and mobility (approximately 8 pounds per gallon).
- Do not store directly on cement or on dirt (to prevent lye leaching). Always store on a pallet or platform.
- Place any large-size water containers where you plan on storing them, BEFORE filling them. A filled 55-gallon barrel weighs about 483 pounds.
- Fill them up using a white "drinking" hose, if possible, as the green or black garden hoses tend to have lead in them.
- Consider where you are storing plastic bottles. After time, they leach the odors around them, causing a toxic flavor in the water. To prevent this, rotate every 3 months, unless treated with a preserver.
  — If you store them in the garage, they could taste like a lawn mower.
  — If you store them in the trunk of the car, they will taste like a car tire.
- Rotate bottles every 2–3 months, if temperatures consistently exceed 120 degrees, like in a hot car over the summertime. The chemical reaction with the heat and plastic can cause health problems.
- Check containers every few months for leaks. At the same time check the water for cloudiness or undesirable appearance or taste. If undesirable appearance or taste has developed the water should be discarded.
- One case of 24 bottles (16.9 ounces) = 3 gallons of water
- When stored in clean containers, away from sunlight, and when free from bacteria at the time of storage, water will remain safe. Most disease-producing organisms tend to die during long storage. Generally, the longer the water is stored, the safer it will become bacteriologically.

Water-Storage Options

5–7 gallon containers

These are ideal for daily use or for bugging out because they are easy to fill, move, and use. Stick with a name brand that says BPA free and has a good seal on the screw-on cap to keep your water fresh and prevent leaking. Seven gallons is about the most you can have for a container that is considered portable—it weights nearly 60 pounds when full.

15–55 Gallon Barrels

These barrels can be purchased inexpensively from food-processing plants or Craigslist; just make sure they are food-grade plastic. Prior to filling, make sure to thoroughly clean any residue out. Over time the previous contents may have leached into the plastic. When stored, the previous flavors may reintroduce themselves to the water; they won't hurt you, but who wants that after taste.

275 Gallon IBC Totes

IBC stands for intermediate bulk container. IBC totes are large tanks that are used to store and transport fluids and other bulk materials. IBC tanks are composed of three primary components—the IBC plastic container bottle, the IBC metal cage, and the container's pallet, which can be made from wood, plastic, or metal. You can purchase them for as little as $65 each from food processing plants and Craigslist. Just make sure they are local and you can pick them up, otherwise the shipping will kill you.

They can be stacked vertically to conserve space, and from what I've read, buried as well. They can be connected to your rain gutter, thus creating an awesome rainwater collection setup.

Cleaning Used Food-Grade Containers

Spray Down

1. Depending on what was previously stored in your 55-gallon drum or tote, you may have the ingredients all over the inside and outside of the container. Clear off all residual matter so that when filled with water, you don't contaminate it. Also, fill-up the inside with about 5 gallons of water and swish it around for a couple of minutes. You want to get most of the easy gunk out so the bleach can break down the tough stuff.

   After swishing it around for about 3–4 minutes, dump it out. If you have remaining ingredients in the container, make sure the water is coming out crystal clear. If it isn't, swish it around a little longer to break-up the ingredients.

   After cleaning out the container, rinse off the bung (if it has one) and the threads around the hole, to get any ingredients off of them as well.

Disinfect with Bleach

2. Fill 1/3 of your drum with water. Add 1 cup of bleach. Secure bung with your bung wrench so you can toss this thing around without the water spilling out. Aggressively shake your drum for 5–10 minutes. Hold it upright and shake it back and forth. Put it on its side and roll it around. Do whatever you have to do to make the water violently hit every square inch of your drum.

   For a tote: add 4–6 cups of bleach, fill to the top with water, then let sit for 20 minutes, then drain.

Dump, Test, and Repeat if Necessary

3. Unscrew your bung and check your drum. Come up with some sort of test to determine if the ingredients have been removed. For example, one of mine contained safflower oil, so I checked the side walls to see if there were any visual remnants of the oil and then smelled inside of the drum to see if I could still pick-up any scent. If I could only smell the bleach, I stopped cleaning it. If I still smelled the oil, I repeated step 2.

   Once you've cleaned your drum appropriately, drain it.

Rinse

4. If you have a high-pressure valve attachment for your hose, screw it on. If not, get ready to use the old thumb to create a high pressure rinse. Spray out the inside of the drum thoroughly. Once it's rinsed out, drain it.

   Replace your bung and spray off the outside of the drum or tote.

   This completes the cleaning process. It should now be as good as new!

7
FIRST AID

Nobody likes to think about medical emergencies and accidents, especially if there are no hospitals available or a wait time that would defeat the purpose. In the course of everyday events, accidents and injuries can happen to anyone. A well-stocked first-aid kit is imperative!

 Everyone should have a well-stocked first-aid kit handy at home, in the car, and in the workplace. The contents of your kit will vary depending upon the number of people it is designed to serve, as well as special circumstances where it will be used.

For example, a first-aid kit in a factory where there may be danger of flying debris getting into the eye should certainly have a sterile eyewash solution in its kit. If a family member is a known diabetic, your kit at home should have glucose or sugar solution. When assembling your first aid kit, whether for use in the home, car, or at work, you should consider possible injuries you are likely to encounter and then select kit contents to treat those conditions. It's also important to check your kit periodically to restock items that have been used and to replace items that have expired.

This is just a basic intro to first aid; I would highly suggest you take a CPR course and pick up the best first-aid book you can find for TEOTWAWKI. Get proper training from a qualified organization in your area. Training from an experienced instructor is the best way to be prepared in an emergency.

Recommended Contents for a First-Aid Kit (Modify to Suit Your Particular Needs)

- CPR kit
- First aid manual
- Required prescription medication
- Activated Charcoal
- 100-proof whiskey
- Hydrogen peroxide
- Isopropyl alcohol
- Alcohol-based hand sanitizer
- Tincture of iodine
- Germicidal hand wipes
- Colloidal Silver
- Latex or vinyl gloves
- Potassium iodide (KI) tablets
- Oral Rehydration Salts
- Pedialyte
- Tylenol, Ibuprofen, Aspirin
- Infant Tylenol drops
- Oscillococcinum
- Cough drops
- Eye drops
- Vicks vapor rub
- Mucus relief
- Benadryl
- Castor oil
- Tea tree oil
- Clove oil
- Anti-diarrhea
- Petroleum jelly
- Caladryl lotion
- Insect-sting wipe-ups
- Bug repellent 100% DEET
- Sunscreen 85 SPF
- Baby powder
- Soap

- Splinter-removal kit
- Dermoplast spray
- Hydrocortisone cream
- Triple antibiotic cream
- Nystatin and Triamcinolone
- Acetonide cream
- Antifungal Cream
- Ipecac syrup
- Condoms
- Pads and tampons
- EpiPen
- Dermabond
- Gauze, telfa pads, 4x4, 2x2
- Roller gauze (self-adhering)
- Mastisol liquid adhesive
- Bandages (assorted sizes)
- Butterfly bandages
- Moleskin
- Universal military splint
- Burn gel
- Quikclot or Celox
- Israeli Bandages
- Tourniquet
- EMT shears
- Tweezers
- Safety pins
- Hypoallergenic tape
- Tongue blades
- Flashlight
- Chemical ice packs
- Chemical hot packs
- Cotton balls
- Cotton swabs
- CPR mask
- Saline solution
- Digital thermometer
- Lace-up ankle brace

- Ace bandages
- Gold Bond foot powder
- Mole skin
- Epsom salt
- Baking soda
- Blood-pressure cuff
- Stethoscope
- Dental instruments
- Magnifying glass
- Duct tape
- Space blankets

Heimlich Maneuver

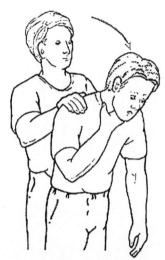

1. Lean the person forward slightly and stand behind him or her.

2. Make a fist with one hand.

3. Put your arms arund the person and grasp your fist with your other hand near the top of the stomach, just below the center of the rib cage.

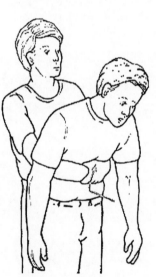

4. Make a quick, hard movement, inward and upward.

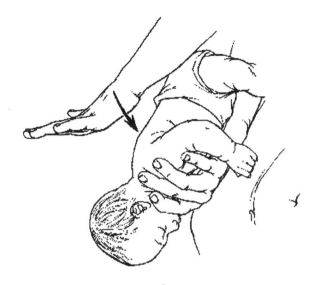

Heimlich Maneuver on Baby

Use the heel of one hand to give up to 5 back slaps between the baby's shoulder blades. If the object does not pop out, support the baby's head and turn him or her face up on your thigh. Keep the baby's head lower than his or her body. Place 2 or 3 fingers just below the nipple line on the baby's breastbone and give 5 quick chest thrusts (same position as chest compressions in CPR for a baby)

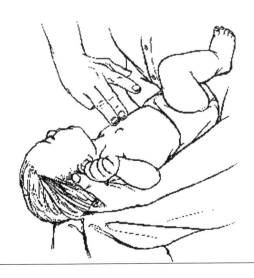

Heimlich Maneuver on Unconscious Victim

For small rescuers and large victims, particularly children rescuing an adult: Instead of standing behind the victim, have the victim lie down on his or her back. Straddle the victim's waist. Place one hand on the belly, halfway between the belly button and the edge of the breastbone. Thrust inward and upward. This is the same technique used in unconscious people.

The main difference in performing the Heimlich maneuver on a pregnant woman is in the placement of the fists. Instead of using abdominal thrusts, chest thrusts are used. The fists are placed against the middle of the breastbone, and the motion of the chest thrust is in and downward, rather than upward. If the victim is unconscious, the chest thrusts are similar to those used in CPR.

The Heimlich Maneuver On Oneself

There are two ways to perform the Heimlich maneuver on one's self. The first method is much like those conducted on others.

- Place balled fists together, about 2 inches above the navel, but below the breastbone. Thrust forcefully upward and into the abdomen. Repeat until the blockage is cleared. This may be difficult, as the angle at which one must place one's arms in order to achieve this compression can be hard to reach, especially with the force required to dislodge a tracheal blockage.
- If not cleared, alternatively lean over a chair or similar prop to attempt compression. One must place himself over a chest-high chair, and if possible, force himself upon it quickly and forcefully, in an attempt to thrust out the blockage. This may, depending upon strength and stature, be more or less effective than the traditional fisted method.

Many people find it difficult to perform the Heimlich maneuver upon one's self, for much the same reason that it is difficult to slap, cut, or otherwise hurt one's self—the natural instinct against self-infliction of pain. However, one must do what is possible to ensure that the necessary force is used, because consciousness will quickly fail in conditions of hypoxia, as with tracheal blockage. To fall unconscious in a room alone with a blocked airway is, needless to say, at best dangerous and at most deadly.

Immediate First-Aid Actions

Remember the **ABC**s of emergency care: **a**irway-**b**reathing-**c**irculation? Well, that's all changed. Now the acronym is **CAB**: **c**irculation-**a**irway-**b**reathing. In 2010, the American Heart Association made a radical change to the recommended CPR process for victims of cardiac arrest. Now, studies have shown that compression-only CPR (no mouth-to-mouth breathing) has equal standing with the traditional **a**irway-**b**reathing-**c**ompression approach. In an attempt to encourage bystanders to perform CPR, the AHA has modified the procedure to **CAB** (**c**ompression-**a**irway-**b**reathing) and stated that individuals can skip the latter two steps as they wait for emergency services to arrive.

1. **Check the scene for dangers.** If you come across someone who is unconscious, you need to quickly make sure there are no dangers to yourself if you choose to help that person. Is there a running car emitting exhaust? A gas stove? Is there a fire? Are electrical lines down?

   - If there is anything that could endanger you or the victim, see if there is something you can do to counteract it.
     Open a window, turn off the stove, or put out the fire if possible. Anything you can do to counteract the danger.
   - However, if there is nothing you can do to counteract the danger, move the victim. The best way to move the victim is by placing a blanket or a coat underneath their back and pulling on the coat or blanket.

2. **Check the victim for consciousness by shaking or tapping their shoulder and saying in a loud, clear voice, "Are you okay? Are you okay?"**

- If they respond, they are conscious. They may have just been sleeping, or they could have been unconscious. If it still appears to be an emergency situation (e.g. they are having trouble breathing, they appear to be fading in between consciousness and unconsciousness, they were unconscious, etc.) call for help and begin basic first aid and take measures to prevent or treat shock.
- If they do not respond, continue with the following steps.

3. Send for help. The more people available for this step the better, however, it can be done alone. Send someone to call the Emergency Medical Services (EMS).

   - Call **911** in North America, **000** in Australia, **112** by cell phone in the EU (including the UK) and **999** in the UK.

4. **Check the victim's pulse**. Do not check for more than 10 seconds. If the victim does not have a pulse, continue with CPR and the next steps.

   - To check the neck (carotid) pulse, feel for a pulse on the side of the victim's neck closest to you by placing the tips of your first two fingers beside his Adam's apple.

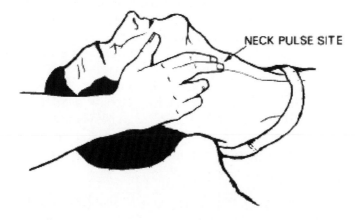

NECK PULSE SITE

- To check the wrist (radial) pulse, place your first two fingers on the thumb side of the victim's wrist.

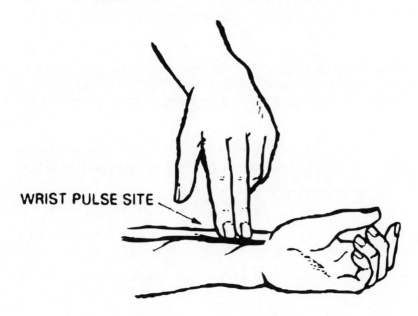

WRIST PULSE SITE

- Other pulse locations are the groin and ankle. To check the groin (femoral) pulse, press the tips of two fingers into the middle of the groin. To check the ankle (posterial tibial) pulse, place your first two fingers on the inside of the ankle.

5. **Perform CPR for one minute (which is about three cycles of CPR) and then call the EMS before resuming with CPR.** If possible, send someone else to get an **AED** (**a**utomatic **e**xternal **d**efibrillator) if there is one in the building.

6. **Remember CAB**: Chest compressions-airway-breathing. In 2010, the AHA changed the recommended sequence to deliver chest compressions before airway opening and rescue breathing. Chest compressions are more critical for correcting abnormal heart rhythms (ventricular fibrillation or pulseless ventricular tachycardia), and because one cycle of 30 chest compressions only require 18 seconds, airway opening and rescue breathing are not significantly delayed.

7. **Give 30 chest compressions**. Place your hands on top of each other and place them on the sternum, or in the center of the chest (on the breastbone) between the two nipples. Your ring finger should be on top of the nipple (this will lower the chances of breaking a rib or ribs).

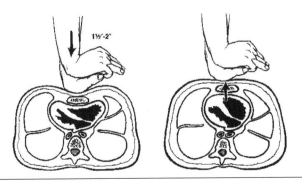

- Compress the chest, with elbows locked, by pushing straight down at least 2 inches deep.
- Do 30 of these compressions, and do them at a rate of at least 100 compressions per minute.
- Allow complete chest recoil after each compression.
- Minimize pauses in chest compression that occur when changing providers or preparing for a shock. Attempt to limit interruptions to less than 10 seconds.

8. **Make sure the airway is open**. Place your hand on the victim's forehead and two fingers on their chin and tilt the head back to open the airway (if you suspect a neck injury, pull the jaw forward rather than lifting the chin). If jaw thrust fails to open the airway, do a careful head tilt and chin lift.

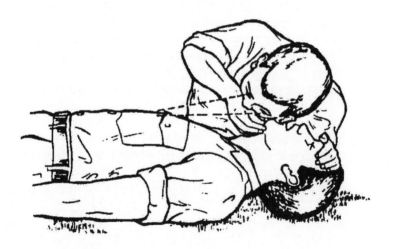

9. **If there are no signs of life, place a breathing barrier (if available) over the victim's mouth.**

10. **Give two rescue breaths**. Keeping the airway open, take the fingers that were on the forehead and pinch the victim's nose closed. Make a seal with your mouth over the victim's mouth and breathe out for about one second. Make sure you breathe slowly, as this will make sure the air goes in the lungs not the stomach. Make sure you keep your eye on the victim's chest.

- If the breath goes in, you should see the chest slightly rise and also feel it go in. If the breath goes in, give a second rescue breath.
- If the breath does not go in, re-position the head and try again. If it does not go in again, the victim may be choking. Give five abdominal thrusts (the Heimlich maneuver) to remove the obstruction.

    1. Straddle the victim.
    2. Place a fist between breastbone and belly button.
    3. Thrust upward to expel air from stomach. Sweep with finger to clear mouth.
    4. Try 2 slow breaths again.
    5. If the airway is still blocked, continue until successful or exhausted.

11. **Repeat the cycle of 30 chest compressions and 2 breaths**. You should do CPR for 2 minutes (5 cycles of compressions to breaths) before checking for signs of life. Continue CPR until someone takes over for you, emergency personnel arrive, you are too exhausted to continue, an AED is available for immediate use, or pulse and breathing return (signs of life).

To Perform CPR on a Child

The procedure for giving CPR to a child age 1 through 8 is essentially the same as that for an adult. The differences are as follows:

1. **If you're alone, perform five cycles of compressions and breaths on the child**—this should take about two minutes—before calling 911 or your local emergency number or using an AED.

2. **Use only one hand to perform heart compressions. Breathe more gently.**

3. **Use the same compression-breath rate as is used for adults: 30 compressions followed by two breaths.** This is one cycle. Following the two breaths, immediately begin the next cycle of compressions and breaths.

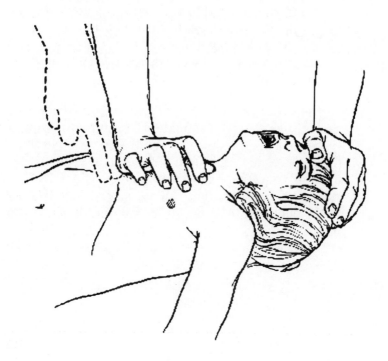

4. **After five cycles (about two minutes) of CPR, if there is no response and an AED is available, apply it and follow the prompts.** Use pediatric pads if available. If pediatric pads aren't available, use adult pads.

5. **Continue until the child moves or help arrives.**

To perform CPR on a Baby

Most cardiac arrests in babies occur from lack of oxygen, such as from drowning or choking. If you know the baby has an airway obstruction, perform first aid for choking. If you don't know why the baby isn't breathing, perform CPR.

1. **If there's no response (DON'T SHAKE the baby to check, though) and you're the only rescuer and CPR is needed, do CPR for two minutes**—about five cycles—before calling 911 or your local emergency number.

2. **Place the baby on his or her back on a firm, flat surface, such as a table.** The floor or ground also will do.

3. **Imagine a horizontal line drawn between the baby's nipples.** Place two fingers of one hand just below this line, in the center of the chest.

4. **Gently compress the chest about 1.5 inches** After 30 compressions, at a rate of at least 100 compressions per minute, gently tip the head back by lifting the chin with one hand and pushing down on the forehead with the other hand.

5. **In no more than 10 seconds, put your ear near the baby's mouth and check for breathing:** Look for chest motion, listen for breath sounds, and feel for breath on your cheek and ear.

6. **Cover the baby's mouth and nose with your mouth. Prepare to give two rescue breaths.** Use the strength of your cheeks to deliver gentle puffs of air (instead of deep breaths from your lungs) to slowly breathe into the baby's mouth one time, taking one second for the breath. Watch to see if the baby's chest rises. If it does, give a second rescue breath. If the chest does not rise, repeat the head-tilt, chin-lift maneuver and then give the second breath.

7. **If the baby's chest still doesn't rise, examine the mouth to make sure no foreign material is inside.** If the object is seen, sweep it out with your finger. If the airway seems blocked, perform first aid for a choking baby.

8. **Give two breaths after every 30 chest compressions.**

9. **Continue CPR until you see signs of life or until medical personnel arrive.**

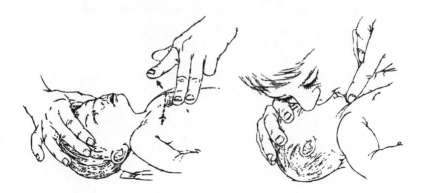

Warnings

- Remember that a baby's lungs are small, so each of your breaths during rescue breathing should not be too big. Lung or stomach damage can occur if you breathe too forcefully during this time.
- Do not perform chest compressions if the infant starts breathing again, since this action can stop the heart.

If Victim is Unconscious, but Breathing

- Keep head and neck aligned with body.
- Roll victim on side (drains the mouth and prevents the tongue from blocking airway).

CAUTION: DO NOT remove an impaled object unless it interferes with the airway. You may cause more tissue damage and increase bleeding. For travel, you may shorten and secure the object.

Control bleeding as follows

1. Apply a pressure dressing

2. If STILL bleeding—

   - Use direct pressure over the wound.
   - Elevate the wounded area above the heart.

3. If STILL bleeding—

   - Use a pressure point between the injury and the heart.
   - Maintain pressure for six to ten minutes before checking to see if bleeding has stopped.

4. If a limb wound is STILL bleeding—

CAUTION: Use of a tourniquet is a **LAST RESORT** measure. Use **ONLY** when severe, uncontrolled bleeding will cause loss of life. Recognize that long-term use of a tourniquet may cause loss of limb.

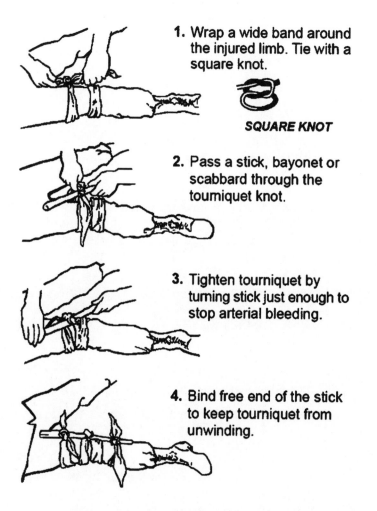

1. Wrap a wide band around the injured limb. Tie with a square knot.

    SQUARE KNOT

2. Pass a stick, bayonet or scabbard through the tourniquet knot.

3. Tighten tourniquet by turning stick just enough to stop arterial bleeding.

4. Bind free end of the stick to keep tourniquet from unwinding.

- Apply tourniquet (TK) band just above bleeding site on limb. A band at least 3 inches or wider is best.
- Follow steps illustrated.
- Use a stick at least 6 inches long.

- Tighten only enough to stop arterial bleeding.
- Mark a **TK** on the forehead with the time applied.

CAUTION: The following directions apply **ONLY** in survival situations where rescue is **UNLIKELY** and **NO** medical aid is available.

5. If rescue or medical aid is not available for over 2 hours, an attempt to SLOWLY loosen the tourniquet may be made 20 minutes after application. Before loosening—

- Ensure pressure dressing is in place.
- Ensure bleeding has stopped
- Loosen tourniquet **SLOWLY** to restore circulation.
- Leave loosened tourniquet in position in case bleeding resumes.

Treat Shock

(Shock is difficult to identify or treat under field conditions. It may be present with or without visible injury.)

1. Identify by one or more of the following:

- Pale, cool, and sweaty skin.
- Fast breathing and a weak, fast pulse.
- Anxiety or mental confusion.
- Decreased urine output.

2. Maintain circulation.

3. Treat underlying injury.

4. Maintain normal body temperature.

- Remove wet clothing.
- Give warm fluids.

- **DO NOT** give fluids to an unconscious victim.
- **DO NOT** give fluids if they cause victim to gag.
- Insulate from ground.
- Shelter from the elements.

5. Place conscious victim on back.

6. Place very weak or unconscious victim on side, this will—

   - Allow mouth to drain.
   - Prevent tongue from blocking airway.

Treat Chest Injuries

A sucking chest wound occurs when the chest wall is penetrated: may cause victim to gasp for breath, may cause a sucking sound, may create bloody froth as air escapes the chest.

- Immediately seal wound with hand or airtight material.
- Tape airtight material over wound on 3 sides only to allow air to escape from the wound but not to enter.
- Monitor breathing and check dressing.
- Lift untapped side of dressing as victim exhales to allow trapped air to escape, as necessary.

Flail Chest

Flail chest results from blunt trauma when three or more ribs are broken in two or more places. The flail segment is the broken area that moves in a direction opposite to the rest of chest during breathing.

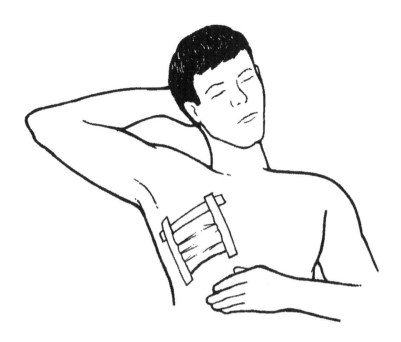

Stabilize the flail segment as follows:

- Place rolled-up clothing or bulky pad over site.
- Tape pad to site
- **DO NOT** wrap tape around chest.
- Have victim keep segment still with hand pressure.
- Roll victim onto side of flail segment injury (as other injuries allow).

Fractured Ribs

Encourage deep breathing (painful, but necessary to prevent the possible development of pneumonia). **DO NOT** constrict breathing by taping ribs.

Treat Fractures, Sprains, and Dislocations

1. Control bleeding.

2. Remove watches, jewelry, and constrictive clothing.

3. If fracture penetrates the skin—

    - Clean wound by gentle irrigation with water.
    - Apply dressing over wound.

4. Position limb as normally as possible.

5. Splint in position found (if unable to straighten limb).

6. Improvise a splint with available materials:

    - Sticks or straight, stiff materials from equipment.
    - Body parts (for example, opposite leg, arm-to-chest).

7. Attach with strips of cloth, parachute cord, etc.

8. Keep the fractured bones from moving by immobilizing the joints on both sides of the fracture. If fracture is in a joint, immobilize the bones on both sides of the joint.

CAUTION: Splint fingers in a slightly flexed position, **NOT** in straight position. Hand should look like it is grasping an apple.

9. Use **RICES** treatment for 72 hours.

    - **R**est
    - **I**ce

- **C**ompression
- **E**levation
- **S**tabilization

10. Apply cold to acute injuries.

11. Use 15–20 minute periods of cold application.

   - **DO NOT** use continuous cold therapy.
   - Repeat three to four times per day.
   - Avoid cooling that can cause frostbite or hypothermia.

12. Wrap with a compression bandage after cold therapy.

13. Elevate injured area above heart level to reduce swelling.

14. Check periodically for a pulse beyond the injury site.

15. Loosen bandage or reapply splint if no pulse is felt or if swelling occurs because bandage is too tight.

Common Injuries and Illnesses

Burns

1. Cool the burned area with water.

   - Use immersion or cool compresses.
   - Avoid aggressive cooling with ice or frigid water.

2. Remove watches, jewelry, and constrictive clothing.

3. **DO NOT** remove embedded, charred material that will cause burned areas to bleed.

4. Cover with sterile dressings.

5. **DO NOT** use lotion or grease.

6. Avoid moving or rubbing the burned part.

7. Drink **extra** water to compensate for increased fluid loss from burns. (Add **1/4 teaspoon** of **salt** [if available] to each quart of **water**.)

8. Change dressings when soaked or dirty.

Heat Injury

1. Heat cramps (cramps in legs or abdomen).

   - Rest in shade.
   - Drink water. Add **1/4 teaspoon** of salt per **quart**.

2. Heat exhaustion (pale, sweating, moist, cool skin).

   - Rest in shade.
   - Drink water.
   - Protect from further heat exposure.

3. Heat stroke (victim disoriented or unconscious, skin is hot and flushed [sweating **may** or **may not** occur], fast pulse):

CAUTION: Handle heat stroke victim gently. Shock, seizures, and cardiac arrest can occur.

   - Cool as rapidly as possible (saturate clothing with water and fan the victim). Remember to cool the groin and armpit areas. (Avoid overcooling.)
   - Maintain airway, breathing, and circulation.

Hypothermia

Hypothermia is a progressive injury. Intense shivering with impaired ability to perform complex tasks leads to:

- Violent shivering, difficulty speaking, sluggish thinking
- Muscular rigidity with blue, puffy skin, and jerky movements
- Coma, respiratory, and cardiac failure.

Protect Victim from the Environment

- Remove wet clothing.
- Put on dry clothing (if available).
- Prevent further heat loss.
- Cover top of head.
- Insulate from above and below.
- Warm with blankets, sleeping bags, or shelter.
- Warm central areas before extremities.
- Place heat packs in groin, armpits, and around neck.

CAUTION: Handle hypothermia victim gently. Avoid overly rapid rewarming which may cause cardiac arrest. Rewarming of victim with skin-to-skin contact by volunteer(s) inside of a sleeping bag is a survival technique (but can cause internal temperatures of all to drop).

Dysentery and Diarrhea

1. Drink extra water.

2. Use a liquid diet.

3. Eat charcoal. Make a paste by mixing fine charcoal particles with water. (It may relieve symptoms by absorbing toxins.)

Constipation (can be expected in survival situations).

- **DO NOT** take laxatives.
- Exercise.
- Drink **extra** water.

Rules for Avoiding Illness

- Purify all water obtained from natural sources by using iodine tablets, bleach, or boiling for five minutes.
- Locate latrines 200 feet from water and away from shelter.
- Wash hands before preparing food or water.
- Clean all eating utensils after each meal.
- Prevent insect bites by using repellent, netting, and clothing.
- Dry wet clothing as soon as possible.
- Eat varied diet.
- Try to get 7–8 hours of sleep per day.

LEAVE THE BULLET ALONE
"In the movies, you'll take your big bowie knife and stick it in a fire, slug down some whiskey and start digging, but that doesn't make a lot of sense," says Dr. Jason Koh, Vice Chairman of the Orthopedic Surgery Department in the NorthShore University Health System. Most of the time, doctors opt to leave the bullet where it is and just repair the damage it's done, Koh says. The risk of infection is surprisingly low. "[Infection] doesn't seem to be that common, in part because the bullet is pretty hot [and therefore sterile]," Koh explains. Put those pliers away: Instead, wash the area, apply pressure to stop the bleeding and hope the bullet didn't shred any vital organs.

DELIVER A BABY

Once again, you shouldn't go imitating what you've seen in the movies. "You don't need to boil any water or tear any sheets," says Dr. Robert Kelsey, Assistant Professor of Obstetrics and Gynecology at Northwestern University Medical School. Instead, get a clean towel, a shoelace, and a turkey baster. Don't rush the little bugger: "You shouldn't pull at all, because you can cause injury to the baby," Kelsey says. Once he's made his grand entrance, Kelsey says, wrap him in the towel and use the turkey baster to gently suck any liquid out of his nose and mouth. Use the shoelace to tie off the umbilical cord, which will stop the flow of blood so the baby doesn't bleed out. Take a 20-minute breather while (hopefully) the placenta delivers, and then cut the umbilical cord. There is no need to sterilize the scissors beforehand: "[The umbilical cord] all dries up and falls off anyway," Kelsey explains.

STITCH YOUR OWN WOUND

"I'd probably use fishing line, because it's smooth," Koh says. Other supplies on the list include a needle (Koh uses curved ones in surgery—a curved quilting needle can be purchased for a couple of bucks at a craft store) and rubbing alcohol. Wash your hands and boil the needle in an inch of water for five minutes while you prep the fishing line. "Wipe down that piece of fishing line with alcohol, so it's sterilized," Koh says. For do it yourself anesthesia, rub a piece of ice on the wound for a couple of minutes. The effect doesn't last long, so hopefully you were the fastest stitcher in home-ec class. Poke the needle into your skin a couple of millimeters from the edge of the cut and down through the flesh in a half circle that comes out on the other side of the cut. Right about now, you'll be wishing you'd bought that curved needle. Keep going over and through, pulling the cut gently closed as you go. "You don't want to leave a hollow pocket—[it] will fill with fluid, and if that fluid gets infected, you've got an abscess," Koh warns. Knot the end and wipe your handiwork with alcohol before you pass out.

8
VETERINARY DRUGS FOR HUMAN CONSUMPTION

In times of uncertainty, we humans like to stockpile and hoard. We seek information that will keep us safe and provide for our well-being. One of these topics will invariably center around medical knowledge or first-aid in case of an accident, sickness, or injury. Many of us already have a well-rounded medical kit or basic skills in how to treat traumatic injuries. Yet we don't have the antibiotics necessary to prevent infection and illness. While small amounts of medications can be obtained by anyone willing to tell their doctor that he or she is going out of the country and would like to avoid "traveler's diarrhea," this approach is probably only good for one or two courses of therapy, but a long-term alternative is required in order to have enough antibiotics to protect the whole family or survival group. This is a common concern in the prepper world. The lack of concrete, factual information when it comes to antibiotics, and specifically, whether it is safe to use animal antibiotics in humans, is going to be given the attention it deserves in this chapter.

Many other questions typically revolve around: "Where can I find prescription-quality medicines?" "What should I do since my doctor won't prescribe me common antibiotics for long-term disasters or bugging out?" "What medicines should I stockpile?"

What this chapter will attempt to provide is the answer to these very questions and more. While Big Pharma isn't the only answer, there are some amazing capabilities of modern medicines.

There are also many home remedies and antibacterials that surround us in nature, and like any medicine, require a bit of know-how and understanding in order to administer correctly. Proper nutrition also plays a vital role in maintaining our health, but what about treating cuts, punctures, or infections when there are no hospitals or pharmaceuticals any longer?

Many people can't convince their doctor into writing extraneous prescriptions for a "what if?" scenario. If that's the case, what's the alternative? Is all hope lost?

It's not a big secret that veterinary antibiotics and drugs do not require a prescription. Drugs such as Fish-MOX clearly state on their label, "For Aquarium and Fish Use Only," but are they truly only for fish? Are these antibiotics any different than what my pharmacist gives me?

When researching this topic, you may become overwhelmed, as there is much debate between pseudo-doctors and "scientists" from all across the internet. There is page after page of conflicting information regarding the human consumption of animal antibiotics. Many people with several initials behind their name give a variety of answers or simply beat around the bush. While one MD would say XYZ, another doctor would say ABC. Some would say that they thought it would be safe to use veterinarian drugs, but only in dire times or as a last resort. Others would warn against it entirely, and yet some would encourage their use in everyday applications. So what is the truth? What is the safety and efficacy of this particular endeavor? Would it be better to buy generic medications from across the border?

Black-Market Drugs
You've likely seen the internet ads for generic versions of prescriptions from Canada or Mexico. They offer great prices and no questions asked. But like anything that seems too good to be true, they mostly are. Health regulations and quality control can be absent, to say the least.

Many of these "pills" are manufactured by an unorthodox "3rd shift" at the normal plant, but have no oversight, and their often-criminal motive is only black-market profit. Some are simply made in a dirty kitchen or backyard shack.

The list of safety risks in using black market medicines is long, but the principal problems involve the use of prescription drugs without the proper knowledge in administration and the danger of buying drugs of unknown origin and quality. Daniel Hancz, Pharm.D., a pharmacist with the Health Authority Law Enforcement Task Force (HALT) in Los Angeles, says, "The drugs could be old, contaminated, or counterfeit. And if you experience some kind of allergic reaction or other side effect, it's hard to trace the problem and treat it."

The FDA Initiative to Combat Counterfeit Drugs estimates that a significant amount of drugs available in Mexico may be counterfeit. Some of these medicines can contain "filler material" in order to lower manufacturing costs, and these can range from excess wood pulp (cellulose), to baking powder, petroleum by-products, or other, potentially dangerous substances. Either way, this is not something that you want in your bug-out bag only to find out it's worthless in your time of need or creates further medical problems that you can't treat!

So go ahead and mark that avenue of prepping off your list. **DO NOT** buy from questionable, fly-by-night, internet-based "doctors" with no business ratings or certifications, and avoid wasting your money while on vacation in Mexico. So where does that leave us? How can we find quality medicines without a prescription for truly legitimate concerns and uses?

Veterinary Drugs
Yes, they might sound more dangerous than buying pills from a Mexican street corner, but they are not. USP-approved animal pharmaceuticals are often made in the same manufacturing plants as human pharmaceuticals and

will contain the same ingredients, but do not require a prescription.

They are the same color, shape, and bare the same markings as human drugs. This likely boils down to cost-effectiveness for Big Pharma, but for once, is also in your best interest.

This needs to be explained. Every "drug" manufactured, sold, or brought into the United States must pass FDA regulations and is listed within the United States Pharmacopeia, or USP. This is a compendium recognized officially by the Federal Food, Drug, and Cosmetic Act that contains descriptions, uses, strengths, and standards of purity for selected drugs and for all of their forms of dosage. Use of the USP Verified Pharmaceutical Ingredient Mark helps ingredient manufacturers assure their customers that the quality of the ingredients they are supplying have been rigorously tested and verified by an independent authority. When the mark appears on an ingredient container or carton, it represents that the USP has evaluated the ingredient and found that:

1. The participant's quality system helps to ensure that the ingredient meets its label or certificate of analysis claims for identity, strength, purity, and quality.
2. The ingredient has been prepared under accepted good manufacturing practices (GMP) that ensure consistency in the quality of ingredients from batch to batch.
3. The ingredient meets its specifications' acceptance criteria.

So what does all of this FDA jargon mean? Overall, it translates into assurance that if you see an animal drug that is labeled, "USP pharmaceutical grade amoxicillin," it is the exact same pharmaceutical-grade amoxicillin that your doctor would prescribe you for various infections.

As for the identification or verification process, should you still feel uneasy, we can look to the FDA. Per the Federal

Food, Drug, and Cosmetic Act, each capsule, tablet, or pill must be uniquely marked. Two tablets with identical colors, shapes, and markings cannot, by law, have different ingredients. This is for a variety of reasons, not limited to assisting Poison Control hotlines, hospitals, doctors, etc., in determining what someone might have ingested, overdosed on, or is causing side effects.

These markings, colors, tablet shapes, and other identifying information can be found in medical reference texts, but now we can use resources such as WebMD, Drugs.com, RxList.com, and many verified smartphone applications such as iPharmacy that can quickly and easily identify drugs should you need to. (You may want to carry a pocket-sized guide to pill identification in your gear bag, as it may prove invaluable when the grid is down, for that matter.)

Are you still not convinced? Above is a picture of a 250 mg amoxicillin capsule. It is imprinted with "Westward 938." This is a pharmaceutical-grade, USP-approved, safe-for-human-consumption antibiotic that can be verified on pill-identification sites, such as Drugs.com. This is also the exact same pill you will find in a bottle of 250 mg Fish-Mox that can be ordered from a veterinarian-supply company. That means it came from the same manufacturer and contains the exact same ingredients as the amoxicillin that can be picked up at your local pharmacy.

Where Do I Find Veterinary Drugs?
So this brings us to the question, "What sort of veterinary drugs do I need, and where can I find them?" Well, this mostly boils down to what you are comfortable with and prepared to use in whatever future, post-SHTF scenario you are prepping for.

You may be familiar with the more common, everyday antibiotics, such as doxycycline, amoxicillin, cephalexin, penicillin, and ciprofloxacin. We will get into this matter in greater detail shortly, but this requires you to exercise caution and take your own risks. Consider that your doctor takes these very same risks when he prescribes you an antibiotic in which you've never had before. There is always a chance of side effects or allergic reactions, therefore, stock only what you need and what you have taken before. It would be wise for whoever is in charge of your medical preps to have a list of everyone's medical allergies and any contraindications.

There are a variety of sources for these antibiotics, but a few of them really stand out as quality, mainstream suppliers. Choose a distributor that has high-quality products, is easy to order from, has top selections, and is cost-effective.

What Do I Need?
Provided below is a short list of some of the more common antibiotics and their veterinary-named counterparts, but tailor these to your specific needs or criteria. These medications are available without a prescription in lots of 30–100 count tablets for less than the same prescription medication at the local pharmacy. It appears that there is no limit to how much you can obtain in order to be prepared for TEOTWAWKI.

Penicillin
Penicillin is an antibiotic in the penicillin group of drugs. Penicillin is used to treat many different types of infections caused by bacteria, such as ear infections, urinary tract infections, septicemia, meningitis, intra-abdominal infections, gonorrhea, syphilis, pneumonia, respiratory

infections, ear, nose, throat infections, skin, and soft tissue infections.

Veterinarian Equivalent: 250 mg Fish Pen and 500 mg Fish Pen Forte

Amoxicillin
This is a penicillin antibiotic. Amoxicillin is used to treat many different types of infections caused by bacteria, such as ear infections, bladder infections, pneumonia, gonorrhea, E. coli, and salmonella infections.

Veterinarian Equivalent: 250 mg Fish Mox (for children) and 500 mg Fish Mox Forte (for adults).

Ampicillin
Ampicillin is an antibiotic in the penicillin group of drugs. It fights bacteria in your body. Ampicillin is used to treat many different types of infections caused by bacteria, such as ear infections, bladder infections, pneumonia, gonorrhea, E. coli, and salmonella infections.

Veterinarian Equivalent: 250 mg Fish Cillin

Ciprofloxacin (Cipro)
Ciprofloxacin is an antibiotic in a group of drugs called fluoroquinolones. It is a potent, broad-spectrum antibiotic that fights bacteria in the body. Ciprofloxacin is used to treat infections of the skin, lungs, airways, bones, and joints caused by susceptible bacteria. Ciprofloxacin is also frequently used to treat urinary infections caused by bacteria, such as E. coli. Ciprofloxacin is effective in treating infectious diarrheas caused by E. coli, Campylobacter jejuni, and Shigella bacteria. It may also be used to prevent or slow anthrax after exposure.

Veterinarian Equivalent: 500 mg Fish Flox Forte

Cephalexin (Keflex)

Cephalexin belongs to a class of antibiotics called cephalosporins. They are similar to penicillin in action and side effects. Cephalexin is used to treat infections caused by bacteria, including upper respiratory infections, ear infections, skin infections, urinary tract infections, and tooth and mouth infections.

Veterinarian Equivalent: 250 mg Fish Flex and 500 mg Fish Flex Forte

Erythromycin

Erythromycin is in a group of drugs called macrolide antibiotics and is used to treat certain infections caused by bacteria, such as bronchitis, diphtheria, Legionnaires' disease, pertussis (whooping cough), pneumonia, rheumatic fever, venereal disease (VD), and ear, intestine, lung, urinary tract, and skin infections. It is also used before some surgery or dental work to prevent infection.

Veterinarian Equivalent: 250 mg Fish Mycin

Metronidazole (Flagyl)

Metronidazole is an antibiotic and antiprotozoal. It works by stopping the growth of bacteria and protozoa (single-celled parasites). Metronidazole is used to treat bacterial infections of the vagina, stomach, skin, joints, and respiratory tract. Metronidazole, sold under the trade name Flagyl, is also effective against infections caused by certain kinds of parasites. Giardiasis is an infection of the intestinal tract by the protozoan parasite Giardia lamblia. Trichomonas vaginalis is a protozoan parasite that causes trichomoniasis, a sexually transmitted infection of the vagina in women and urethra in men. Flagyl is used to treat trichomoniasis and can also be used to treat the most common type of vaginal bacterial infection, making it a good choice when the diagnosis is uncertain. This medication will not treat a vaginal yeast infection, however.

Veterinarian Equivalent: 250 mg Fish-Zole and 500 mg
Fish Zole Forte

Ketoconazole

Ketoconazole is used to treat fungal infections. Ketoconazole
is most often used to treat fungal infections that can spread
to different parts of the body through the bloodstream such
as yeast infections of the mouth, skin, urinary tract, and
blood, and certain fungal infections that begin on the skin or
in the lungs and can spread through the body. Ketoconazole
is also used to treat fungal infections of the skin or nails that
cannot be treated with other medications. Ketoconazole is in
a class of antifungals called imidazoles. It works by slowing
the growth of fungi that cause infection.

Veterinarian Equivalent: 200 mg Fish Fungus

Tetracycline

Tetracycline is used to treat bacterial infections, including
pneumonia and other respiratory tract infections, acne,
infections of skin, genital and urinary systems, and the
infection that causes stomach ulcers (Helicobacter pylori). It
also may be used as an alternative to other medications for
the treatment of Lyme disease and for the treatment and
prevention of anthrax (after inhalational exposure).
Tetracycline is in a class of medications called tetracycline
antibiotics. It works by preventing the growth and spread of
bacteria. Antibiotics will not work for colds, flu, or other viral
infections.

Veterinarian Equivalent: 250 mg Fish Cycline and 500
mg Fish Cycline Forte

Doxycycline

Doxycycline is a tetracycline antibiotic. It may be substituted
in place of penicillin to treat common infections in those
people who are allergic to that particular drug. Doxycycline
is used to treat may different bacterial infections, such as

urinary tract infections, acne, gonorrhea and chlamydia, Lyme disease or tick-bite infections, anthrax infections, cholera, periodontitis (gum disease), and other bacterial infections.

Exercise caution with any and all expired tetracycline-family drugs. There has been some documentation of liver damage, and some have even labeled it toxic if used past the expiration date. However, doxycycline provides a great alternative to penicillin medications for those who are allergic.

Veterinarian Equivalent: 100 mg Bird Biotic

Dosages and Notes Regarding Veterinary Drugs
Joseph Alton, MD, is a medical doctor and Fellow of the American College of Surgeons and the American College of Obstetrics and Gynecology. He is also a prepper and writes:

> These antibiotics are used at specific doses for specific illnesses; the exact dosage of each and every medication is beyond the scope of this [chapter]. Suffice it to say that most penicillin and cephalosporin (Keflex and other cephalexin) medications are taken at 500 mg dosages, 3-4 times a day for adults, and 250 mg dosages for children, whereas Metronidazole (250 mg) and Doxycycline (100 mg) are taken twice a day.

It's important to have as much information as possible on medications that you plan to store for times of trouble, so consider purchasing a hard copy of the latest Physician's Desk Reference (PDR). This book comes out yearly and has just about every bit of information that exists on a particular medication, including those that do not require a prescription. You may also purchase a PDR for Herbal Medicines, a definitive guide to herbal remedies used throughout history. Indications, dosages, risks, and side effects are all listed for both the standard guide and herbal.

In Closing

Dr. Alton reminds us of the state of affairs that we might one day find ourselves in:

> If we ever find ourselves without modern medical care, we will have to improvise medical strategies that we perhaps might be reluctant to consider today. Without hospitals, it will be up to the [field] medic to treat infections. That responsibility will be difficult to carry out without the weapons to fight disease, such as antibiotics.
>
> Alternative therapies should be looked at carefully, as well. Honey and garlic have known antibacterial actions, as do a number of herbs and essential oils. Be sure to integrate all medical options, traditional and alternative, and use every tool at your disposal to keep your community healthy.

Please verify and check all medications that you order with a reputable pill-identification book or website in order to make sure you truly receive what you ordered. The advice herein is contrary to standard medical practice and is only appropriate in the event of societal collapse.

9
EMERGENCY HEATING
AND COOKING

During emergencies every facet of our lives becomes disrupted. Things which we normally take for granted suddenly become of major importance in sustaining our lives or in making life much more comfortable. One of the most basic of all the elements around us, and which we probably take for granted the most, is fuel. Fuels are used to keep us warm in the winter, cool in the summer, prepare our food, and light our homes. In our modern society we are used to just flipping a switch and having the lights come on. This action has become so common place in our lives that we do it automatically upon entering a dark room without even realizing we have done it. At the flip of another switch our furnace comes on to keep us warm. The constant vigilance of our furnace thermostat even makes it so convenient that we only have to turn the furnace on once at the beginning of the winter and then forget about it until the spring when we turn it off again. Cooking is just as easy: the turning of a dial on a gas range, the pressing of a button on an electric range, or the use of a microwave oven.

During even a minor emergency one or all of these conveniences may be unusable. For many of us this may cause true panic. How do you keep warm when it is below freezing and the furnace is out of commission? How do you get a hot meal when your stove or microwave doesn't work? Remember that in an emergency your home will probably not be the only one affected, so you may not be able to simply run to the neighbors' homes for temporary help. Let's examine the alternatives which you can pursue now so that proper preparations can eliminate the chaos and panic which lack of planning will surely create. Proper planning can also

keep your family safe from improper use of fuels—preventing
fires and asphyxiation.

Heating

During the winter it is essential that adequate heat be
provided. The human body, unlike that of animals, is not
capable of producing sufficient internal heat to keep alive
when the temperature drops below about 50 degrees.
Therefore you must assist the body with either insulation to
retain the heat—such as blankets, coats, sleeping bags, etc.—
or you must provide an outside source of heat, such as fire.
Unfortunately, many of us have had no experience in proper
fire building and would therefore become totally frustrated
by our attempts, give up, and then die of exposure and
hypothermia; or we would succeed in burning the house
down and then die of exposure and hypothermia.

Coal stores well if kept in a dark place and away from
moving air. Air speeds deterioration and breakdown, causing
it to burn more rapidly. Coal may be stored in a plastic-lined
pit or in sheds, bags, boxes, or barrels, and should be kept
away from circulating air, light, and moisture. Cover it to
lend protection from weather and sun.

Wood: Hardwoods such as apple, cherry, and other fruit
woods are slow burning and sustain coals. Hardwoods are
more diffcult to burn than softer woods, thus requiring a
supply of kindling. Soft woods such as pine and cedar are
light in weight and burn very rapidly, leaving ash and few
coals for cooking. If you have a fireplace or a wood/coal
burning stove, you will want to store several cords of
firewood. Firewood is usually sold by the cord, which is a
neat pile that totals 128 cubic feet. This pile is 4 feet wide, 4
feet high, and 8 feet long. Some dealers sell wood by the ton.
As a general rule of thumb, a standard cord of air-dried
dense hardwood weighs about two tons and provides as
much heat as one ton of coal. Be suspicious of any alleged
cord delivered in a ½- or ¾-ton pickup truck. For best
results, wood should be seasoned (dried) properly, usually at

least a year. A plastic tarp, wood planks, or other plastic or metal sheeting over the woodpile is useful in keeping the wood dry. Other types of fuels are more practical to store and use than wood or coal.

Newspaper logs make a good and inexpensive source of fuel. You may prepare the logs in the following manner: Use about eight pages of newspaper and open flat. Spread the stack, alternating the cut sides and folded sides. Place a one inch wood dowel or metal rod across one end and roll the paper around the rod very tightly. Roll it until there are six to eight inches left to roll, and then slip another eight pages underneath the roll. Continue this procedure until you have a roll four to six inches in diameter. With a fine wire, tie the roll on both ends. Withdraw the rod. Your newspaper log is ready to use. Four of these logs will burn about 1 hour.

Propane is another excellent fuel for indoor use. Like kerosene, it produces carbon dioxide as it burns and therefore, is not poisonous. It does consume oxygen, so be sure to crack a window when burning propane. Propane stores indefinitely, having no known shelf life. Propane stoves and small, portable heaters are very economical, simple to use, and comes the closest to approximating the type of convenience most of us are accustomed to using on a daily basis. The storage of propane is governed by strict local laws. Please check the laws governing propane in your city or county. The primary hazard in using propane is that it is heavier than air, and if a leak occurs it may "pool," which can create an explosive atmosphere. Furthermore, basement natural-gas heating units CANNOT be legally converted for propane use. Again, the vapors are heavier than air and form "pockets." Ignition sources such as water heaters and electrical sources can cause an explosion.

White Gas (Coleman fuel): Many families have camp stoves which burn Coleman Fuel or white gasoline. These stoves are fairly easy to use and produce a great amount of heat. However, they, like charcoal, produce vast amounts of carbon monoxide.

NEVER use a Coleman Fuel stove indoors. It could be a fatal mistake to your entire family. Never store fuels in the house or near a heater. Use a metal storage cabinet that is vented on top and bottom and can be locked.

Kerosene (also known as Range Oil No. 1) is the cheapest of all the storage fuels and is also very forgiving if you make a mistake. Kerosene is not as explosive as gasoline and Coleman fuel. Kerosene stores well for long periods of time and by introducing some fuel additives, it can be made to store even longer. However, do not store it in metal containers for extended periods of time unless they are porcelain lined, because the moisture in the kerosene will rust through the container, causing the kerosene to leak out. Most hardware stores and home improvement centers sell kerosene in 5-gallon plastic containers, which store for many years. A 55-gallon drum stored in the backyard, or 11 plastic containers, 5 gallons each, will provide enough fuel to last an entire winter if used sparingly.

CAUTION: To burn kerosene you will need a kerosene heater. There are many models and sizes to choose from, but remember that you are not trying to heat your entire home. The larger the heater, the more fuel you will have to store. Most families should be able to get by on a heater that produces about 9,600 BTUs of heat, though kerosene heaters are made that will produce up to 25,000 to 30,000 BTUs. If you have the storage space to store the fuel required by these larger heaters, they are excellent investments, but for most families, the smaller heaters are more than adequate. When selecting a kerosene heater, be sure to get one that can double as a cooking surface and source of light.

Then when you are forced to use it, be sure to plan your meals so that they can be cooked when you are using the heater for heat rather than wasting fuel used for cooking only. When kerosene burns it requires very little oxygen, compared to charcoal. You must crack a window at least ¼ of an inch to allow enough oxygen to enter the room to prevent asphyxiation. During combustion, kerosene is not poisonous and is safe to use indoors. To prevent possible fires you should always fill it outside.

The momentary, incomplete combustion during lighting and extinguishing of kerosene heaters can cause some unpleasant odors. To prevent these odors from lingering in your home, always light and extinguish the heater out of doors. During normal operation a kerosene heater is practically odorless.

Charcoal should never be burned indoors. When charcoal burns it is a voracious consumer of oxygen and will quickly deplete the oxygen supply in your little "home within a home." Furthermore, as it burns it produces vast amounts of carbon monoxide, which is a deadly poison and could prove fatal to your entire family.

Cooking

Whether an emergency should happen during winter or summer, preparation and cooking of food will always require fuel. There is much greater flexibility in choosing the source of fuel for cooking than there is for heating the home. Cooking, even in the most miserable of weather, can be done out of doors and can therefore be done using fuels that could not safely be used inside.

To conserve your cooking-fuel storage needs, always do your emergency cooking in the most efficient manner possible. Don't boil more water than you need, extinguish the fire as soon as you're finished, plan your meals ahead of time to consolidate as much cooking as possible, during the winter cook on top of your heating unit while heating your home, and cook in a pressure cooker or other fuel-efficient container as much as possible. Keep enough fuel to provide cooking for at least 7–10 days.

It is even possible to cook without using fuel at all. For example, to cook dry beans you can place them inside a pressure cooker with the proper amount of water and other ingredients needed and place it on your heat source until it comes up to pressure. Then turn off the heat, remove the pressure cooker, and place inside a large box filled with newspapers, blankets, or other insulating materials. Leave it for 2½ hours and then open it; your meal will be done, having cooked for 2½ hours with no heat.

If you don't have a large box in which to place the pressure cooker, simply wrap it in several blankets and place it in the corner. **Store matches in a waterproof, airtight container with each piece of equipment that must be lit with a flame.**

Sterno fuel, a jellied-petroleum product, is an excellent source of fuel for inclusion in your bug-out bag. Sterno is very light weight and easily ignited with a match or a spark from flint and steel, but is not explosive. It is also safe for use indoors. A Sterno stove can be purched at any sporting-goods store. They fold up into a very small, compact unit ideal for carrying in a pack.

One can, about the diameter of a can of tuna fish and twice as high, will allow you to cook six meals if used frugally. Chafing dishes and fondue pots can also be used with Sterno. It is not without some complications. It will evaporate very easily, even when the lid is securely fastened. If you use Sterno in your bug-out bag, you should check it every 6–8 months to insure that it has not evaporated beyond the point of usage. Because of this issue, it is not a good fuel for long-term storage. It is a very expensive fuel to use compared to others fuels available, but is extremely convenient and portable.

White gas, or Coleman fuel, when used with a Coleman stove, is another excellent and convenient fuel for cooking. It is not as portable or as lightweight as Sterno, but produces a much greater BTU value. Like Sterno, Coleman fuel has a tendency to evaporate even when the container is tightly sealed, so it is not a good fuel for long-term storage. Unlike Sterno, however, it is highly volatile and will explode under the right conditions; therefore, it should **NEVER** be stored in the home. Because of its highly flammable nature, great care should always be exercised when lighting stoves and lanterns that use Coleman fuel. Many serious burns have been caused by carelessness with this product. Always store Coleman fuel in the garage or shed.

Charcoal is the least expensive fuel per BTU that the average family can store. Remember that it must always be used outside because of the vast amounts of poisonous carbon monoxide it produces. Charcoal will store for an extended period of time if it's stored in air-tight containers. It readily absorbs moisture from the surrounding air, so don't store it in the paper bags it comes in for more than a few months, or it may be difficult to light. Transfer it to airtight metal or plastic containers, and it will keep almost indefinitely. Fifty or sixty dollars' worth of charcoal will provide all the cooking fuel a family will need for an entire year if used sparingly. The best time to buy briquettes inexpensively is at the end of summer. Broken or torn bags of briquettes are usually sold at a big discount.

Charcoal Starter
You will also want to store a small amount of lighter fluid or kerosene. Newspapers will also provide an excellent ignition source for charcoal when used in a funnel-type lighting device. To light charcoal using newspapers, use two or three sheets, crumpled up, and a #10-tin can. Cut both ends out of the can. Punch holes every two inches around the lower edge of the can with a punch-type can opener (for opening juice cans). Set the can down so the punched holes are on the bottom. Place the crumpled newspaper in the bottom of the can and place the charcoal briquettes on top of the newspaper. Lift the can slightly, and light the newspaper. Prop small rocks under the bottom edge of the can to create a good draft. The briquettes will be ready to use in about 20–30 minutes.

When the coals are ready, remove the chimney and place them in your cooker. Never place burning charcoal directly on concrete or cement because the heat will crack it. A wheelbarrow or old metal garbage can lid makes an excellent container for this type of fire. One of the nice things about burning charcoal is that you can regulate the heat. Each briquette will produce about 40 degrees of heat. If you are baking bread, for example, and need 400 degrees of heat for your oven, simply use ten briquettes.

Baking in a Cardboard Box

To conserve heat, and thereby get the maximum heat value from your charcoal, you must learn to funnel the heat where you want it, rather than letting it dissipate into the air around you. One excellent way to do this is to cook inside a cardboard oven. Take a cardboard box, about the size of an orange crate, and cover it with aluminum foil inside and out. Be sure that the shiny side is visible so that maximum reflectivity is achieved. Turn the box on its side so that the opening is no longer on the top, but is on the side.

Place one pie plate upside down at the base of the oven, and the second one right-side up on top of it. This will hold the charcoal briquettes that are used as a heat source.

The lower pan prevents the briquettes from burning the floor of the cardboard box.

Create a baking shelf about 1/3 down from the top, by straightening and cutting wire coat hangers into straight pieces and pushing them through the box from left to right. Use a ruler to ensure that the shelf is level. After installed, bend the ends of the wires to keep them from pulling out.

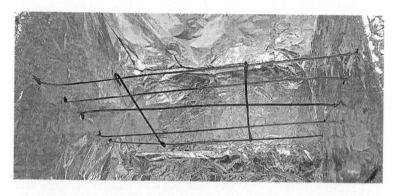

If the wires sag, you can strengthen the shelf by weaving a few additional wires back and forth.

Preheat the briquettes outside the oven and then place them in the top pie plate and your baked goods on the rack in a disposable foil pan. A small shovel can be used to transfer preheated coals into the oven. You may need to experiment with the heat, but usually 4–6 briquettes, preheated until they are mostly white, will give you 350 degree baking capability on a clear, warm day.

In theory, you should be able to bake just about anything in this oven, with the only constraint being the oven's small size and lightweight construction, which will by no means support a heavy load. Simple to prepare items, such as canned foods, shish-kebob, and muffins or cornbread from a pre-packaged mix, are perfect for this use. Really anything that could be heated in a conventional toaster oven could also be prepared in this manner as well.

How to Make Charcoal Briquettes

To make your own charcoal, select twigs, limbs, and branches of fruit, nut, and other hardwood trees; black walnuts and peach or apricot pits may also be used. Cut the wood into small chunks and split them. If you really want them to look like briquettes, you will need to chunk them into very small pieces. The wood should be dry and preferably seasoned for 3 months or more.

Get a metal barrel or bucket with a lid. Remove any rubber gaskets, as they will just melt. Punch a few holes in the bottom for air intake. They will need to be about 1.5 inches wide and somewhat close to the center. Place the bucket or barrel on top of some bricks or concrete blocks to raise it above the ground.

Wad up a bunch of newspaper or cardboard and place it into the bottom of the barrel or bucket. Fill it with kindling, and then light it on fire. While allowing it to come to a full flame, add some longer sticks of hardwood. Begin adding the prepared wood once the fire is going strong. Don't pack it in too lightly or it will have a hard time charring.

Watch the smoke. Once the smoke has changed from a billow of yellowish-white smoke to a wispy-blue smoke and there is more heat than smoke, start shutting it down. Put the lid on the container and kick out the bricks holding it up off the ground. Place a weight on the top of the lid to close off any air passage, and then kick some dirt around the base if necessary. It is this action of depriving the wood of oxygen that will stop the burn and cause the charring.

Let it sit for 24 hours; by then it should be cool to the touch. Open the lid and carefully pick out your charcoal chunks and store in a moisture-proof container. The charcoal will burn hot and long with very little smoke or ash. Be careful not to breathe in the charcoal dust at the bottom of the barrel and remember to only burn charcoal in a well-ventilated area.

Tip: Cook up a batch of cornstarch and water until it becomes a thick paste. Stir in any charcoal dust and finely crushed charcoal bits until this mixture can be made into a briquette mold. Spoon this into Styrofoam egg cartons and let dry for several days. Now these are ready for use as any commercially made briquettes would be—almost totally smokeless.

Wood and coal burning stoves have a built-in cooking surface. These are excellent to use indoors during the winter, because you may already be using it to heat the home. In the summer, however, they are unbearably hot and impractical for indoor use. If you choose to build a campfire outside, be sure to use caution and follow all the rules for safety. Little children, and even many adults, are not aware of the tremendous dangers that open fires may pose.

Kerosene heaters will also double as cooking units. Only purchase a kerosene heater that can be used to cook on as well. Follow the same precautions for cooking, as was discussed under the section on heating with kerosene.

Propane camp stoves are generally a family's first choice. They are the most convenient and easy to use of all emergency-cooking appliances available. They may be used indoors or outdoors. As with any other emergency-fuel source, cook with a pressure cooker whenever possible to conserve fuel.

10
EMERGENCY LIGHTING
AND POWER

Alternative sources of lighting and power must be stored in advance in order to prepare for a temporary lapse in electrical power. Before the event, this is relatively inexpensive and easy, but after the event, it becomes very difficult, perhaps impossible. In most emergencies with a several-day time span (hurricanes, ice storms, etc.), battery-operated lighting will often see us through. With a major emergency, however, the duration can be much greater. There are many products on the market that will serve well for long-term emergencies.

Be sure to have a good quality fire extinguisher in each room where candles, kerosene, and gas are being used. Most of the alternatives require a fire or flame, so use caution. More home fires are caused by improper usage of fires used for light than for any other purpose.

Use extra caution when children are in the house. Teach them the proper safety procedures to follow under emergency conditions. Allow them to practice these skills under proper adult supervision now, rather than waiting until an emergency strikes.

Cyalume sticks are the safest form of indoor lighting available, but very few people even know what they are. Cyalume sticks can be purchased at most sporting-goods stores for about two dollars per stick. They are plastic sticks about 4 inches in length and a ½ inch in diameter. To activate, simply bend them until the glass tube inside them breaks, then shake to mix the chemicals inside. They will glow a bright light for up to eight hours. Cyalume is the only

form of light that is safe to use inside a home after an earthquake. After a serious earthquake, one of the great dangers is ruptured natural gas lines. If you flip on a light switch or even turn on a flashlight, you run the risk of causing an explosion. Cyalume will not ignite natural gas. Cyalume sticks are so safe that a baby can even use them as a teether.

Two-Mantle Gas Lantern: A gallon of Coleman-type fuel utilized with a two-mantle gas lantern has a burning time of approximately 40 hours. Light output is approximately the same as a 200W light bulb. Assuming an operating or burning time of five hours per day, the following estimated amounts of fuel would be consumed. White gas may be substituted in some camping equipment, but read and follow the specific instructions of the equipment manufacturer. A gas lantern gives a high intensity light and lots of heat too—though the pressurized gas delivery system is quite noisy when operating.

Five Hours per Day Fuel Consumption

Day	1 pint
Week	1 gallon
Month	4 gallons
Year	50 gallons

Kerosene Lanterns

Given today's technology, a kerosene lantern seems a bit old-fashioned and out of place. However, a kerosene lantern with a 1-inch wick will burn approximately 45 hours per quart of kerosene, saving lots of natural resources and utilizing approximately one-fourth as much fuel as a gas lantern. Kerosene lanterns are inexpensive, effective, and fairly-safe lighting sources.

Now there are scented lamp oils which replace kerosene. This lamp oil is generally available in retail stores. Make sure the oil is approved for use in your lamp. There is a difference in lighting quality and quantity, as the kerosene lantern is quite dim when compared to the two-mantle gas lantern. The light output of a kerosene lantern is comparable to a 40W-60W light bulb. As a rule of thumb, the typical kerosene lantern burns approximately one ounce of fuel per hour.

The main problem with using them is failure to properly trim the wicks and using the wrong size chimney. Wicks should be trimmed in an arch, a "V," an "A," or straight across the top. Failure to properly trim and maintain wicks will result in smoke and poor light.

Aladdin-type lamps that use a circular wick and mantle do not need trimming and produce much more light than conventional kerosene lamps. These lamps, however, produce a great amount of heat, getting up to 750 degrees Fahrenheit. If placed within 36 inches of any combustible object (wooden cabinets, walls, etc.) charring can occur. Therefore great caution should be exercised to prevent accidental fires.

The higher the elevation the taller the chimney should be. Most chimneys that come with kerosene lamps are made for use at sea level. At about 4,500 feet above sea level the chimney should be about 18–20 inches high. If your chimney isn't tall enough you can extend it by wrapping aluminum foil around the top. This enables the light to penetrate the bottom portion and still provide proper drawing of air for complete combustion. If the chimney is too short it will result in smoke and poor lighting. Be sure to store extra wicks, chimneys, and mantles.

Five Hours per Day Fuel Consumption

Day	1/4 pint
Week	1 quart
Month	1 gallon
Year	12 gallons

Tallow candles burn brighter, longer, and are fairly smoke-free when compared to wax candles. Tallow candles are generally available in specialty stores only, unless you make your own. Wax candles are available almost anywhere housewares are sold. Store tallow candles in a cool, dry location. Candles stored in the freezer will burn slower and without dripping.

Height	Diameter	Hours of burning time
6"	1/2"	3
6"	1"	8
9"	2"	48

Candles

Every family should have a large supply of candles. Three hundred sixty-five candles, or one per day, is not too many. The more you have the better. Fifty-hour candles are available in both solid and liquid form. White or light colored candles burn brighter than dark candles. Tallow candles burn brighter, longer, and are fairly smoke free when compared to wax candles. Their lighting ability can be increased by placing an aluminum foil reflector behind them or by placing them in front of a mirror. However, candles are extremely dangerous indoors because of the high fire danger—especially around children. For this reason, be sure to store several candle lanterns or broad-based candle holders. Be sure to store a substantial supply of wooden matches.

Save your candle ends for emergency use. Votive candles set in empty jars will burn for up to 15 hours. Non-candles (plastic dish and paper wicks) and a bottle of salad oil will provide hundreds of hours of candle light. The type made of hardened wax in a can has the capability of utilizing several wicks simultaneously. The other type is a liquid paraffin-filled bottle with a wick for easy lighting. The liquid paraffin burns without odor or smoke. This candle has a minimum 100-hour burning time and indefinite shelf life.

Improvised Olive-Oil Lamp

If you have some olive oil (other cooking oils will work in a pinch), some stiff, flexible wire, a mason jar (or just about any glass or fire-proof container), and some cotton-cord material (shoelaces, mop strands, yarn, etc.), you can make an expedient oil lamp.

Our ancestors have been using oil lamps for thousands of years. The earliest (the Canaanite lamp) dates as far back as 1500 B.C. People have relied on oil lamps in general up until the last few generations. One of the advantages to using olive oil for your lamp instead of more traditional lamp oils like kerosene is that olive oil has a much higher flash point, meaning that it's not a very flammable material, making your lamp safer. A wick soaked in olive oil will burn steadily, but if the flame comes in contact with the oil reservoir or if the vessel is knocked over, the flame will simply be extinguished. These lamps are reliable, plus they burn bright and long. A few ounces of olive oil can burn for several hours, so if you are concerned about the cost, it is much cheaper than most candles (and safer too).

While you can burn other cooking oils in your improvised lamp, such as vegetable, canola, corn, etc., olive oil burns with the least amount of smoke and odor. If you have any store-bought kerosene lamps or lanterns, you can use olive oil in those as well. Adaptability is the key to survival, and it's always good to identify items that serve a dual purpose. You can cook with the oil and eat your dinner by the light of it! (Don't forget to save your used cooking oil too!)

You can make a lamp out of a can of tuna (packed in oil), and then eat the tuna when all the oil has been used up!

Making your lamp is relatively easy, and most likely you will have many of the materials on hand already. You'll need:

- A glass jar, such as a quart-size, wide-mouthed canning jar works best.
- A short length of flexible steel wire (two times the height of the jar).
- A wick.
- Olive oil.

1. Form one end of the steel wire into a long hook, about the same height as the jar. This hook holds the wire on the jar and doubles as a handle to pull the wick up for lighting.

2. Take the other end of the wire and wrap it into a coil, creating a wick stand about an inch or two tall that sits on the bottom of the jar.

3. Pinch the top of the metal coil onto about two inches of wick length so that about a quarter inch or less of the wick is sticking up above the wire coil. Any longer and the wick will smoke. The other end of the wick will be soaking in the olive oil.

4. Add enough olive oil to your jar so that the level is just under where the wick is pinched by the wire. Any higher and you risk putting out the lamp with the oil.

How the Lamp Works

The olive oil is drawn up the wick where it vaporizes and gets burned by the flame. If you can find lampante oil (olive oil not suitable for eating, but for burning), you can save money by buying that instead of culinary olive oil.

If you are having problems with it smoking when you blow it out, use wet fingers to put out the flame, or just douse it with the oil in the jar.

Notes on Materials

One of the benefits of using a canning jar is that when the oil lamp is not in use you can put a canning lid on top for storage. A wide-mouthed, pint-sized jar will also work well; you just need to adjust the size of the wick holder. For your wick, you can use 100-percent cotton string or twine and salt it to ensure that it burns longer.

To salt your wick, take your cotton twine, put it in a bowl with a little water and then cover with table salt. Squeeze it thoroughly and let it dry overnight or until it is no longer damp.

If you need or want your lamp to produce more light, try using a braided, flat wick (1/2 inch or narrower), adjusting the way the wire supports this kind of wick by crimping it to accommodate the extra girth. You can buy flat wicks from stores that carry supplies for oil lamps, or you can cut up an old 100-percent-cotton tea towel into strips and use that instead.

Electric lighting has several advantages and one main disadvantage. It's more portable and safer than fire-based light. It can be extremely light weight and reliable. Its major drawback is the requirement of a power source. The most portable and available power source we currently have on the market is the traditional battery.

EDC is short for "every day carry." This light should be small enough that you don't mind carrying it around with you daily. You never know when you might need a light in an emergency, and it will determine where you can and can't go. You should always have it with you. Ideally it will run off a single battery. LED should be your first choice, and the runner-up would be a flashlight with krypton or halogen light bulbs, because they last much longer and give off several times more light than regular flashlight bulbs with the same energy consumption. Store at least two or three extra bulbs in a place where they will not be crushed or broken.

Low Level
You can get away with this kind of lighting when traveling through known territory, around camp, through your house, a night trip to the outhouse, reading, etc. Conserved batteries last a long time. Size is probably not important. This type of light is easiest to obtain, helpful in most basic situations, and important because of these reasons.

Thrower
This is your big light. You may need it for search and rescue, a security patrol around a camp site, illuminating an area a long distance away (hence the name, since it "throws" light afar). You probably won't use it daily, and it will eat batteries fast, so you will not want to run it all the time anyway. It's likely to be a larger light and only carried when a need is anticipated. This is probably the least important, but when you need it, you need it.

Headlamp
This light will be used for night work or work in the dark where you need both hands free. If you've ever tried to do the dishes by hand, with-

out power, or any other such similar chore, you will quickly appreciate what a headlamp can do for you. You may not have the ability to ask someone to hold a flashlight for you as you accomplish a task. It should be reasonably small and use small batteries. It is possible to rig up a flashlight to perform this role, for example, an EDC and a holder for it in a hat. A lantern can also perform this role to a degree; however, an actual headlamp still is a good idea.

Small Lantern
Sometimes you need to light up a room for socialization or reading. Lanterns mostly give light to a small group of people. Other possibilities are using a flashlight in "candle mode", which is either with the bezel off the light exposing the lamp or just standing the flashlight on its tail and letting the light reflect off the ceiling.

Large Lantern
When more light is required than a small lantern can provide, allow a group of people to have light in a small, usually stationary place. Eating a meal at night or socializing would be good examples.

Incandescent/Halogen/Krypton
These are not recommended for general flashlight use. They are not very durable, prone to break easily—especially when dropped. They are inefficient, consume batteries rapidly, and generally get dim quite quickly with use. Really they are only suitable for use in a thrower type of light, and even then should probably be avoided due to their fragility.

LED
These are outstanding for almost all uses and much more efficient than incandescent or halogen bulbs. Highly durable, they only get more efficient as batteries deplete. You really get what you pay for with these

lights. Do some research and get what fits inside your budget and meets your needs. They are getting better every year and now come in super-high outputs of 200 or more lumens.

Fluorescent
This is a decent choice for large lanterns on a budget. Fluorescent lights last a reasonably long time and aren't very expensive, so you should own a few. The major drawback is they can't be dimmed to save power and don't work as well in cold weather. I would recommend spending a few more dollars and going with LED.

Self-Powered Lights
These are generally not recommended for several reasons. They are usually bulky and prone to mechanical failure. This is especially true since they are very cheaply made, making them more of a novelty item than actually useful. If you're really interested in these, I would recommend a shake light. They appear quite durable; the mechanical part is only a lose magnet that goes back and forth inside a sealed container. Though not prone to breakage, the light level is low. Be aware that there have been reports of shake lights on the market that have coin-cell batteries in them so that they look nice and bright when you pick them up, but once the internal batteries die (in a few hours), they run on shake power only, which is nowhere near as bright as the batteries were. Nowadays there are several solar products that can provide lighting, even on cloudy days. There are solar lanterns, solar flashlights, and even solar-battery chargers. The solar walkway lamps that line outdoor paths are available in home-improvement stores. These can be used at night to provide ambient lighting. Solar-photovoltaic panels or wind generators, hooked to batteries, can provide lighting and cost as little as $100 per light. With solar or wind, once the power is restored, you still have free, non-polluting lighting. Solar lights are nice, but first buy a solar battery charger; otherwise you'll have to carry the bulk of a solar cell around with you when using the light. Internally, a solar light is going to have a battery anyway. Self-powered lights can probably only fill the role of a low-level light, though.

How to Make Your Own Electricity

As a part of energy independence, generating electricity is the easiest and most flexible thing you can do. One of the easiest ways to generate electricity is to purchase solar panels. You can do anything from generate power to run a gate or garage door opener, put lights and power in an outbuilding, sell power back to the grid to cut your electric bill, or even completely live without power from a utility company.

Examine Your Needs:

- Be realistic—don't deny yourself if it's important to you.
- Plan for future extension if you underestimate.
- Don't neglect well pumps and other necessities in your planning.
- Do you want to be prepared for disasters?
- Do you want to be self-sufficient?

Evaluate what you need the power for:

- Water/Well
- Lights
- Refrigeration
- Appliances
- Entertainment
- Electric Vehicles

Incremental Growth

It's possible to install in stages, so that you don't bite the huge cost all at once. You can start small, then learn and build confidence so that you can go bigger.

1. Many grid-attached rooftop systems can be expanded—this is something to make sure of when you shop.

2. An automatic gate can be run off solar power, whether the grid is up or not.

3. Any RV or trailer that has deep-cycle batteries should have at least 60W of solar power just to keep the batteries up when it's not in use, but more like 200–400W if you are going to use it and not run a generator every day.

4. An outbuilding (a detached garage or shed) that doesn't have lights or power, or that "needs" an electric door opener, can be run off solar for less than the cost of having it wired to the main building by an electrician.

5. A well pump is important, so you will still have water if the power is out.

6. Certain circuits in your home can be isolated and put on a battery/inverter such as:

   - The one that has your computer room, for a truly uninterruptable power supply
   - The lighting circuits only, so your home is always well lit.
   - The alarm system.
   - Gas/propane-powered heaters or pellet stoves.
   - Circulating fans.
   - Gas/propane powered stoves/ovens/water heaters with electric "brains."

Conservation

While it's possible to run everything you can think of from solar, wind, or water, it would be prohibitively expensive for most people to afford to install a system that could handle all of it. Large-household air conditioners, electric heaters, electric ranges, etc., all draw high amounts of current that reasonably-scaled renewable systems just can't handle.

Your local solar dealer (assuming there is one) may run their whole business off the panels and keep it 59 degrees Fahrenheit (15 degrees Celsius) in the peak of summer and 85 degrees Fahrenheit (29 degrees Celsius) in the dead of winter, but consider how much hardware they had to buy (wholesale) and install (themselves) to manage that trick.

- Every dollar you spend on conservation means two or more dollars less on generation equipment to make the home work.
- You may want to consider comfort vs. luxury vs. ideology.
- Realistically, photovoltaic panels, wind, and micro-hydro power will not heat or cool your home for a reasonable installation budget.
  If you have the money they CAN, but you will probably be looking at a grid-tie solution since you will be generating excess power much of the time that batteries can't soak up fast enough.
- There are solar water and air heaters that work well, but these heat the water or air directly from sunlight, not via an electrical circuit.
- Generally speaking, you won't be able to air condition or heat your home with the size of a solar and/or wind system that you could reasonably afford without a second mortgage on the house.
- Highly-efficient refrigerators tend to be smaller, and the most energy efficient ones open from the top. Consider what you will need (and want) to keep cold, and whether you can put some things in a chest freezer, or re-arrange your conventional kitchen layout.
- Another option is a gas-absorption (gas/electric/heat powered) refrigerator.

- On non-grid systems, 12V or 24V lighting and appliances, such as refrigerators and washing machines, can save substantial power over their AC counterparts by cutting the inverter "middle man" out of the equation. That 10–15% load is a walk in the park for an inverter.

Inverters
While it's possible to run the whole household off DC, it's far less expensive and far more convenient to get AC appliances and run them off an inverter.

- With grid-tie systems the inverter is integrated into the system that ties the power to the grid and is connected between the power company's meter and the house. These can usually be chained together to handle power-output requirements.
- Many smaller inverters can be more efficient and less expensive than one large inverter. These can run individual-household circuits.

Unreliable Backup
The natural elements that self-contained power systems rely on are not reliable. The sun is not always shining, the wind is not always blowing, and the water is not always flowing.

Grid
This is the least expensive solution for most people, especially those who are already power customers. They install one sort of power (solar) and tie the package to the grid. Then when there isn't enough power coming in, the grid makes up the shortfalls, and when there is excess power, the grid buys it. Larger systems can consistently run the power meter backwards.

Generator

- If there is no grid, or you want disaster/blackout backup, a generator may be required.

- You don't want to draw batteries dead, so you'll need a way to make power when all else fails, then you won't deep-cycle your batteries to the point where you end up replacing them too frequently or end up with no power.
- Even with a generator, batteries are required in an off-grid system. Charging batteries will put a reasonable load on the generator so it works efficiently for the fuel it consumes, while simply running lights will put mostly light loads, which are very inefficiently handled by most generators.
- Many generators are very slow to react to load changes (switching on a power-hungry device causes the power to falter).
- Small, commonly available generators at your hardware store are made for occasional emergency use. They will generally fall apart if used for daily power.
- Large-household generators cost a LOT of money. They can run off of gasoline (diesel or LPG too) and usually have a self-starting mode where they kick on when the grid power is interrupted. These can kill electricians who pop a service disconnect and don't know there's also a backup generator.
- Generators made for RV/trailer/marine use are small, quiet, made for continuous/daily duty, and affordable (at least compared to household generators). They can run off of gasoline, as well as diesel or LPG, and are made to run on demand for hours at a time for a period of years.

Solar Power

Solar panels should have south-facing exposure to the sun (north-facing in southern hemisphere, up-facing near the equator).

- Relatively clear weather most of the year is helpful, but light overcast conditions are sometimes beneficial.
- The best angle needs to be adjusted according to your latitude.
- If necessary, they can point straight up at any latitude, but will lose some efficiency, and then you'll need more panels.
- Fixed mounts can be built onto their own structure (which may house batteries and charge controller beneath) or placed on an existing roof. They are easy to mount and maintain if near the ground and have no moving parts.
- Tracking mounts follow the sun and add efficiency, but can be more expensive than simply adding a couple more panels to a fixed installation to make up for the difference. They are mechanical contraptions that are easily damaged by severe weather and have moving parts that wear out.
- Just because a solar panel is rated for 100W, it doesn't mean it will deliver that much because of the way it was mounted, because of weather, or because the sun is riding lower on the horizon (during winter). You'll need more power.

Wind Power

- There are many kinds of wind generators.
- They can be home fabricated from old car alternators, but need relatively high wind to operate.
- They can be bought pre-packaged and less expensively than equivalent solar output.
- Wind power can be noisy, so shop around.
- Occasionally, birds fly through the propeller blades, but only pieces come out the other side.

- Windmills need consistent wind. Open, desolate areas work best, as they have the fewest things blocking the wind. Wind power generally supplements solar power, by making energy whenever the wind is blowing, like at night and on cloudy days.

Micro-Hydro

There are various types, ranging from a homemade propeller connected to a car alternator to fairly robust and intricately engineered systems.

- This needs flowing water. If you don't have river-front property or year-round streams/springs, it's just not going to work for you.

What You Should Consider

- If you live in a sunny environment, consider solar energy.
- If you live in a windy environment, consider wind energy.
- If you have access to flowing water, micro-hydro may work better than solar and wind combined.
- A combination of power sources works best.
- If your home is connected to the grid (has electrical power delivered from a utility company), consider a grid-tie solution.
- If your home is remote and/or not connected to the electrical grid or you want renewable power backup, consider a self-contained solution.

Things You'll Need

- Inverter(s)
- Charge controller(s)
- Deep-cycle batteries
- Power source(s)

- Solar (photovoltaic) panels
- Wind generator(s)
- Micro-hydro generator(s)
- Motor(s)

Warnings

- Check with local building codes, zoning laws, and CC&Rs.
- Whatever you install, make sure your homeowner's insurance covers it. Make no assumptions.
- If you have no working electrical theory or safety knowledge, consider this a list of what to find out about for somebody else to do.
- You can cause severe property damage (fry your set-up, cause roof leaks, or burn down the house).
- You can cause severe injury or death (electrocution, falling off the roof, or materials improperly secured falling onto people).
- Shorted or unvented batteries can cause an explosion.
- Splashed battery acid can cause severe burns and/or blindness.
- Even DC power at these amps can stop your heart or cause severe burns should jewelry come into contact with it.
- **This is the real deal**! That innocent spinning wheel and those purple panels can *kill* you until you *die* from it!

11
BOB INCH GHB REK EDC MPL

Surviving a tough situation involves using your brain to tap into a reservoir of knowledge and maintain emotional control. That said, having the right equipment goes a long way too. All the will in the world won't light a fire like a match can, and having survival supplies can support your outlook and build the necessary confidence and optimism you need to survive.

BOB

What exactly is a bug-out bag? A bug-out bag is a collection of basic-survival gear that might be required in a disaster scenario, natural or even manmade, for 72 hours. It is transportable and combined into a single pack so that you can grab it and evacuate rapidly if disaster should strike.

It is also known as a 72-hour kit, a grab bag, a battle box, and other popular names include GO bag and GOOD (**g**et **o**ut **of d**odge) bag. The focus is on evacuation, rather than long-term survival. Distinguishing the bug-out bag from a survival kit, I like to keep one at home and one in each vehicle, but how you implement your bug out bag is up to you.

The actual bag could be as simple as an extra backpack or

duffel bag, or as elaborate as a framed military surplus ALICE pack. The best bug-out bag is one that you can pack the most in and still carry comfortably for an extended time.

The bug-out bag offers you a CHANCE at survival when all else seems lost. This is its purpose. The more ingenuity invested in the design of your BOB, the better your chance will be. Finding items and tools that streamline efficiency, space, weight, or serve two or more functions at once is crucial in organizing a high-performance pack. In this way, building a BOB becomes a sort of art form.

To properly pack your bug out bag, anticipate a worst-case scenario, but choose only the essential items. Imagine no running water, no food, no electricity, and no city services for days. What type of things would you need to survive?

The Essential BOB Items

Water
It should go without saying that water is a survival basic for any situation. In a survival situation water quickly becomes the most precious commodity. One liter per person per day is really the bare minimum. Thus, your 3-day BOB should have at least three liters of water. To expand your capability or survive longer than a couple of days, you will need a water purification system. This can be as simple as boiling water, using purification tablets, or better yet, a Katadyn Pocket Water Microfilter.

Food
For a three-day BOB, backpack meals and energy bars can be sufficient. Backpack meals are freeze-dried meals that you just add boiling water to. They are light weight and last a long time, but if you can spare the extra weight, MRE's are just that, "meals ready to eat" and have far more calories.

Clothing
Your BOB clothes' list should be similar to the way you would pack for a weekend backpacking trip.

- Plan for the Season
- Pair of sturdy boots
- Pair of long pants (in earth tones)
- Two pairs of socks (not cotton)
- Two shirts, one long sleeved and one short sleeved for layering (in earth tones)
- Jacket (Gore-Tex in earth tones)
- Poncho
- Gloves
- Long underwear
- Hat
- Shemagh

Shelter

If you are going to survive for three days, you are going to need protection from the elements and a warm, dry place to sleep. You need at least a:

- Tent or tarp with items needed to set it up.
- Emergency Bivvy.
- U.S. Military Gore-Tex Modular Sleep System.

First-Aid Kit

I recommend that you build your own first-aid kit instead of buying one of those prepackaged, first-aid kits that claim to have 1001 things to get you through any emergency. While some are OK, in my experience these types of kits are usually filled with a lot of stuff you are unlikely to need and not enough of the things you will probably need the most of. Plus, building your own first-aid kit gives you an intimate knowledge of what it contains and how to use it. Most people buy one of those pre-made set ups and just assume they are prepared because there's so much crap in it. Add things like QuikClot, Israeli battle dressing, butterfly stitches, moleskin, Telfa pads, ect. Refer to my first-aid list for suggested items.

Rain Gear: A poncho and Gore-Tex coat are good coupled with your tent/shelter to keep you dry in the rain.

Fire: The best way to start a fire is the easiest way. That's why I stress to carry several lighters, and as backup, magnesium bars or storm-proof matches.

Cooking: U. S. army mess kit and canteen cup are small, lightweight, and almost indestructible. If you have room, a small backpacking stove and fuel would be a nice addition.

Light resources include the Nuwick 120-hour candle, at least two dependable LED flashlights, a LED headlamp, and extra batteries for each.

Survival knife
The most used and versatile tool in your BOB is your knife. Most survival knives fall within the range of 6–12 inches. Any less and it might not be big enough to chop wood, amongst other things. Sure, it would work a lot better with a hatchet or saw, but if you bug out, you might not have anything else. Make sure its full tang for maximum strength. Stainless steel is...well, stainless steel. It's virtually indestructible, and lasts a long time without rusting. However, many people say stainless blades lose an edge pretty fast. Whereas carbon- steel knives are usually known to hold a good edge longer than stainless steel, but will rust faster in the elements. My favorite brand is Tops.

Weapons
You are preparing for a WROL, "Without Rule of Law," situation, so being prepared to defend yourself is part of the survivalist mindset. A handgun in a large caliber with four loaded magazines and a small cleaning kit is a must. If this isn't possible in your area, carry pepper spray, a slingshot, or even wasp spray.

Here is a broad list of items you will want to consider for your BOB, in no particular order. It goes beyond the urban environment, because you might be bugging out of the city.

- Gas mask (extra filters)
- Stormproof lighter
- Magnesium bar
- NATO-stormproof matches
- Military-gel fuel
- Canteen and cup
- Snare wire
- Fishing kit
- Compass
- Compact binoculars
- Local/topographical map
- U. S. army mess kit
- Spoon, fork, spork
- Handgun (extra magazines)
- 150+ rounds of ammo
- Night-vision monocular
- Pocket knife
- Survival knife
- Combat knife
- Knife-sharpening stone
- Leatherman multi-tool
- Pepper spray
- Slingshot
- Goggles (military style)
- Wire saw
- Folding camp saw
- Compact Ax
- 550 paracord
- Plastic zip ties
- Carabiners
- Small sewing kit
- GI-issued, tri-fold shovel
- Backpacking stove and fuel
- Re-rolled toilet paper
- Poncho
- Emergency thermal blanket
- U.S. military, Gore-Tex modular sleep system

- Emergency water packets
- Water purification tablets
- Oral-rehydration salts
- Katadyn water filter
- Glow sticks
- LED tactical flashlight
- LED headlamp
- Batteries
- Clothing (as listed previously)
- Tactical gloves
- Pocket radio
- Two-way radios
- Small pry bar
- Re-rolled duct tape
- Hygiene kit
- First-aid kit
- Camp soap
- Hoo-Ahhs
- Prepaid phone card
- Cash (small bills)
- Sun screen
- Insect repellant
- Extra pair of glasses/contact lens
- Can opener P-38
- 1-gallon Ziploc bags
- Whistle
- This book

INCH

The "I'm never coming home" (INCH) variant is designed to support the life of its owner indefinitely, as opposed to other BOBs, which are oriented toward sustaining life for a fixed length of time. These bags tend to be much larger, contain a wider array of tools and supplies, and are also much heavier.

"I'm never coming home" or INCH bag confronts the idea that society has completely imploded, and you need to be as self-sufficient as possible. We'll refer to this as the "post-apocalyptic world" or PAW scenario. The INCH bag is basically a large survival kit containing items critical to your survival following a disaster or other SHTF scenario. An INCH bag should differ from a BOB or GOOD bag in that it must sustain you indefinitely. The mindset is, "What good will a BOB do for you after 72 hours?" After 72 hours, the average BOB turns into a SOL bag. In this type of situation, I have a modified version of an old saying; "Give a man a fish; you have fed him for today. Teach a man to fish and you will not have to listen to his incessant whining about how hungry he is."

The focus should be on hard supplies that last a long time, rather than on consumable goods. The idea is that eventually you are going to run out of consumables and will still have needs. The tools which allow you to gather these resources will be more of a priority in this situation, meaning that the ability to purify water is going to be worth more than having water that's already clean (of course you will need enough bottled water to get you to the open-water source). Therefore, if you only have room for 1 type of item in your kit, I would pick the one that's going to last the longest.

There are, of course, a few key points to remember when building a kit like this, and for the most part, they will correspond to your basic needs that are beyond the BOB list.

Water: Mid-size pot to boil water in

Food: Non-hybrid seeds (Don't forget you can sprout them, thus, eating is right away.)

Shelter: Sturdy tent (until you can find or build something better)

Battle rifle: AR or AK, six extra magazines, and as much ammo as you can carry

U.S. Survival AR-7: (Don't leave civilization without one.) Since 1959, the respected AR-7 has been the choice of U.S. Air Force pilots who need a small-caliber rifle they can count on for survival, should they have to punch out over a remote area. The AR-7 has a reputation for portability, ease of operation, and reliability. This semi-automatic rifle is lightweight (just 3.5 pounds) and highly portable. At just 16½ inches in length (when all the components are stowed), it fits easily into a backpack; and because it's chambered in .22LR, you can carry a few thousand rounds of ammunition without adding much weight to your gear.

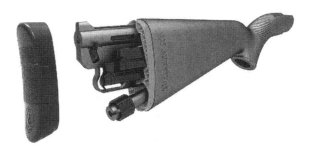

When disassembled, the pieces fit inside the impact-resistant, waterproof stock. Assembly is as easy as attaching the receiver to the stock, inserting the barrel, and screwing on the barrel nut, all within a few seconds, without the need for any tools. The AR-7 is your best bet for dispatching those "uncatchable" chickens for the stew pot, for shooting small game/pests, as well as for small incursions. You may not need more than a .22 for most conflicts—without available hospitals, a gunshot wound is going to be fatal regardless of caliber. No one is going to think "ah, it's only a .22, so I don't care if I get shot." I saw a ballistics test that showed a .22LR round go through a ½-inch piece of pine wood at 400 yards!

A .22, stainless-steel Ruger Mark II is a noteworthy SHTF INCH-bag addition if your bag space is too limited for an AR-7.

Survival books: Wild edibles, medicinal plants, trapping, shelter building, etc. (You can photo copy only parts of the books that are relevant to your area, so that you don't have to carry all of the books.)

Predetermined Caches

Part of your INCH plan should include finding predetermined bug-out locations, where you can bury a mono-vault burial tube with extra ammo, some MRE's, and anything else too heavy to carry ahead of time. Remember: "Loose lips sink ships!"

Beyond that, most other things are going to be considered "luxury" items, things that are good to have but not completely necessary to survive. Of course the idea that you're never going home also means you are probably going to be thinking about setting up shop somewhere new, so your destination is going to have a significant impact on the rest of your kit. Where you end up should determine what else you want to bring with you, but you have to consider its benefit vs. how much it weighs.

My Bag

My pack is a cross between a BOB and an INCH, mainly because I live in the inner city, but have mountains that can be reached with little effort. I feel that most bug-out bags you see on the Internet are too limiting for urban escape and evasion, as 72 hours is going to come and go. The BOB contents that I have listed as suggestions are a good middle ground for short and long-term solutions. That is why I added less common BOB items, like a tri-fold shovel, small pry bar, fishing kit, and snare wire.

Let your immediate surroundings dictate what you will pack in your bag, not some slick YouTube video or even what I suggest. If you live in Kansas, you probably don't need 500 feet of rock-repelling rope and equipment; and if you live in Los Angeles, you don't need bear spray... wait a minute, that may come in very handy when encountering ferocious man-imals!

CART

You always see local bums with shopping carts, as well as refugees on the news with makeshift carts, and there are logical reasons for this.

The novice and the out-of-shape all begin by assuming that they can fill their pack with everything that they've read is necessary and still perform a prolonged panic hike of some 20+ miles per day. Many an Old-West, wagon-train movie illustrated a trail dotted with belongings, discarded when times got hard, animal power to haul having sickened, weakened, or died, or other trail hazards and dilemmas arose.

That's why, if you are not bugging out alone and have kids, you might want to consider adding a cart to your plan. Unless you see the early warning signs, it is going to be very difficult to leave a large city in a fully-loaded vehicle. Unfortunately, if you are forced out of your survive-in-place plan, you will want to carry all that you can. I suggest either building a cart or purchasing a game carrier that will accommodate your family's bug-out bags and food and water supplies. Using a tarp to cover your load will keep prying eyes astray, keep your goods from the elements, and shelter you and your family at night.

Bug-Out Bikes

Bikes are an option, and anyone saying otherwise doesn't know anything about survival. Every option has its pros and cons, but survival is all about options, not just locking on to any one thing. If you are healthy enough to ride a bike, you would do well to have one in good condition with extra parts, EVEN if you own a car. If you own a bike as a secondary option, make sure you ride it at least one a month (preferably once a week), so that you will be aware of any maintenance that it requires.

Since I'm a mountain bike enthusiast, I believe that mountain bikes would be a most excellent alternative to gas-operated vehicles in a SHTF or bug-out scenario for a variety of reasons. For instance, at least in my area, there's enough street construction currently happening that gridlock is guaranteed in the event of an emergency (not to mention we have THE worst drivers!!) and the likely possibility of gas shortages will make having/using a bike indispensible. I could see myself rolling past all the "sheeple," bumper-to-bumper, in their cars on the I-10 trying to make their way out.

I was thinking about attaching a deer-game cart or a kiddie-carrier to haul supplies behind the bike. They're both lightweight enough to carry a great deal of supplies and are rugged enough to ride off-road trails with. I have also considered a mountain-bike set-up with carry packs.

GHB

Imagine this: you're 15 miles away from home running some last minute errands before dinner and disaster strikes. The grid goes down, crippling communication, all road ways have become jammed, and your family is home alone and scared. You need to get home immediately. But there's just one thing...

Do you have the resources to make the trek back home on foot? Are you going to remain where you are, just hoping the government will assist you in getting home. This is where you need your get-home bag.

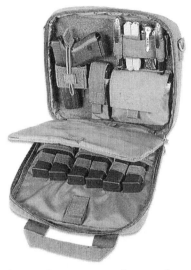

The purpose of a get-home bag is to get you to your home or to some other shelter safely and as quickly as possible. A get-home bag is different than a bug-out bag in that it is designed to be carried with you at all times (or at least readily accessible) any time you're away from home.

While a typical bug-out bag is stocked full of items to support you for at least three days, a get-home bag should contain the minimal amount of items to support you in getting home within a 24-hour period.

What Type of Bag Should I Choose?

If you are caught in a situation where looting and other forms of lawlessness are breaking out (Remember Hurricane Katrina?), the last thing you want to do is stand out in the crowd. It's at those times that you want to be the "gray man" and fade into the background.

If your get-home bag screams tactical or looks expensive, you could be a target. For this reason, you want to ensure that your bag looks very ordinary.

If you're a female, you've got it made. A purse doesn't draw any strange attention and you can even get away with a large, plain-looking hand bag; guys are used to seeing women carry 15 pounds of survival, beauty products.

For the guys, a simple messenger bag works well. Especially in the cities, messenger bags are seen being carried by guys more and more, so they blend in well. If you can't deal with the "man purse," go for a standard back pack. Just be sure not to abuse its size with a crap load of gear. Keep it under 15 pounds. Anything over that and you'll soon give up carrying it around on a day-to-day basis.

In most cases, try to stay away from the Alice Pack or MOLLE Pack type of look. If it's overly military looking or you have a bunch of MOLLE webbing with all sorts of gear riding on it, you'll attract undesired attention since it looks like you've got a bunch of supplies on you (and they'd be right). Give it a KISS: "Keep it simple, stupid!"

What Should Your Get-Home Bag Contain?

What you pack in your get-home bag is obviously dictated by personal preference and what your needs are. However, if you're unsure as how to organize it, perhaps I can share what I carry in my get-home bag and hopefully it'll give you some tips on how best to organize yours.

Essential GHB Items

Personal Security

If you have the option to carry a concealed firearm in your state and you're comfortable with that, by all means I would recommend doing so. Otherwise, if it's not an option, you can carry a knife, pepper spray, wasp spray, stun gun, or any other item that can protect you from animals of both the four-legged and two-legged-walking-upright kind.

Suggestions

- Handgun and two loaded magazines with hollow-point ammunition
- Tactical folding knife
- Compact pepper spray
- Tactical LED flashlight
- Mini-trauma kit containing QuikClot Combat Gauze, Israeli bandage, pain killers, and nitrile gloves.

Shelter

Since carrying a tent around with you 24/7 is totally unrealistic, my GHB contains one of the simplest and lightest shelters available: a space blanket. These ingenious devices are waterproof, windproof, and can reflect up to 97% of the radiated heat your body throws off. The down side is that they are so reflective that they aren't very discreet and can tear easy, but for a 24-hour survival pack, they are about the best you can do.

Water

If you are forced into a 24-hour trek back home, dehydration will quickly become a real issue. That's why it's so important that you have either water on you or some means of getting, storing, and purifying it.

Suggestions

- Several emergency water packets
- Rolled-up water bladder
- Water-purification tablets
- Aquamira filtration straw

Fire

I wouldn't recommend packing some obscure, "cool" fire-making implement, like a battery and steel wool or a fire piston. Remember, this isn't about impressing your friends, but about survival. Instead, pack something you know you'll be able to start a fire with, like a lighter.

Suggestions

- Lighters
- NATO Stormproof matches
- Magnesium bar and dryer lint

Food
For the food part of your get-home bag, you'll want to avoid any high-water-content containing foods like canned goods or fresh foods. Instead, pack some simple, dense, calorie-rich foods that save space and take no extra preparation beyond tearing open a wrapper. Dehydrated foods and dense candy bars are more along the lines of what you want.

For my bag, I carry four energy bars. It's not gourmet, but it will carry me through until I get home.

Beyond the Essentials
The elements of your GHB should be the minimum required to get you home, but if your bag still has some room in it, may I suggest a few more things which can greatly aid you in the getting-home process.

- Maps: I carry foldable topographical maps (homemade from MyTopo via Google Maps) of my area. This encompasses where I work, my home, and the areas in-between. This way, I can figure out how best to navigate around potentially unsafe or inaccessible areas.
- GPS: This would be my primary means of navigation if satellite coverage is available.
- Compass: This would be back-up in case my GPS were to go down (via EMP or otherwise).
- Survival knife
- 550 paracord
- Flashlight: Surefire E2D LED Defender
- Multi-tool: Leatherman
- Small hand sanitizer

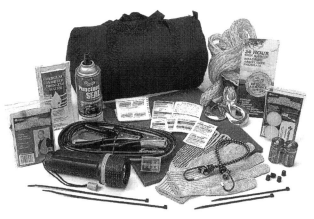

REK

Have you ever been in this scenario? It's 11:00 p.m.; you're driving on a lonely country road that's dark and desolate. You know in an instant that something is wrong. Controlling the vehicle becomes increasingly difficult and you ease the car to the side of the road. Getting out, you see that the left, rear tire is flat, and you're already running on your spare.

If you're lucky, you have an account with AAA and your cell phone has service in that area. If not, you're either faced with a long walk until you flag down a passing motorist or spend a night in the boonies, hoping you don't hear banjo music. That is, unless you have a well-stocked, emergency-roadside kit in the trunk of your car.

When it comes to commuting or traveling any lengthy distance, a roadside-emergency kit can mean the difference between getting back on the road or being stuck for a long period of time. A roadside-emergency kit is the one item that every vehicle should have; yet most of us never carry any of the basic items to help get us back onto the road quickly and safely.

Vehicle Check List

- Battery and ignition systems should be in top condition and battery terminals clean.
- Ensure antifreeze levels are sufficient to avoid freezing.
- Ensure the heater and defroster work properly.
- Check and repair windshield-wiper equipment, and ensure proper washer-fluid level.
- Ensure the thermostat works properly.
- Check all lights for serviceability.
- Check for leaks and crimped pipes in the exhaust system and repair or replace as necessary. (Carbon monoxide is deadly and usually gives no warning.)
- Check breaks for wear and fluid levels.
- Check oil for level and weight. Heavier oils congeal more readily at low temperatures and don't lubricate as well.
- Consider snow tires, snow tires with studs, or chains.

Roadside-Emergency Kit

- 5-gallon can
- Small fire extinguisher
- Food (non-perishables: MREs, power bars, etc.)
- Water (1-gallon, plastic jug)
- Sleeping bag or blanket (wool is best)
- Sturdy shoes or boots and a pair of thick socks should be stuffed in each shoe.
- Cigarette lighter and storm-proof matches
- LED flashlight with spare batteries
- Auto-size fire extinguisher
- First-aid kit
- Your medication (72-hour supply)
- Spare glasses (even if it's your old prescription)
- Work gloves
- Portable radio (AM/ FM/weather radio with spare batteries)

- Maps (Thomas Guide/maps within last five years)
- Notebook (pocket-size with pen and pencil in Ziploc bag)
- Garbage bags (large, heavy duty—doubles as rain suits by cutting holes in the corners and center of top for arms and head)
- Clothing (old coat and pants)
- Fix-A-Flat
- Bungee Cord (twenty-four inch)
- Roadside flares (four 15 minutes each) or reflective triangle
- Hose (6-foot garden hose or siphon kit)
- Tire-pressure gauge
- Two quarts of oil
- Radiator fluid
- Starting fluid
- WD-40
- Pry bar
- Extra fuses
- Zip ties
- Duct tape and electrical tape
- Wire clothes hanger (Two is minimum)
- Tool kit: pocket knife, Leatherman multi-tool, water-pump pliers, needle-nose pliers, wire cutter, diagonal cutter, Phillips screwdriver, standard screwdriver, zip ties, electrical tape, medium-grit sand paper, crescent wrench, vise grips, metric and standard ratchet kit, Allen-wrench set, metric and standard open wrenches, hammer, ice scraper, and safety glasses
- Folding shovel
- Folding saw
- 550 paracord (for a quick fix-tie job)
- Paper towels or clean rags
- Cash in small bills, credit card, and pre-paid phone card
- Jump-N-Carry portable battery charger
- Jumper cables (proper length and type)

- Tow straps and rope
- Car keys (extra set outside of trunk/interior wired in place or use magnetic key hider)
- Evaluate: Do you have everything you need?

Several companies offer pre-assembled, emergency-roadside kits that you can find in most automotive departments for under $40. While these kits contain the basics in a small, convenient carrier, you might want to augment them with a few of the items I have just listed to suit your needs.

Before you actually use your kit in an emergency situation, take some time to familiarize yourself with the items you've collected and how to use them properly. Also remember that the MOST important item is your own good judgment.

In a real SHTF situation, when out of fuel, you are going to roll up to abandoned cars, punch a hole in the gas tank with a screw driver and hammer, fill your containers, and roll away as quickly as possible.

EDC

Every day carry refers to a small collection of tools, equipment, and supplies that are carried on a daily basis to assist in tackling situations ranging from the mundane to the disastrous. The term EDC also refers to the philosophy or spirit of preparedness that goes along with the selection and carrying of these items.

Implicit in the term is the sense that an EDC is an individual's personal selection of equipment, arrived at after deliberation, rather than a standardized kit.

EDC items will normally fit in your pockets, or small pack, or be attached to clothing. Emphasis is placed on the weight, usefulness, accessibility, and the reliability of these items. Here is a list of different items you might consider when putting together your EDC.

Suggestions

- Tactical folding knife with pocket clip, karambit, or spring-assisted knife
- KA-BAR TDI Law Enforcement Last Ditch Knife
- Multi-tool
- Gerber Artifact
- Handcuff key
- 550-paracord bracelet or lanyard
- LED tactical flashlight or LED pen light
- Tactical pen
- Compact Pepper Spray
- Water purification tablets
- Extra medication
- "Altoids survival tin"
- Stormproof lighter
- USB flash drive

MPL

This master-preparedness list is a suggestion of supplies and items to have on hand, but of course, you'll add to this list depending on your preferences. Imagine all stores being closed for several months.

Take an inventory of the non-grocery commodity items in your kitchen, bathroom, laundry room, and garage. Determine how much of each item your family needs per month or per year. Based upon the estimated consumption rates, establish a stocking level of your essential and desirable household supplies. Be sure it's adequate to see your family through a long-term economic disruption.

Acquire both over-the-counter and prescription medications for as many common medical conditions as possible, even if you and your family are perfectly healthy right now.

Obtain personal-protection equipment, such as respirators, face masks, disposable gloves, sanitation supplies, and any items that will help you care for someone with an infectious disease.

Hospitals are not prepared to care for the vast numbers of people who will become sick, so you must accept the fact that it will be completely up to you to provide medical care in your home for every family member who becomes sick. Assume that you will not have access to a medical care facility for several months.

Clothing

- Boots
- Tennis shoes
- Sweatpants
- Sweatshirts
- Coats
- Hats/beanies
- Long and short sleeved shirts
- Long underwear
- Denim pants
- Rubberized rain gear
- Snow jackets
- Socks (heavy)
- Underwear
- Bras (athletic)
- Bandanas
- Winter gloves

- Work gloves
- Shoelaces
- Patches

Communication

- CB radio
- Two-way radio
- Police scanner
- Frequency list
- AM/FM/weather-band radio
- Hand-crank radio
- Map of area
- Topographical maps
- Road flares
- Signal mirror
- Signal whistle
- Compass

Fuel and Power

- Barrels (55 gal)
- Gas cans (5 gal)
- Charcoal
- Fire wood
- Gasoline
- Kerosene
- Sterno fuel
- Lighter fluid
- Propane
- Gas stabilizer
- Anti-bacterial diesel additive
- Starter fluid
- White gas
- Strike-anywhere matches

Hardware and Building Supplies

- Chains
- Padlocks
- Fencing material
- Chicken wire
- Barbed wire
- Duct tape
- Electrical tape
- Lumber
- Woodworking tools
- Common tools
- Drill (hand-operated)
- Hammer
- Nails
- Nuts
- Bolts
- Screws
- Files
- Plumbing repair supplies
- Cable
- Rope
- Pulleys
- Shovel
- Axe
- Pick
- Machete
- Sledgehammer
- Wood saw
- Hacksaw
- Ladder
- Spare keys to all locks
- Tarps
- Wire

Household Items

- Batteries (AA, AAA, C, D, 9V, CR123A, rechargeable)
- Solar-battery recharger
- Candles (10 and 36 hour)
- Candles (100-hour liquid paraffin)
- Candle holders
- Non-electric can opener
- Bottle opener
- Corkscrew
- Clock (wind-up)
- Watches wind up/solar
- Solar calculator
- Broom and mop
- Fire extinguisher
- LED flashlights
- LED headlamp
- Propane heater
- Kerosene heater
- Kerosene lamps
- Lamp wicks
- Waterproof matches
- Lighters
- Glow sticks
- Scissors
- Mosquito net
- Sleeping bags
- Bed roll
- Large first-aid kit
- Wash board
- Wash tub
- Clothes line
- Clothes pins
- Needles
- Sewing supplies
- Bleach
- Soap (hand and dish soap)

- Clothing detergent
- Liquid plumber
- Bottled lye
- Baking soda
- Camping toilet
- Toilet paper
- Paper towels
- Ziploc bags in various sizes
- Aluminum foil
- Manual-grain mill grinder
- Cast-iron Dutch oven
- Pressure cooker
- Kettle
- Pots, pans, cast iron skillet, bread pan
- Food grade 5-gallon buckets with lid
- Mylar bags in various sizes
- Oxygen absorbers
- Canning jars and lids
- Timer
- Flour sifter
- Measuring cups and spoons
- Thermos bottles
- Plastic utensils
- Disposable cups
- Paper plates
- Tents
- Smoke detectors
- Carbon-monoxide alarm
- Trash bags
- Wool blankets

Baby Items

- Baby powder, shampoo, lotion, ointments
- Bottles with extra nipples
- Formula and baby food
- Portable crib, blankets, sheets

- Extra clothes
- Diapers
- Baby wipes
- Teething rings
- Toys

Miscellaneous

- 275-gallon IBC tote tank w/steel cage (water storage)
- Water-storage barrels (55 gallon)
- Water-storage containers (7 gallon)
- Water filters
- Solar shower
- 5-gallon emergency toilet
- Bug-spray concentrate
- Binoculars
- Burning barrel
- Fishing tackle
- Knives
- Metal bucket
- Night vision
- 550 cord
- Safe
- Glue (various types)
- Window screen
- Guns, ammunition, and magazines
- Gun-cleaning equipment
- Ammo cans
- Military web gear
- Bug out bag
- Gas masks with extra filters
- Smoke hood
- N95-particulate respirator mask
- Perimeter alarms
- Solar-powered perimeter lights
- Chainsaw
- Pry bar

- Generator
- Fuel filter for generator
- Gardening tools
- Wheel barrel
- Welding equipment and supplies
- Bolt cutters
- Camouflage netting
- 16-mil, UV-treated tarps
- Black paint for widows
- Sand bags
- Solar panels and inverter
- WD-40
- Board games, deck of cards, coloring books, etc.
- Recipe books/cooking with home-storage books
- Books on edible plants
- How to books
- Home-school curriculum
- Musical instruments
- Bicycles with spare parts
- Automotive replacement parts/fluids
- Birth control
- Feminine-hygiene supplies
- Extra glasses/contact lenses with solution
- Mirror
- Magnifying glass
- Money in small bills
- Pre-1965 silver dimes
- Mouse/rat traps
- Pesticides
- NukAlert
- Potassium Iodide (KI)
- Non-hybrid seeds
- Vitamins and minerals
- Wheelchair and crutches
- Paper, note pads, pencils, and pens
- Non-electric pencil sharpener
- Birth, death, and marriage certificates

- Deeds and contracts
- Home and life-insurance policies
- Medical records
- Passports
- Bible!

12
SECURITY AND DEFENSE

In a massive social collapse, most people will be able to keep only that which they can defend. This includes their lives, their homes, their food, their money, and if they're male, even their wives and children. This is a thought that may disturb many people who are doing serious emergency planning; many do not have a "survivalist" background or mindset, and they've never had any reason to think about physically defending that which is precious to them. A major disaster may change all that, just as it may change nearly everything else in the world for those living through it.

In an orderly, productive society, with a stable division of labor, the harsh realities of life are not so obvious. You have laws that most people obey, and you have professional police who enforce those laws. It's their job to defend the lives and property of the average citizen; if there's any violence to be done in that defense, the police handle that. The average person never has to consider defending what is his, unless he is personally threatened by a criminal. The threat of force by the police keeps order in society and tends to discourage aggressive, criminal behavior. It also tends to hide a basic truth about the nature of human relations.

In a massive social collapse, law and public order break down, and the truth about human rights is revealed: An individual has rights only as long as he can defend them. This is the subtle logic of violence. It has always been true but it's something to which most of us have never given a moment's thought. However, unless you understand and accept this basic fact of life, you may not survive the coming challenges.

If a disaster crashes down hard upon us, it will destroy all the illusions and most of the rules we have lived by for the past hundred years or more. It will create harsh new rules. When the fundamental order of a society changes and new rules arise, those who fail to understand the new rules suffer the most. It's not just having a weapon that's important, or even knowing how to use one; it's knowing full well why you need to use it and therefore not hesitating to use it when needed. A gun in your hand is totally worthless against an assailant unless you're fully willing to use it to defend yourself. You must understand that the new rules brought on by a major disaster may require you to defend your life personally.

After TSHTF, only an idiot would believe that the police will protect them from the crime wave that will follow the collapse. A lot of people that are antigun now will run to the gun shops, seeking advice on how to defend themselves and their families. They will buy a firearm, a box of ammo, and leave it in the closet, probably believing that it will magically protect them from intruders. Maybe you don't think that firearms are really necessary or your beliefs do not allow you to buy a tool designed to kill someone. You probably ask yourself, is a gun necessary when TSHTF? Will it truly make a difference? YES, it surely will! You need a gun, pepper spray, a machete, a battle axe, club with a rusty nail sticking out of it, or whatever weapon you can get hold of. I personally drew a line in the sand a few years ago deciding, after a long, serious conversation with my wife, that no one would be allowed inside our home uninvited, no matter what. There are worse things than death. Having decided that, I make sure I always have a weapon on me. They'll have to pay dearly for my life, plus interest. If someone does invade your home—killing them is probably the best way to go—that way there is only one story, and it's YOURS.

Defense inside Your Home or Close-Quarters Combat

Shotgun

The best weapon for home defense is a shotgun with a short barrel. There are three reasons why this is true. First, there is nothing scarier than looking at that big, black hole at the end of the barrel of a shotgun when it's pointed at you. Second, when you fire a shotgun at close range, it's impossible to miss; you're going to hit what you're aiming at. Third, when you hit someone with a shotgun, that person doesn't get up and come after you. A short-barrel gun is easier to handle than one with a long barrel.

There are several good, basic shotguns on the market. One of the best is a 12-gauge Remington Pump 870 Express Magnum with an 18-inch barrel. Just hearing the unmistakable click of a pump-action shotgun being cocked will scare off most intruders. The Remington costs about $350 new. Mossberg also makes a good pump 12 gauge, along with several other manufacturers. If you want to stop somebody, a nice riot shotgun should do the trick. The blast won't go through too many walls like a large-caliber rifle round, so a much less chance of killing your neighbor—its range is very suitable for inside a house, and its pattern leaves little chance of you missing someone shooting down a long hallway or from upstairs to down. The sound alone will cause people to panic and run. If there's a good gun store in your area, stop by and look at what's available. Ask questions; most gun-shop employees are very knowledgeable and willing to share that knowledge with you.

Dedicated Light Mount

As with any tactical/defensive weapon, a light mount is a must. Not having a light mount is like a car without headlights. You can still get around, but you're not going to be very effective or safe once it gets dark. For most weapons, you can get by with a powerful LED, handheld flashlight, but shotguns, especially pumps, are extremely difficult to shoot with a handheld light. Fortunately, Surefire makes a dedicated replacement forend light mount/housing for all of the popular shotguns. If they don't make one for your gun, they make great universal mounts that will fit just about any shotgun.

Sling

All shotguns must have a sling. That is a serious rule. A long gun without a sling is like a handgun without a holster. When your weapon stops working, whether it be a malfunction or you've simply run out of ammo, your first response should always be to get rid of that weapon and immediately transition to your backup sidearm. You don't have time to fool around trying to reload or clear a malfunction when people are trying to kill you; your active coverage of an area of responsibility is critical to the safety of a family member. A sling on your weapon allows you to simply "let it hang" while you go for your back up.

Buttstocks

The biggest complaint about shotguns is their recoil. Yes, they do recoil quite a bit, but this recoil can be managed to a surprising degree through proper training in recoil management. However, no amount of training will help if the buttstock isn't properly configured to the shooter. You don't hear it discussed much, but for a large majority of shooters a simple adjustment to the length of pull on the shotgun will drastically reduce felt recoil and improve their ability to better handle the weapon. Nearly all shotgun manufacturers produce shotguns with buttstocks designed to fit the typical six-foot tall North American man.

Not everyone fits that profile, however. If you don't, in order to mount the weapon and acquire the sights, the buttstock must be moved out of the proper shoulder pocket and usually comes to rest right on top of the radial nerve. This is a very bad place for any buttstock to be, but especially bad for one of the heaviest recoiling weapons. When the weapon is fired, the shooter experiences a great deal of pain. Shooters who've had this happen to them tend to shy away from the shotgun from that point on. Simply having the buttstock shortened will eliminate this problem and allow you to place the buttstock of the shotgun into the proper shoulder pocket. You'll find that afterward the recoil isn't too bad and that it's much easier to manipulate the weapon, making you much faster on the gun. This is a worthy modification to consider.

Handgun
The other useful weapon for home or personal defense is a handgun. An automatic shoots faster and loads quicker than a revolver, and you can have extra magazines pre-loaded, ready to run and gun. Like any firearm, handguns are encumbered by a number of limitations, namely low power and limited range compared to a rifle or shotgun—but a handgun can be easily concealed and drawn quickly. Remember the "rule of 3s." Most handgun battles are within 3 feet of your opponent, with only 3 seconds of reaction time, taking 3 rounds to completely end the threat.

One of the best for the money is the Smith & Wesson M&P .45 ACP, and the runner up is a Glock 21 .45 ACP. If money isn't a concern, then SIG SAUER makes very fine handguns. I chose a .45 over a 9mm, because there's more mass and less velocity, meaning more take down power and less chance of the bullet going beyond the target and hitting an unknowing passerby.

A 9mm takes several shots to take a person down and the rounds could easily travel into a neighbor's home. Going from a .45 to a 9mm you trade mass for velocity. Going from a 9mm to a .45, you trade velocity for mass.

Things to Consider with Your Handgun
- For now, get a license to carry a concealed weapon (CCW). After TSHTF, keep it loaded and on you at all times, and forget about any restricting gun laws.
- Shoot with both eyes open, and shoot as soon as you see your target in the front sight. This is a little sloppy, but the fastest way in a gun fight.
- Learn to shoot with either hand.
- Shoot first and as much as needed to take your opponent down. Waiting till he aims and shoots at you may be the last mistake you ever make.
- If you're out of ammo or suffered a jam, use it as a blunt-hitting object.
- Nine times out of ten, the physical presence of a gun defuses any intended attack.
- When you draw your gun for self-defense, think about where your wife and kids are or innocent bystanders in relation to your intended target.
- If you get caught in a Mexican standoff where neither side is willing to shoot for fear of being shot in return, try to talk the attacker into just leaving as a way out. If you must shoot, quickly drop to the ground while shooting or rapidly move to the right or to the left to get off your base and be a much harder target to hit. Unload your magazine on the attacker until you're sure he can't fire back.

Defense outside Your Home or Urban Warfare

Assault Rifles
You know, the *evil black rifles* that *kill, kill, kill* and should be banned just for looking so frightening are being demon-

ized by many politicians, media-types, and other anti-gun folk who actually have no idea what it is they are demonizing. Most people who hear the truth are quite surprised to find out just how off-base and factually wrong these naysayers are.

Many of the national leaders in the gun banning community know they are lying to the public. Josh Sugarmann, author of the 1988 book *Assault Weapons and Accessories in America,* laid out the strategy for all to see.

Assault weapons—just like armor-piercing bullets, machine guns, and plastic firearms—are a new topic. The weapons' menacing looks, coupled with the public's confusion over fully-automatic machine guns versus semi-automatic assault weapons—anything that looks like a machine gun is assumed to be a machine gun—can only increase the chance of public support for restrictions on these weapons.

True automatic assault rifles such as the Sturmgewehr 44 were first developed by the Germans in WWII and further refined by the Russians immediately post-war as defined by the AK-47. America's eventual version, the M16/M4, wasn't too bad either, but certainly wasn't universally loved by soldiers. They tried to meet the needs of the soldiers who were actually fighting, so the weapons tended to:

- Be lightweight.
- Have a larger-capacity magazine.
- Have a smaller caliber.
- Be easier to maintain.
- Be rugged.
- Shoot from the hip if necessary.
- Be more accurate to a reasonable distance.
- Fire in three different modes: single, 3-shot, and full automatic.

The guns sold to the civilian market that "look like" the military weapons all fire ONE SHOT at a time, just like virtually every other gun on the market. It's nothing special, and it's the way civilian rifles have been made for almost 140 years. What many in the anti-gun movement are trying to do is to get you to believe that if you put racing stripes and decals on your dad's Oldsmobile, you can take it out to the NASCAR track and compete equally.

These rifles can be used with magazines that hold up to 30 rounds in some states, but if one can shoot three, 10-round mags in 30 seconds or one, 30-round mag in 24 seconds, it is not really any more dangerous. When the King riots were happening in L.A., there were many Koreans on their rooftops with their AR-15s and multiple-round mags. They kept their neighborhood from burning down. That's a pretty impressive reason for wanting any weapon.

The civilian models have been made more accurately than the military models, because the majority of the guns sold are simply used as target rifles. It's a huge sport and tens of thousands compete across the country to see who can maintain the most accurate rifle. Go to most outdoor ranges and you'll see all kinds of guys with their AR-15s, AK-47s, and other look-alikes at the line. These guys are just average, everyday guys (and some women) who like to put little holes in paper with things that go bang, but don't be fooled, they will be ready when the SHTF. Now that you know the truth of the matter, you can spot when someone is ignorant about assault weapons, yet is still willing to give their opinion about something they know nothing about.

AR-15
Made of machined aluminum, the AR-15 has tight tolerances.

Reliability
Known to fail to feed or fail to eject when exposed to extremely cold temperatures and sandy environments. Proper cleaning is required to ensure reliability. The gas system leaves a lot to be desired and should be cleaned regularly, or it will cause reliability issues. When properly maintained, it functions flawlessly.

Stopping Power
The standard 5.56 NATO lacks stopping power when using ball ammo. However, the AR-15 is available in many calibers, from 22LR to 308 Winchester to 50 Beowulf.

Accessories
Tons of accessories (particularly optics) made specifically for the AR-15 work "out of the box."

Price
Range from $850 to as much as you want to spend. Magazines run between $15 and $25.

Accuracy
Tight tolerances of the machined parts yield a more accurate rifle. The AR is known to be accurate at 600 yards.

Ergonomics
The AR-15 offers proper cheek-weld. Its controls (selector, safety, bolt release, and magazine release) are convenient to the shooter's hands. Some folks find the charging-handle design is a bit odd.

Sights
Military peep sights are rugged and durable.

Trigger Pull
Military-style trigger is crisp, but not the smoothest.

AK-47

Made mostly from stamped sheet metal, it has loose tolerances.

Reliability

Due to low mechanical tolerances, it will fire every time you pull the trigger. It doesn't matter where it's at or what you just did to it. I have heard reports of it firing while the bolt was rusted shut. It fired, ejected the round, and chambered the next one (don't try that at home, kids). Cleaning, though a good idea, is generally not required.

Stopping Power

The standard 7.62X39 round is battle tested and proven. The AK is also available in many calibers from 22LR to 308 Winchester.

Accessories

There are tons of accessories for the AK as well. However, there are issues with optics in that the stock AK lacks a good platform to mount them. The receiver side mounts are a nuisance. Many common accessories require modifications to the weapon.

Price

AKs can be had for as little as $550. Some high-end, custom jobs can be pricey. Mags can be had for less than $10.

Accuracy

It may be accurate at 300 yards on a good day.

Ergonomics
The AK is an awkward design in terms of ergonomics. There is no cheek weld to speak of (it's more like a chin-weld), which affects sight picture. Removing the magazine requires losing sight picture. The safety requires the shooter to remove their trigger hand from the pistol grip. There is no bolt release.

Sights
AK sights are not the most durable and consist of a front post and a rear blade.

Trigger Pull
The loose tolerances really show in the trigger pull. It is not crisp or smooth. Also, they are prone to trigger slap.

Ammo and Gun Safety

No matter which guns you get, be sure to get lots of ammunition. Any ammo you don't use or need could be a great bartering item after a disaster. Wal-Mart and www.cheaperthandirt.com generally have decent prices on ammunition. Gun shows are always a good place to shop for ammo deals, as well as the internet if they will ship to your state.

If you know someone who has a good bit of knowledge and experience with guns, get them to teach you how to shoot safely. It is a terrible mistake to have a gun and not know anything about proper shooting and gun safety. If there is a gun course offered in your area, take it; ask about this at your local gun shop. Be sure to keep your guns away from your children! Put them where you can get to them quickly if needed, but in a place to which they don't have access. There are lockable gun boxes on the market that are quick to get into if you know how, but impossible for a child to open; again, ask at the gun shop.

SHTF Weapons That Don't Require a License

With the high likelihood that an SHTF scenario will happen in the near future, learning about means of self-defense and what weapons you can use to protect yourself is very important. Not every situation calls for guns, and certainly nobody has a gun available every single minute of the day. So what are some other weapons that can be used to protect you and your family? Some simple techniques and some readily available items you may already have around the house, coupled with some awareness, will give you the SHTF weapons that will keep you safe in the tough times ahead.

Kubotan

Kubotans are highly accessible, extremely durable, and very effective self-defense weapons. They can be used for stabilizing your fist, applying pressure to sensitive parts of an assailant's body, or gaining leverage on an assailant's wrist or fingers. A Kubotan is made of aluminum and comes in various colors. They measure about 5½ inches long, about a ½ inch in diameter, and weigh about 4 ounces. Kubotans can have either pointed or flat tips. Attach your Kubotan to your keychain so you will always have it with you. This is a very popular martial arts weapon.

The Kubotan is designed to be used against bony surfaces, soft tissue, and nerve points. It is effective because of the temporary paralysis or extreme pain it causes. Even for those without experience in a martial art, the Kubotan provides an inexpensive and easily learned method of self-defense. It comes with the key ring so you can attach it to your regular keychain.

The Kubotan increases the power of any strike. It is not necessary to waste time or miss an opportunity by trying to be overly precise. It's better to react naturally. Good targets are the groin, stomach, solar plexus, throat, the arm, the shin, hip bone, collarbone, ankle, and kneecap. A sharp strike to a bony part of the body will encourage an assailant to stop his attack. A harder, well placed blow can easily break bones—especially if the force of the blow is not hindered by clothing.

The most basic applications involve striking or poking vulnerable areas of the body with the Kubotan. Generally speaking, swinging strikes work better against bony surfaces, while fleshy areas are more susceptible to pokes and jabs with the ends of the Kubotan. With this concept in mind, a person avoids the confusion and frustration of trying to remember specific strikes for specific targets. Instead, one simply remembers to strike bones and poke soft tissue and pressure points.

There is no wrong strike. Just hit the closest body part as you can. The strike does not have to be perfect. Since nerves are close to the surface of most bony parts, even a glancing blow will inflict enough pain to make your assailant think twice about continuing his attack.

You can also use the keys that you have attached to the Kubotan. You can hold the Kubotan and swing the keys. This is most effective when hitting the face. The keys will scrape into the flesh and cause pain and bleeding.

The Kubotan is legal and entirely unregulated. To most people, the Kubotan is little more than a nondescript key ring. While the Kubotan is not particularly intimidating, it remains an effective self-defense instrument. It really can save your life.

Screwdriver

A screwdriver can certainly be as deadly as a knife, but unlike carrying a concealed knife or gun without a permit, possession of a screwdriver is not a crime. If you carry a hidden knife, it's a concealed weapon, but a screwdriver is just a tool. Screwdrivers also serve a dual purpose: to break into abandoned cars and houses after "it" hits the fan. Transients sometimes carry them for protection against assaults from other street people

ASP Baton

The ASP baton has proven itself "virtually indestructible." ASP expandable batons offer significant advantages over other intermediate-force weapons.

- Easily carried and readily at hand
- Unparalleled psychological deterrence
- No maintenance required
- No sharp edges
- Better balance than traditional impact weapons

The ASP baton is famously enjoyed by law enforcement due to the ease with which it may break surface bones and the ability to rapidly flick and unflick it, allowing the wielder great intimidation through direct threat of physical harm.

Pepper Spray

Pepper spray, oleoresin capsicum (OC), is a natural substance derived from the oily resins found in cayenne and other varieties of pepper. Contact with OC in a sprayed mist induces an immediate and intense burning sensation of the skin, but especially impacts the eyes, causing them to slam shut, burn, tear, and swell. Also, the mucous membranes of the nose, throat, and sinuses burn, swell, and make breathing difficult. In fact, even though tear gas is fairly nasty, it does not have the same inflammation and swelling effects of OC. Plus, OC will not degrade over time like tear gas. People under the influence of drugs or who are otherwise oblivious to pain may be able to keep their eyes open when sprayed with tear gas, but not so with OC. When sprayed in the eyes, they will involuntarily shut instantly, whether they feel pain or not. This temporary blindness causes fear and disorientation, allowing you to escape and get help.

An Alternative to Pepper Spray

A great weapon that you can use either in your home or from your car is a can of wasp spray. It shoots a stream about 30 feet and will allow you to defend yourself against multiple attackers at the same time. The good thing about wasp spray is that it does not "fog" an area like pepper spray can, so if you spray it at a home invader, the entire room will not be filled with noxious fumes.

A shot to the face will cause immediate blinding, pain, respiratory distress, and blistering. It's also effective against dogs. It may seem ugly, brutal or cruel, but so is getting attacked or killed. I'm not saying go out and grab it right now and pack it in a holster. I'm saying it has its uses as an expedient device and is worth consideration if you have nothing else.

Slingshot
When one thinks of a slingshot, the image of the forked stick and rubber band hanging out of the back pocket of Dennis the Menace is usually what comes to mind. Often overlooked in the survival community, the slingshot can be a valuable addition to any survival kit.

Slingshots are an excellent choice to distract others or defend you while roaming the urban jungle. The IRA has infamously used slingshots as weapons during the war in Northern Ireland. A .38-caliber slingshot ball is just as effective as a bullet in the right spot, but a lot less noisy. Although it has no guarantee of a lethal shot, a strong strike to the face, neck, or groin from a hefty lead fishing sinker or ball bearing will put the brakes on any attacker looking for an easy target. Granted, you will need to be alert to possible danger in order to utilize it, but if you aren't paying attention to your surroundings, you're going to get owned no matter what you're packing.

Mastering the slingshot is as simple as taking an empty cardboard box in the back yard and drawing a bulls-eye in magic marker. After about an hour of plinking, with a wide array of ammo and at various distances, you should have a firm grasp of the abilities and limitations of your slingshot. Aiming is a simple affair. The two most common methods deal with whether or not you have a forearm support. For those who do have a forearm support, hold the slingshot upright with a strong grip, pull back the sling, center your target between the tops of the braces, and let go.

For the older "Dennis the Menace" style, hold the slingshot sideways with your thumb in the notch of the supports. Draw back like a mini-bow, aim, and fire. This position allows you to get a stronger draw without putting too much tension on your wrist.

There are differences between modern slingshots with rubber tubing and biblical slingshots like the one that David used to slay Goliath. The biblical slingshot is nothing more than a strip of rawhide about 5-feet long with a pouch in the middle. One end had a loop that went over the middle finger while the other end was pinched between the thumb and index finger. You spun it either beside you or over your head to build up momentum and then let fly.

For those who are interested in a more primitive way of hunting, the biblical slingshot is worth a look. Keep in mind that it requires much more skill than the modern sling shot, does not allow for a quick follow up shot, and is not as quiet. Another great thing about slingshots is the multiple uses for their parts. The surgical tubing scavenged off a slingshot can be uses as a drinking straw or as a tourniquet.

Knives
Laws concerning carrying knives for self-defense are often more lax than those concerning carrying handguns. For this reason, I can't imagine not carrying it at all times. Have one that is dedicated just for self-defense, that way it will be

razor sharp for cutting through clothing, fat, muscle, and tendons with ease.

You don't have to buy the most expensive, but I would suggest sticking to name brands like Cold Steel, Ka-bar, Spyderco, Tops, and Benchmade.

Some of the definite benefits of a knife are:

- They won't jam.
- They won't run out of ammo.
- It's nearly impossible to take away from an experienced person.
- At very close range, the person with a knife has an advantage even if the other person has a gun.
- The only expense is the purchase price, and then you can practice with it indefinitely. I would recommend putting some thick tape over the blade while sparring with it.
- They are bare necessities when the DHTRO (defecation hits the rotating oscillator).

Practice finding and opening your folding knife until you can get it open and ready to use smoothly and quickly. Practice retrieving and blocking your opponent's knife until you're sure you will be able to do so quickly in a self-defense situation.

Defending Your Life and Property

No doubt, there are plenty of nice people in this country, and I think that in small towns and rural areas, people are going to find ways to cooperate and get along. I also think that some cities will suffer complete social breakdown and violence will rule. If you happen to be stuck in one of these cities, you're going to need to use force to defend your home. The section that follows discusses extreme responses to violence in the direst of situations. Hopefully, you won't find yourself in these circumstances, but if you do, this information may be valuable.

Defending your house is a crucial element in your stay-in-the-city plan. Make your house your fortress and hold drills to help other family members practice some of the more common activities such as hiding, defending, and evacuating.

Some useful items for home defense include:

- A guard dog
- Pepper spray
- Firearms
- Smoke bombs (military-grade)
- Molotov cocktail
- Trip wires
- Man traps

A Guard Dog
The guard dog is certainly a welcome addition to any family trying to defend their dwelling place. Although he'll probably eat a lot of food, the investment will be well worth it. Dogs also tend to sleep light, so let them sleep right next to the food-storage areas, and make sure you sleep within earshot. If the dog barks, don't consider it an irritation, consider it an INVASION.

Pepper Spray
Pepper spray is a great alternative to the firearm. It will incapacitate people and certainly give them a painful experience to remember. On the downside, it might just remind them that next time they come back for food, they better kill you first, so understand the limitations of pepper spray.

Firearms
Firearms are useful for obvious reasons. In the worst-case scenario, when looting is rampant, you may have to actually

shoot someone to protect yourself or your family. If you're squeamish about pulling the trigger under these circumstances, don't plan to stay in the city. Use the "bug-out" plan instead.

Smoke Bombs
Smoke bombs can be useful for covering a planned escape from your house. You can purchase high-volume smoke bombs that will quickly fill up any house with an un-breathable cloud of military-grade white smoke.

Molotov Cocktail
A Molotov cocktail is the quintessential urban-decay weapon. The Molotov cocktail, also known as the petrol bomb, gasoline bomb, Molotov bomb, fire bottle, fire bomb, or simply Molotov, is a generic name used for a variety of improvised, incendiary weapons. A breakable glass bottle is used, containing a flammable substance, such as gasoline, with some motor oil added, and usually a source of ignition, such as a burning cloth held in place by the bottle's stopper. The wick is usually soaked in alcohol or kerosene, rather than gasoline.

Molotov cocktails may be a psychologically effective method of disabling fighting vehicles by forcing the crew out or damaging external components. Be aware that marauders may try to burn your house down using this method to force you out.

Trip Wires
Trip wires are great perimeter defenses. They are early warning signs if someone is approaching. You can connect the tripwires to flares, blank shotgun shells, light sticks, or other warning devices. In this way you can have an audible or visible alert (your choice).

Man Traps
Man traps are used to capture, or even kill, your enemy without your involvement or to signal the presence of an

intruder. The ones used by the Viet Cong guerrillas were simple but inhumane.

Defense-Style Improvements for Your Home

- Replace glass windows with non-breakable Plexiglas.
- Add steel bars to windows. They must be easily removable from the inside, in case of fire or other emergency.
- Replace all outside door locks with heavy-duty deadbolts.
- Replace all outside doors with steel doors, preferably without windows.
- Remove bushes and other shrubs where people might hide.
- Entirely black out windows to avoid light escaping at night (similar to what residents of London did during the WWII bombing raids).
- Build secret hiding places for food, coins, or even people.
- Create escape hatches or passageways.
- Remove and securely store ladders and other tools and equipment that could be stolen or could be used by criminals to break into your house. Remember a shovel is quite effective at forcing a door open or breaking a window.
- Make vehicles as secure as possible. Put the car in the garage even if you are going out later the same day. Make it harder for the criminal to "read" your property, so that it isn't known if the absence of a car means you are out or just that the car is in the garage and the whole family is actually in.
- Depending on the location and conditions, consider installing lighting that may be operated by a switch, timer, or automatically triggered by movement sensors. A criminal won't want to be floodlit while he tries to attack your property.

- Add noise makers. At a modest cost, it is possible to add alarms or noise makers to a boundary. For example, stretch thin lines attached to tins, which contain a handful of gravel, along the perimeter. If an intruder tries to climb the wall, he will catch the line, pull it, and make a disturbance. When the racket starts, he will quickly be gone to avoid detection and the boom stick.
- Locks give you security; keys give you access. Remember that unless you are very careful with your keys, you might as well not bother installing locks and locking things up in the first place.
- Avoid fixed schedules and routines, as well as routes of travel.

Doors

- The weakest part of a door is the entry-lock mechanism. Install a steel door in a steel frame with deep deadbolts top and bottom.
- Create a secondary barrier by installing slots for 2x4s on either side of the door that tie into the door frame and frame of the house. Place one near the top of the door and one near the bottom for best effectiveness. When you drop a 2x4 into that slot, it prevents the door from swinging in without your consent.
- Use a security door bar—a metal bar that you jam under the door knob and against the floor.
- Install a security peep-hole. Never open a door to a stranger.

Windows

- Reinforce your windows by using security film on both sides of the windows. Do this on every first and second floor window.
- If you don't want to install security bars, consider stocking them for future use when conditions warrant.

- Set a couple of nails on the sides of the window frame so that the window can only be opened six inches.
- Store pre-cut, ¾-inch-thick plywood panels that can easily be placed over windows from the inside. Provide view slits so you can see outside without exposing yourself. This is effective for large picture windows and sliding glass doors.
- Multi-story urban buildings have fire escapes that can be used for easy access to your home and other parts of your building. Install a hinged metal grate in the inside of all windows that have access to fire escapes. These should be easily opened from the inside, but impossible to open from the outside.

Options for Passive Home Defense

Appearance: During an extended crisis in which there is a breakdown in law enforcement, making your property look less attractive and better protected is the first step toward a good, passive defense. In an extended crisis, people will be looking for resources to loot. Hide anything that may be attractive to thieves.

Visitor Control: Implement a procedure to keep visitors at the edge of your property and as far away from your buildings as possible. Meet people at the edge of your parameter and send them away if necessary.

Rural Organic Fences: Create an "organic" barrier, such as a wide-perimeter strip of blackberry thickets and other fast, dense growing thorny-vine plants.

Guard Animals: Keep a few dogs, geese, or peacocks inside the fence line. Animals will provide a great alarm system. Be sure to provide them with available shelter, food, and water.

Lighting: Install solar-powered floodlights with motion detectors on all sides of the house, other structures, and further away for more coverage. These can also be modified so that they come on at night and stay on. They put out about the same light as a 45-watt, incandescent light bulb. Test them regularly.

Broken Glass: In urban areas, covering alleys and other approach areas with broken glass will help keep people out. Folks just don't like walking on broken glass even with shoes on. It's something about the noise and "feel" that keeps them off.

No Place to Hide: Remove hiding places at the approach to your property and around your house. You must be able to have a good field of vision at all times.

Information Security: Don't discuss your group's capabilities, plans, supplies, or weapons' capabilities with others.

Active Home and Neighborhood Defense

During a breakdown of the rule of law, the main emphasis of an active home and neighborhood defense plan should be to establish and control conditions so that use of firearms for protection is not needed, but includes their potential use in extreme survival situations where lawlessness creates life-threatening situations.

A highly pro-active defense that includes the intent to use lethal force as a response to threat of violence may not be palatable for every person, group, or neighborhood. To implement such a plan requires close-group training and psychological "hardening" to actually execute a plan that could result in killing or wounding another human being.

Involve Neighbors
It's easier to defend your neighborhood with your neighbor than to protect just your single home. Design and implement a "Neighborhood Watch" style program. Creating

an extended-defense plan that includes your immediate neighbors or extended neighborhood can be a very effective strategy. Of course, for this plan to be most effective, others in your neighborhood must have prepared and be willing to work together. Be ready to hold meetings with your neighbors to discuss mutual aid for protection including:

- Communication.
- Visual identification and recognition of neighbors.
- Sharing of resources.
- Establishing 24/7 control of all points of access to the area.
- Group training.

Neighborhood defense is a more complex and extended version of home defense, requiring a strong command and control structure, as well as individual training.

Lookouts and Patrols
Post well-hidden lookout posts that can see all approaches to the property or neighborhood. If one lookout cannot see all areas, add more. Lookouts must have a means of contacting the interior of your home or neighborhood command center to warn of approaching people and provide a status report of the potential for hostility. Whenever possible, lookouts and patrols should be done in pairs.

Property/Neighborhood Access Control
If safe, a single person (greeter) should go out to meet all unarmed visitors and delay or prevent further encroachment into your property or neighborhood. Warning signs include a group attempting to move closer to and/or spreading out near the greeter.

The armed lookouts should continue to scan all areas of approach and not lock onto just the active-approach area. If hostile intent is suspected, other group members should move to pre-arranged areas out of sight to provide defensive weapons' coverage. Do not allow strangers into your home.

Neighborhood-perimeter control should include defended chokepoints and roadblocks manned by groups of two or three people in communication with a command center. Active patrols provide a visible deterrent.

Evacuation

Have a plan that provides for evacuation of children from your home before things get ugly. Practice evacuation from all exits, so they can leave from a door that is furthest away from potential hostilities. Provide an adult leader. Select several pre-designated rally points. They may have to move silently in the dark. Hardened "safe rooms" are not a good idea. You will place yourself in a siege/captive situation with no means of escape, which can make rescue difficult.

Communication

Develop, implement, and practice radio, hand, and audible single-word communication procedures that convey "all safe," "danger," or "engage." Develop prearranged arm signals for communication, for up to a distance of 50 feet or more, between group members if radios are not an option.

Tactical Plan

In the most hazardous phases of a crisis during a breakdown of the rule of law, all firearm-trained group members should carry at least a sidearm at all times inside and outside. Conduct practice exercises for both approach of hostiles and friendlies until everything goes smoothly, then add a few more wrinkles to find any problems with the plan. A well designed and executed plan can save your life. All group members need to be well drilled in the hazards of independent actions in a potentially deadly, hostile situation.

Fortunately, roving bands of bad guys will probably not be able to act in any coordinated fashion. They will generally rely on fear and intimidation to succeed. You don't want to get into a fire fight unless it becomes absolutely necessary to protect the lives of group members.

Weapons Deployment
During times when active protection must be implemented, keep your weapons and spare clips/ammunition at strategic locations. Everyone should be trained to use every weapon on hand.

If your intention is to simply scare-off an individual or group, use warning shots if verbal warnings don't work. A quick, rapid volley of three shots from every weapon will drive off anyone but the most determined and trained group. All members of your group need to be drilled in tactical firing scenarios.

My Rant
These aren't as absurd as they might at first sound. Many people living in rough cities already have steel bars covering their windows, and removing extra bushes and shrubs is a well-known tactic for making your home a safer place. The question I have is, "Are you willing to kill to save your life and/or the lives of your family members?" I pity the person who doesn't love life enough to fight or even kill for it. You should consider the possibility of having to kill a violent criminal in order to save your children. I understand that there are people who think differently than me.

Some people have been so mentally castrated by a lifetime of liberal, politically-correct brainwashing that they wouldn't be able to pull the trigger if their entire family was being tortured in front of them. It's also a matter of principle. Free men own guns; dictators and authoritarian governments have always tried to disarm them.

Wild Animals

Train Your Group
If your group has children or people unfamiliar with the wild animals in your area, be sure to train them in the hazards and precautions that must be taken to avoid contact with

wild animals. Small children who have grown up with household pets may think that any animal is tame, especially wild dogs and feral cats.

Live-Animal Food Stocks
If your survival plan includes raising chickens or other small food animals, be sure to have a design to protect them against predators, such as bobcats, foxes, and wolves. This can include having dogs inside the perimeter of your property (but outside the livestock fence line), anti-climb fencing, and anti-burrowing design around fences, along with live and spring traps.

When using traps, never get close enough to allow the captured animal to claw or bite. Kill them with a well-placed head shot while still in the trap. Be sure they are dead before emptying the trap. Use the animal for food or bury or burn the carcass.

Gardens
In the Southwest and Southeast United States, armadillos are a significant hazard to your garden. They are efficient burrowers and can destroy a garden overnight. Raccoons will dig up food plants that have been buried under hay and soil for wintering over.

Camp Sites
In the event that you have to establish even a temporary outdoor camp, protecting your group and its food supply takes center stage, especially in bear or wolf country. Keep people close to camp.

Only go out armed and very aware. Food needs to be hung up away from the living area in "bear-bags" such that they can't be reached by bears from the ground or from the major branches/trunk area of the tree (bears can climb trees). Use of "bear bangers," camp fires, and nighttime armed guards will keep your group safer.

Outbuilding Storage

When storing food in outbuilding structures and root cellars, be sure to design them to prevent access by whatever type of wild animals you have in your area. Rats, mice, squirrels, and chipmunks can get through even the smallest cracks.

Dog Packs

When society breaks down you can expect abandoned pet dogs to naturally join into roaming packs and revert to wild behavior. Never trust a dog that has been abandoned. Rabid dogs may become common in an extended crisis. Be prepared to kill any dogs that are unknown and exhibit aggressive behavior.

Feral Cats

Cats turn feral very quickly when abandoned. They can contract and carry many diseases that are highly infectious to humans.

Protection When Traveling

When moving about, either on foot or in a vehicle, learn and practice safe-travel tactics:

- Never travel alone. A group of three is best, but more than that may draw unwanted attention.
- Have preplanned alert words for your group.

- Be as inconspicuous as possible—no boisterous behaviors or conversations. This is survival, not a Sunday stroll.
- Stay hyperaware of all conditions and situations ahead and behind you.
- Read faces and body language to determine a person's intent.
- Be prepared to implement your self-defense plan without hesitation.
- Avoid, don't confront.
- Have a prearranged rally point if you get separated.
- Don't display firearms, except for immediate defense.
- Practice high-speed defensive driving maneuvers with your vehicle.
- Don't look or act as a perceived threat to others.
- Don't present yourself as an easy or attractive target.
- Never accept "help" from a stranger—be prepared and self-reliant.
- Don't stop to help "stranded" motorists. This is an old and time-tested trap.
- Don't pick-up hitchhikers.

You're Vehicle

Keep your vehicle in excellent repair. Check lights, fluid levels, hoses, tire wear, spare tire, tire inflation, wipers, and battery every week. Be very familiar with what's under your hood and in your trunk. For those who can do minor repairs with hand tools (and everyone should know how), keep a set of extra fan and alternator belts with the appropriate tools in your car. Know how to change tires, both front and rear. Stock your glove box with LED flashlights and extra batteries. Know how to disable the interior lights to prevent them from coming on when you open a car door. In a crisis, if your vehicle dies, you might too!

Stopping for the Night

Assuming motels are full or as dysfunctional as the rest of society, if you must stop for the night, pick an easily defendable, out of the way location that has limited access, so you can monitor anyone approaching.

Don't show lights or make noise. Pick one person out of your group as a watchman, and rotate this duty throughout the night. When ready to leave, check the area silently and thoroughly before you move out.

Encountering Others
In the early stages of a crisis, others may be just as wary of you as you are of them. Don't approach in a threatening manner: smile, have a friendly demeanor, and give a kind greeting. Stop well away from other groups to allow you time to evaluate them and time for them to do the same. Groups with children are generally safer than groups of young men. Don't feel obligated to stop and compare notes or share your supplies. Don't focus solely on one group you meet, as there may be others close by, so be hyper vigilant. Remember, you have an objective to meet when you are out and about. Don't tell others where you are going, where you have come from, or your objective. If they want to give you information, listen politely without judgmental or evaluative comments. Be pleasant and non-committal, then watch your back as you leave. The best strategy is to let them move on first.

13
URBAN MOVEMENT, COVER, AND CONCEALMENT TECHNIQUES

Movement techniques must be practiced until they become second nature. To reduce exposure to enemy fire, you should avoid open areas, avoid silhouetting yourself, and select your next covered position before movement. The following paragraphs discuss how to move in urban areas.

Avoiding Open Areas

Open areas such as streets, alleys, and parks should be avoided. They are natural kill zones for enemy, crew-served weapons, or snipers. They can be crossed safely if the individual applies certain fundamentals. Before moving to another position, you should make a visual reconnaissance, select the position offering the best cover and concealment, and determine the route to get to that position. You need to develop a plan for movement. You should always select the shortest distance to run between buildings, and move along covered and concealed routes to your next position, reducing the time exposed to enemy fire.

Moving Parallel to Buildings

You may not always be able to use the inside of buildings as routes of advance and must, therefore, move on the outside of buildings. Smoke, suppressive fires, and cover and concealment should be used as much as possible to hide movement. You should move parallel to the side of the building, maintaining at least 12 inches of separation between yourself and the wall to avoid rabbit rounds (ricochets and rubbing or bumping the wall).

Stay in the shadows, present a low silhouette, and move rapidly to your next position. If an enemy gunner inside the building fires, he exposes himself to fire from other squad members providing overwatch.

Moving Past Windows

Windows present another hazard. The most common mistakes are exposing the head in a first-floor window and not being aware of basement windows. When using the correct technique for passing a first-floor window, you must stay below the window level and near the side of the building. Ensure you do not silhouette yourself in the window. An enemy gunner inside the building would have to expose himself to covering fires if he tries to engage you.

The same techniques used in passing first-floor windows are used when passing basement windows. You should not walk or run past a basement window, as this will present a good target for an enemy gunner inside the building. Ensure you stay close to the wall of the building and step or jump pass the window without exposing your legs.

Moving Around Corners

The area around a corner must be observed before you move. The most common mistake you can make at a corner is allowing your weapon to extend beyond the corner, exposing your position; this mistake is known as flagging your weapon. You should show your head below the height an enemy would expect to see it. You must lie flat on the ground and not extend your weapon beyond the corner of the building. Only expose your head (at ground level) enough to permit observation. You can also use a mirror, if available, to look around the corner. Another corner-clearing technique that is used when speed is required is the pie-ing method. This procedure is done by aiming the weapon beyond the corner into the direction of travel (without flagging) and side stepping around the corner in a circular fashion with the muzzle as the pivot point.

Fighting Positions

How do you find and use a fighting position properly? You have to know this: whether you are attacking or defending. Your success depends on your ability to place accurate fire on the enemy—with the least exposure to return fire.

- Make maximum use of available cover and concealment.
- Avoid firing over cover; when possible, fire around it.
- Avoid silhouetting against light-colored buildings, the skyline, and so on.
- Carefully select a new fighting position before leaving an old one.

- Avoid setting a pattern. Fire from both barricaded and non-barricaded windows.
- Keep exposure time to a minimum.
- Begin improving your hasty position immediately after occupation.
- Use construction material that is readily available in an urban area.
- Remember: positions that provide cover at ground level may not provide cover on higher floors.

Hasty Fighting Positions

A hasty fighting position is normally occupied in the attack or during the early stages of defense. It is a position from which you can place fire upon the enemy while using available cover for protection from return fire. You may occupy it voluntarily or be forced to occupy it due to enemy fire. In either case, the position lacks preparation before occupation. Some of the more common hasty fighting positions in an urban area are corners of buildings, behind walls, windows, unprepared loopholes, and the peak of a roof.

Corners of Buildings

You must be able to fire your weapon (both right and left-handed) to be effective around corners. A common error made in firing around corners is firing from the wrong shoulder. This exposes more of your body to return fire than necessary. By firing from the proper shoulder, you can reduce exposure to enemy fire. Another common mistake when firing around corners is firing from the standing position. If you expose yourself at the height the enemy expects, then you risk exposing the entire length of your body as a target for the enemy.

Walls

When firing from behind walls, you must fire around cover and not over it.

Windows

In an urban area, windows provide convenient firing ports. Avoid firing from the standing position, which would expose most of your body to return fire from the enemy and could silhouette you against a light-colored interior background. This is an obvious sign of your position, especially at night when the muzzle flash can be easily observed. To fire from a window properly, remain well back in the room to hide the flash, and kneel to limit exposure and avoid silhouetting yourself.

Loopholes

You may fire through a hole created in the wall and avoid windows. You must stay well back from the loophole so the muzzle of the weapon does not protrude beyond the wall, and the muzzle flash is concealed.

Roof

The peak of a roof provides a vantage point that increases field of vision and the ranges at which you can engage targets. A chimney, smokestack, or any other object protruding from the roof of a building should be used to reduce the size of the target exposed.

No Position Available

When subjected to enemy fire and none of the positions mentioned are available, you must try to expose as little of yourself as possible. You can reduce your exposure to the enemy by lying in the prone position as close to a building as possible, on the same side of the open area as the enemy. In order to engage you, the enemy must then lean out the window and expose himself to return fire.

No Cover Available

When no cover is available, you can reduce your exposure by firing from the prone position, by firing from shadows, and by presenting no silhouette against buildings.

Prepared Fighting Positions

A prepared firing position is one built or improved to allow you to engage a particular area, avenue of approach, or enemy position, while reducing your exposure to return fire. Examples of prepared positions include barricaded windows, fortified loopholes, and sniper positions.

Barricaded Windows

The natural firing port provided by windows can be improved upon by barricading the window, leaving a small hole for you to use. Materials torn from the interior walls of the building or any other available material may be used for barricading. Barricade all windows, whether you intend to use them as firing ports or not. Keeps the enemy guessing. Avoid making neat, square, or rectangular holes, which clearly identify your firing positions to the enemy. For instance, a barricaded window should not have an obvious firing port. The window should remain in its original condition so that your position is hard to detect. Firing from the bottom of the window gives you the advantage of the wall because the firing port is less obvious to the enemy. Sandbags are used to reinforce the wall below the window and to increase protection.

All glass must be removed from the window to prevent injury. Lace curtains permit you to see out and prevent the enemy from seeing in. Wet blankets should be placed under weapons to reduce dust. Wire mesh over the window keeps the enemy from throwing things in.

Individual Movement Techniques

- Stop, look, listen, and smell (SLLS) before moving. Look for your next position before leaving a position.
- Look for covered and concealed routes on which to move.
- Stop, look, and listen when birds or animals are alarmed (the enemy may be nearby).
- Smell for odors such as petroleum, smoke, and food; they are additional signs of the enemy's presence.
- Cross roads and trails at places that have the most cover and concealment (large culverts, low spots, curves, or bridges).
- Avoid steep slopes and places with loose dirt or stones.
- Avoid cleared, open areas and tops of hills and ridges. Walking at the top of a hill or ridge will skyline you against the sun or moon, enabling the enemy to see you.

Sights to Look For

- Enemy personnel, vehicles, and aircraft
- Sudden or unusual movement
- New local inhabitants
- Smoke or dust
- Unusual movement of farm or wild animals
- Unusual activity—or lack of activity—by local inhabitants, especially at times or places that are normally inactive or active
- Vehicle or personnel tracks

- Movement of local inhabitants along uncleared routes, areas, or paths
- Signs that the enemy has occupied the area
- Evidence of changing trends in threats
- Recently cut foliage
- Muzzle flashes, lights, fires, or reflections
- Unusual amount (too much or too little) of trash

Sounds to Listen For

- Running engines or track sounds
- Voices
- Metallic sounds
- Gunfire (by weapon type)
- Unusual calm or silence
- Dismounted movement
- Aircraft

Feel For

- Warm coals and other materials in a fire
- Fresh tracks
- Age of food or trash

Smell For

- Vehicle exhaust
- Burning petroleum products
- Food cooking
- Aged food in trash
- Human waste

Other Considerations

- Homes and Buildings: Condition of roofs, doors, windows, lights, power lines, water, sanitation, roads, bridges, crops, and livestock.

- Infrastructure: Functioning stores, service stations, and so on.
- People: Numbers, gender, age, residence, apparent health, clothing, daily activities, and leadership.
- Contrast: Has anything changed? For example, are there new locks on buildings? Are windows boarded up or previously boarded up windows now open, indicating a change in how a building is expected to be used? Have buildings been defaced with graffiti?

Low Crawl

The low crawl gives you the lowest silhouette. Use it to cross places where the cover and/or concealment are very low and enemy fire or observation prevents you from getting up. Keep your body flat against the ground. With your firing hand, grasp your weapon sling at the upper sling swivel. Let the front hand guard rest on your forearm (keeping the muzzle off the ground), and let the weapon butt drag on the ground. To move, push your arms forward and pull your firing side leg forward. Then pull with your arms and push with your leg. Continue this throughout the move.

High Crawl

The high crawl lets you move faster than the low crawl and still gives you a low silhouette. Use this crawl when there is good cover and concealment, but enemy fire prevents you from getting up. Keep your body off the ground and resting on your forearms and lower legs. Cradle your weapon in your arms and keep its muzzle off the ground. Keep your knees well behind your buttocks so your body will stay low. To move, alternately advance your right elbow and left knee, then your left elbow and right knee.

Rush

The rush is the fastest way to move from one position to another. Each rush should last from 3–5 seconds. Rushes are kept short to prevent enemy machine gunners or riflemen from tracking you. However, do not stop and hit the ground in the open just because 5 seconds have passed. Always try to hit the ground behind some cover. Before moving, pick out your next covered and concealed position and the best route to it. Make your move from the prone position as follows:

- Slowly raise your head and pick your next position and the route to it.
- Slowly lower your head.
- Draw your arms into your body (keeping your elbows in).
- Pull your right leg forward.
- Raise your body by straightening your arms.
- Get up quickly.
- Rush to the next position.

Movement with Stealth

Moving with stealth means to move quietly, slowly, and carefully. This requires great patience. To move with stealth, use the following techniques:

- Ensure your footing is sure and solid by keeping your body's weight on the foot on the ground while stepping.
- Raise the moving leg high to clear brush or grass.

- Gently let the moving foot down toe first, with your body's weight on the rear leg.
- Lower the heel of the moving foot after the toe is in a solid place.
- Shift your body's weight and balance the forward foot before moving the rear foot.
- Take short steps to help maintain balance.

Avoid making noise at night and when moving through dense vegetation. Hold your weapon with one hand, and keep the other hand forward, feeling for obstructions.

Prone Position:

- Hold your rifle with one hand and crouch slowly.

- Feel for the ground with your free hand to make sure it is clear of mines, tripwires, and other hazards.
- Lower your knees, one at a time, until your body's weight is on both knees and your free hand.
- Shift your weight to your free hand and opposite knee.
- Raise your free leg up and back, and lower it gently to that side.
- Move the other leg into position the same way.
- Roll quietly into a prone position.

Crawling:

- Crawl on your hands and knees.
- Hold your rifle in your firing hand.
- Use your non-firing hand to feel for and make clear spots for your hands and knees.
- Move your hands and knees to those spots, and put them down softly.

If the enemy can see you and you are within range of his weapon system, he can engage and possibly kill you; for that reason, you must be concealed from enemy observation and have cover from enemy fire. When the terrain does not provide natural cover and concealment, you must prepare your cover, and use natural and man-made materials to camouflage yourself, your equipment, and your position.

Cover
Cover is made of natural or man-made materials, gives protection from bullets, fragments of exploding rounds, flame, nuclear effects, biological and chemical agents, and enemy observation

Natural Cover

Natural cover includes logs, trees, stumps, rocks, and ravines; whereas, man-made cover includes fighting positions, trenches, walls, rubble, and craters. To get protection from enemy fire in the offense or when moving, use routes that put cover between you and the enemy. For example, use ravines, gullies, hills, wooded areas, walls, and any other cover that will keep the enemy from seeing and firing at you. Avoid open areas. Never skyline yourself on a hilltop or ridge. Any cover—even the smallest depression or fold in the ground—can help protect you from direct and indirect enemy fire.

Concealment

Concealment is anything that hides you from enemy observation. Concealment does not protect you from enemy fire. Do not think that you are protected from the enemy's fire just because you are concealed. Concealment, like cover, can also be natural or soldier made.

Natural Concealment

Natural concealment includes bushes, grass, and shadows. If possible, natural concealment should not be disturbed. Man-made concealment includes Army combat uniforms (MultiCam), camouflage nets, face paint, and natural materials that have been moved from their original location. Man-made concealment must blend into natural concealment provided by the terrain.

Actions as Concealment

Light, noise, and movement discipline, and the use of camouflage, contributes to concealment. Light discipline is controlling the use of lights at night by such things as not smoking in the open, not walking around with a flashlight on, and not using vehicle headlights. Noise discipline is taking action to deflect sounds generated by your unit (such as operating equipment) away from the enemy and, when possible, using methods to communicate that do not generate sounds (arm-and-hand signals). Movement discipline includes not moving about fighting positions unless necessary and not moving on routes that lack cover and concealment.

In the defense, build a well-camouflaged fighting position and avoid moving about. In the offense, conceal yourself and your equipment with camouflage, and move in woods or on terrain that gives concealment. Darkness cannot hide you from enemy observation in either offensive or defensive situations. The enemy's night vision devices (NVD) and other detection means allow them to find you in both daylight and darkness.

Colors

If your skin, clothes, or equipment colors stand out against the background, the enemy can obviously detect you more easily than he could otherwise, so camouflage yourself and your equipment to blend in with the surroundings. Study the terrain and vegetation of the area in which you are operating. Change camouflage as needed to blend in with the surroundings when moving from one area to another. Take grass, leaves, brush, and other material from your location; apply it to your clothes and equipment, and put face paint on your skin.

Camouflage Patterns

Blotch pattern

- Temperate deciduous (leaf shedding) areas
- Desert areas (barren)
- Snow (barren)

Slash pattern

- Coniferous areas (broad slashes).
- Jungle areas (broad slashes).
- Grass (narrow slashes).

BLOTCH   SLASH

Personal Camouflage Application

1. **Face:** Use dark colors on high spots and light colors on any remaining exposed areas. Use a hat, netting, or mask if available.

2. **Ears:** The insides and the backs should have two colors to break-up outlines.

3. **Head, neck, hands, and the under chin:** Use scarf, collar, vegetation, netting, or coloration methods.

4. **Light colored hair:** Give special attention to conceal with a scarf or mosquito head net.

5. **Combinations:** Blotched and slash may be used together.

Satellite Maps

A commander with superior intel will have an advantage on the battlefield. In fact, billions are spent by the military every year developing ways for commanders and soldiers on the ground to gather valuable intel. One of the most basic and ancient forms of intel is an accurate and current MAP!

I'd like to take the traditional map idea one step further by saying that everyone should play around with Google Satellite Maps. Print out a few different vantage points of the location you are most likely to hole up in, should a disaster strike. I myself have several printouts that show my entire town, as well as a few that show close-up views of my immediate neighborhood. If you're not already familiar with Google Earth, you'll be amazed by this interactive tool that produces actual, detailed satellite photos (zooming in on my house reveals my dog sleeping on the back lawn). Simply put, this is similar to a military-style, high-tech reconnaissance product that is available to anyone with a computer and an internet connection.

To do this, go to Google Maps and Google Map Maker. Printouts colorized aerial maps of your AO, then take to your local printer and have blown-up to 11×17 or larger, then laminate. Use a dry-erase marker (those used on white boards) and mark the map as needed, with the ability to erase and edit!

I think these close-up pictures are extremely valuable, as they not only show streets and highways, but actual houses, fences, backyards, swimming pools, wooded areas, etc. Just imagine how useful it would be to know where all of the swimming pools (excellent sources of water) are in your vicinity or the location of a small pond that doesn't show up on a store-bought map. Your homemade map should be marked with all local water sources (creeks, rivers, springs and pools), high grounds (potential tactical positioning), low grounds (potential flood areas), and areas for placing road blocks, scouting locations, etc. For those of us bugging-in, our AO (area of operations) will be the roughly 1-mile surrounding of our home or retreat.

Encourage your neighbors to do the same thing. When the SHTF, strategically collaborate with them by setting up neighborhood defenses and daily briefings with your team. Determine patrol points, areas for procurement and gathering, and coordinate the systematic searching and scavenging of abandoned homes in your neighborhood.

These maps could also become very useful for your back-up, bug-out plan. By looking at satellite photos, you may be able to find a route to GOOD that avoids most streets. With a decent four-wheel-drive vehicle, you could make use of numerous trails and paths that don't show up on traditional road maps. If you were on foot you, this would enable you to find cover and places to shelter much more easily.

I would bet that most folks have already played around with this tool at least once or twice, but I would encourage more familiarity with it since the information garnished may prove to be lifesaving one day. Printout those maps while the power is still on, rather than wishing you had after the power is off.

14
COMBATIVES

Anyone who has been in a real blood-and-snot, violent confrontation will know what I am talking about when I say thirty seconds on the street is worth three years in the dojo. Multiply that by a million when you have a complete collapse and an "every man for himself" attitude. Not every fight can be won with a gun or a knife. You need a less lethal option for when you are in a situation where a physical response is not only required, but is your only option.

For example, you spot a potentially violent and aggressive individual walking behind you, and your street-smart instincts tell you that he has already sized you up as his next victim. This makes you decide to take the first step by rounding the corner and running like a bat out of hell in order to escape. Is that considered self-defense? Of course it is.

If, however, you have no chance of evasion, then the only option left is a physical one. In such a case you must not hesitate to turn that individual into a grease mark on the pavement.

The bottom line in achieving such a goal is to be first and hit hard. If at any time you can get away, do so without hesitation. If not, continuously attack until the threat is eliminated—then flee to safety at the first opportunity.

Combatives is the belief that self-defense training needs to be based on defending against the ways you are most likely going to be attacked and counter attacking in such a way that makes it hard for your attacker to defend himself.

Basic Principles
There are basic principles that the hand-to-hand fighter must know and apply to successfully defeat an opponent. The ones listed are just a few of these. After years of study they will become intuitive to a highly-skilled fighter.

Physical Balance
Balance refers to the ability to maintain equilibrium and to remain in a stable, upright position. A hand-to-hand fighter must maintain his balance, both to defend himself, and to launch an effective attack.

Without balance, the fighter has no stability with which to defend himself, nor does he have a base of power for an attack.

How to Move to Regain Balance
A fighter develops balance through experience, but usually he keeps his feet about shoulder-width apart and his knees flexed. He lowers his center of gravity to increase stability.

How to Exploit Weaknesses in an Opponent
Experience also gives the hand-to-hand fighter a sense of how to move his body in a fight to maintain his balance while exposing the enemy's weak points.

Mental Balance
The successful fighter must also maintain a mental balance. He must not allow fear or anger to overcome his ability to concentrate or to react instinctively in hand-to-hand combat.

Position
Position refers to the location of the fighter (defender) in relation to his opponent. A vital principle when being attacked is for the defender to move his body to a safe position—that is, where the attack cannot continue unless the enemy moves his whole body.

To position for a counterattack, a fighter should move his whole body off the opponent's line of attack. Then, the opponent has to change his position to continue the attack. It is usually safe to move off the line of attack at a 45-degree angle, either toward the opponent or away from him, whichever is appropriate. This position affords the fighter safety and allows him to exploit weaknesses in the enemy's counterattack position. Movement to an advantageous position requires accurate timing and distance perception.

Timing

A combatant must be able to perceive the best time to move to an advantageous position in an attack. If he moves too soon, the enemy will anticipate his movement and adjust the attack. If the fighter moves too late, the enemy will strike him. Similarly, the fighter must launch his attack or counterattack at the critical instant when the opponent is the most vulnerable.

Distance

Distance is the relative distance between the positions of opponents. A fighter positions himself where distance is to his advantage. The hand-to-hand fighter must adjust his distance by changing position and developing attacks or counterattacks. He does this according to the range at which he and his opponent are engaged.

Momentum

Momentum is the tendency of a body in motion to continue in the direction of motion unless acted on by another force. Body mass in motion develops momentum. The greater the body mass or speed of movement, the greater the momentum. Therefore, a fighter must understand the effects of this principle and apply it to his advantage.

Leverage

A combatant uses leverage in hand-to-hand combat by using the natural movement of his body to place his opponent in a position of unnatural movement.

The fighter uses his body or parts of his body to create a natural mechanical advantage over parts of the enemy's body. He should never oppose the enemy in a direct test of strength; however, by using leverage, he can defeat a larger or stronger opponent.

- The fighter can use his opponent's momentum to his advantage, that is, he can place the opponent in a vulnerable position by using his momentum against him.
- The opponent's balance can be taken away by using his own momentum.
- The opponent can be forced to extend farther than he expected, causing him to stop and change his direction of motion to continue his attack.
- An opponent's momentum can be used to add power to a fighter's own attack or counterattack by combining body masses in motion.
- The fighter must be aware that the enemy can also take advantage of the principle of momentum. Therefore, the fighter must avoid placing himself in an awkward or vulnerable position, and he must not allow himself to extend too far.

Throw From Rear Choke

1. The opponent attacks the defender with a rear strangle choke. The defender quickly bends his knees and spreads his feet shoulder-width apart. (Knees are bent quickly to put distance between you and your opponent.)

2. The defender reaches as far back as possible and uses his right hand to grab his opponent by the collar or hair. He then forces his chin into the V of the opponent's arm that is around his neck. With his left hand, he grasps the opponent's clothing at the tricep and bends forward at the waist

3. The defender locks his knees and, at the same time, pulls his opponent over his shoulder and slams him to the ground.

4. He then has the option of spinning around and straddling his opponent or disabling him with punches to vital areas. (It is important to grip the opponent tightly when executing this move.)

Throw from rear choke

Headlock Escape

1. If a defender is in a headlock, he first turns his chin in toward his opponent's body to prevent choking

2. Next, he slides one hand up along the opponent's back, around to the face, and finds the sensitive nerve under the nose. He must avoid placing his fingers near his opponent's mouth, or he will be bitten.

3. The defender can now force his opponent back and then down across his own knee to the ground and maintain control by keeping pressure under the nose. He can finish the technique with a hammer fist to the groin.

Headlock escape

In medium-range combatives, two opponents are already within touching distance. The arsenal of possible body weapons includes short punches and strikes with elbows, knees, and hands. Head butts are also effective; do not forget them during medium-range combat. A soldier uses his peripheral vision to evaluate the targets presented by the opponent and chooses his target. He should be aggressive and concentrate his attack on the opponent's vital points to end the fight as soon as possible.

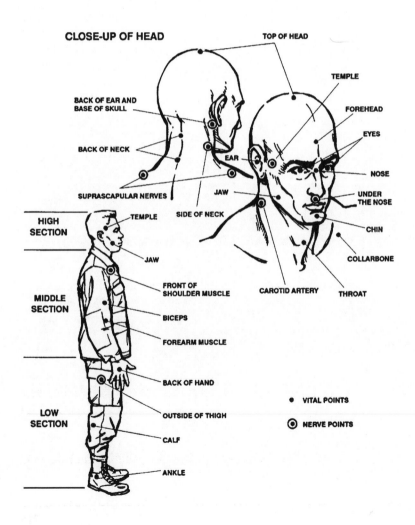

CLOSE-UP OF HEAD

TOP OF HEAD

TEMPLE

BACK OF EAR AND BASE OF SKULL

FOREHEAD

EYES

BACK OF NECK

EAR

NOSE

SUPRASCAPULAR NERVES

JAW

UNDER THE NOSE

CHIN

HIGH SECTION

TEMPLE

SIDE OF NECK

JAW

COLLARBONE

JAW

FRONT OF SHOULDER MUSCLE

CAROTID ARTERY

THROAT

MIDDLE SECTION

BICEPS

FOREARM MUSCLE

BACK OF HAND

● VITAL POINTS

LOW SECTION

OUTSIDE OF THIGH

◉ NERVE POINTS

CALF

ANKLE

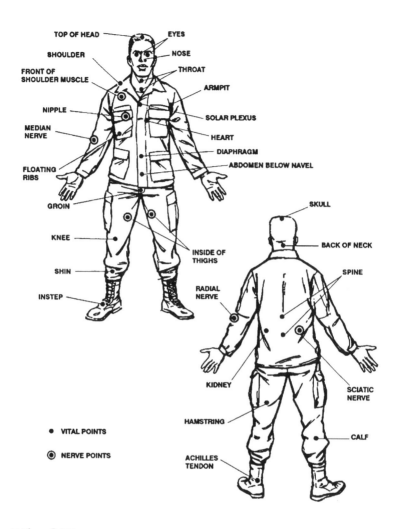

TOP OF HEAD
EYES
SHOULDER
NOSE
FRONT OF
SHOULDER MUSCLE
THROAT
ARMPIT
NIPPLE
SOLAR PLEXUS
MEDIAN
NERVE
HEART
DIAPHRAGM
ABDOMEN BELOW NAVEL
FLOATING
RIBS
GROIN
KNEE
INSIDE OF
THIGHS
SHIN
INSTEP
RADIAL
NERVE

SKULL
BACK OF NECK
SPINE
KIDNEY
SCIATIC
NERVE
HAMSTRING
CALF
ACHILLES
TENDON

• VITAL POINTS

◉ NERVE POINTS

Vital Targets

The body is divided into three sections: high, middle, and low. Each section contains vital targets. The effects of striking these targets follow:

High Section: The high section includes the head and neck; it is the most dangerous target area.

Top of the head: The skull is weak where the frontal cranial bones join. A forceful strike causes trauma to the cranial cavity, resulting in unconsciousness and hemorrhage. A severe strike can result in death.

Forehead: A forceful blow can cause whiplash; a severe blow can cause cerebral hemorrhage and death.

Temple: The bones of the skull are weak at the temple, and an artery and large nerve lie close to the skin. A powerful strike can cause unconsciousness and brain concussion. If the artery is severed, the resulting massive hemorrhage compresses the brain, causing coma and/or death.

Eyes: A slight jab in the eyes causes uncontrollable watering and blurred vision. A forceful jab or poke can cause temporary blindness, or the eyes can be gouged out. Death can result if the fingers penetrate through the thin bone behind the eyes and into the brain.

Ears: A strike to the ear with open-fisted hands can rupture the eardrum and may cause a brain concussion.

Nose: Any blow can easily break the thin bones of the nose, causing extreme pain and eye watering.

Under the nose: A blow to this nerve center, which is close to the surface under the nose, can cause great pain and watery eyes.

Jaw: A blow to the jaw can break or dislocate it. If the facial nerve is pinched against the lower jaw, one side of the face will be paralyzed.

Chin: A blow to the chin can cause paralysis, mild concussion, and unconsciousness. The jawbone acts as a lever that can transmit the force of a blow to the back of the brain where the cardiac and respiratory mechanisms are controlled.

Back of ears and base of skull: A moderate blow to the back of the ears or the base of the skull can cause unconsciousness by the jarring effect on the back of the brain. However, a powerful blow can cause a concussion or brain hemorrhage and death.

Throat: A powerful blow to the front of the throat can cause death by crushing the windpipe. A forceful blow causes extreme pain and gagging or vomiting.

Side of neck: A sharp blow to the side of the neck causes unconsciousness by shock to the carotid artery, jugular vein, and vagus nerve. For maximum effect, the blow should be focused below and slightly in front of the ear. A less powerful blow causes involuntary muscle spasms and intense pain. The side of the neck is one of the best targets to use to drop an opponent immediately or to disable him temporarily to finish him later.

Back of neck: A powerful blow to the back of one's neck can cause whiplash, concussion, or even a broken neck and death.

Middle Section: The middle section extends from the shoulders to the area just above the hips. Most blows to vital points in this region are not fatal, but can have serious, long-term complications that range from trauma to internal organs to spinal-cord injuries.

Front of shoulder muscle: A large bundle of nerves passes in front of the shoulder joint. A forceful blow causes extreme pain and can make the whole arm ineffective if the nerves are struck just right.

Collarbone: A blow to the collarbone can fracture it, causing intense pain and rendering the arm on the side of the fracture ineffective. The fracture can also sever the brachial nerve or subclavian artery.

Armpit: A large nerve lies close to the skin in each armpit. A blow to this nerve causes severe pain and partial paralysis. A knife inserted into the armpit is fatal, as it severs a major artery leading from the heart.

Spine: A blow to the spinal column can sever the spinal cord, resulting in paralysis or in death.

Nipples: A large network of nerves passes near the skin at the nipples. A blow here can cause extreme pain and hemorrhage to the many blood vessels beneath.

Heart: A jolting blow to the heart can stun the opponent and allow time for follow-up or finishing techniques.

Solar plexus: The solar plexus is a center for nerves that controls the cardio-respiratory system. It can be found right in the middle of the upper half of the trunk of the torso, where the rib cage comes together at the stomach level, in front of the diaphragm. A blow to this location is painful and can take the breath from the opponent. A powerful blow causes unconsciousness by shock to the nerve center. A penetrating blow can also damage internal organs.

Diaphragm: A blow to the lower front of the ribs can cause the diaphragm and the other muscles that control breathing to relax. This causes loss of breath and can result in unconsciousness due to respiratory failure.

Floating ribs: A blow to the floating ribs can easily fracture them, because they are not attached to the rib cage. Fractured ribs on the right side can cause internal injury to the liver; fractured ribs on either side can possibly puncture or collapse a lung.

Kidneys: A powerful blow to the kidneys can induce shock and possibly cause internal injury to these organs. A stab to the kidneys induces instant shock and can cause death from severe internal bleeding.

Abdomen below navel: A powerful blow to the area below the navel and above the groin can cause shock, unconsciousness, and internal bleeding.

Biceps: A strike to the biceps is most painful and renders the arm ineffective. The biceps is an especially good target when an opponent holds a weapon.

Forearm muscle: The radial nerve, which controls much of the movement in the hand, passes over the forearm bone just below the elbow. A strike to the radial nerve renders the hand and arm ineffective. An opponent can be disarmed by a strike to the forearm; if the strike is powerful enough, he can be knocked unconscious.

Back of hand: The backs of the hands are sensitive. Since the nerves pass over the bones in the hand, a strike to this area is intensely painful. The small bones on the back of the hand are easily broken, and such a strike can also render the hand ineffective.

Low Section: The low section of the body includes everything from the groin area to the feet. Strikes to these areas are seldom fatal, but they can be incapacitating.

Groin: A moderate blow to the groin can incapacitate an opponent and cause intense pain. A powerful blow can result in unconsciousness and shock.

Outside of thigh: A large nerve passes near the surface on the outside of the thigh about four finger-widths above the knee. A powerful strike to this region can render the entire leg ineffective, causing an opponent to drop. This target is especially suitable for knee strikes and shin kicks.

Inside of thigh: A large nerve passes over the bone in the middle of the inner thigh. A blow to this area also incapacitates the leg and can cause the opponent to drop.

Knee strikes and heel kicks are the weapons of choice for this target.

Hamstring: A severe strike to the hamstring can cause muscle spasms and inhibit mobility. If the hamstring is cut, the leg is useless.

Knee: Because the knee is a major supporting structure of the body, damage to this joint is especially detrimental to an opponent. The knee is easily dislocated when struck at an opposing angle to the joint's normal range of motion, especially when it is bearing the opponent's weight. The knee can be dislocated or hyperextended by kicks and strikes with the entire body.

Calf: A powerful blow to the top of the calf causes painful muscle spasms and also inhibits mobility.

Shin: A moderate blow to the shin produces great pain, especially a blow with a hard object. A powerful blow can possibly fracture the bone that supports most of the body's weight.

Achilles' tendon: A powerful strike to the Achilles' tendon on the back of the heel can cause ankle sprain and dislocation of the foot. If the tendon is torn, the opponent is incapacitated. The Achilles' tendon is a good target to cut with a knife.

Ankle: A blow to the ankle causes pain; if a forceful blow is delivered, the ankle can be sprained or broken.

Instep: The small bones on the top of the foot are easily broken. A strike here will hinder the opponent's mobility.

ANGLES OF ATTACK

Any attack, regardless of the weapon type, can be directed along one of nine angles. The defense must be oriented for each angle of attack.

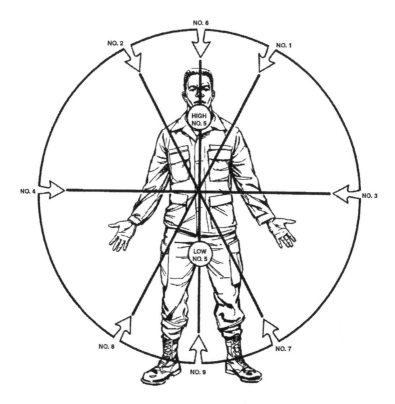

Angles of attack

No. 1 angle of attack is a downward, diagonal slash, stab, or strike toward the left side of the defender's head, neck, or torso.

No. 2 angle of attack is a downward, diagonal slash, stab, or strike toward the right side of the defender's head, neck, or torso.

No. 3 angle of attack is a horizontal attack to the left side of the defender's torso in the ribs, side, or hip region.

No. 4 angle of attack is the same as No. 3, but to the right side.

No. 5 angle of attack is a jabbing, lunging, or punching attack directed straight toward the defender's front.

No. 6 angle of attack is an attack directed straight down upon the defender.

No. 7 angle of attack is an upward, diagonal attack toward the defender's lower-left side.

No. 8 angle of attack is an upward, diagonal attack toward the defender's lower-right side.

No. 9 angle of attack is an attack directed straight up (i.e., to the defender's groin).

Low No. 5 Angle of Defense–Parry

1. A lunging thrust to the stomach is made by the attacker along the No. 5 angle of attack.

2. The defender moves his body off the line of attack and deflects the attacking arm by parrying, or warding off the weapon or blow, with his left hand. He deflects the attacking hand toward his right side by redirecting it with his right hand.

3. As he does this, the defender can strike downward with the left forearm or the wrist onto the forearm or wrist of the attacker.

4. The defender ends up in a position to lock the elbow of the attacking arm across his body if he steps off the line of attack properly.

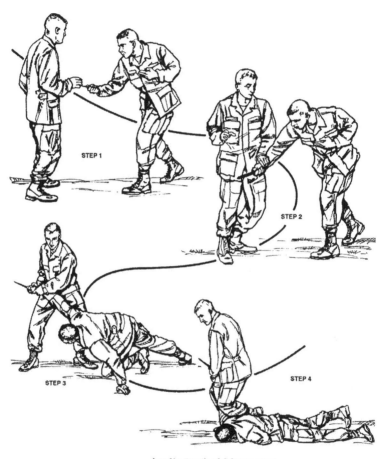

Low No. 5 angle of defense - parry

High No. 5 Angle of Defense

1. The attacker lunges with a thrust to the face, throat, or solar plexus.

2. The defender moves his body off the line of attack, while parrying with either hand. He redirects the attacking arm so that the knife clears his body.

3. He maintains control of the weapon hand or arm and gouges the eyes of the attacker, driving him backward and off balance. If the attacker is much taller than the defender, it may be a more natural movement for the defender to raise his left hand to strike and deflect the attacking arm. He can then gouge his thumb or fingers into the jugular notch of the attacker and force him to the ground.

4. Still another possibility for a high No. 5 angle of attack is for the defender to move his body off the line of attack while parrying. He can then turn his body, rotate his shoulder under the elbow joint of the attacker, and lock it out.

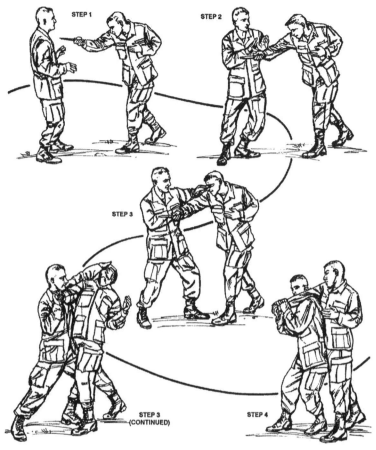

STEP 1

STEP 2

STEP 3

STEP 3
(CONTINUED)

STEP 4

High No. 5 angle of defense

Belgian Takedown

In the Belgian take-down technique, the unsuspecting sentry is knocked to the ground and kicked in the groin, inducing shock. The soldier can then kill the sentry by any proper means. Since surprise is the essential element of this technique, the soldier must use effective stalking techniques. To initiate his attack, he grabs both of the sentry's ankles. Then he heaves his body weight into the hips of the sentry, while pulling up on the ankles. This technique slams the sentry to the ground on his face. Then, the soldier follows with a kick to the groin.

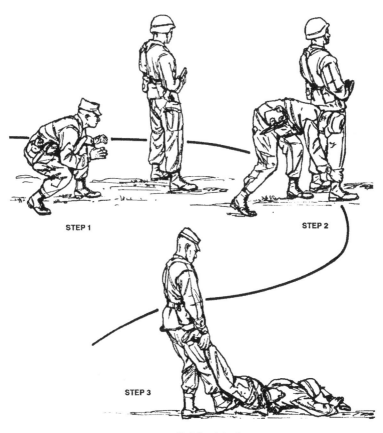

STEP 1

STEP 2

STEP 3

Belgian takedown

Shoulder Dislocation

1. If the opponent applies a choke from the rear, the defender places the back of his hand against the inside of the opponent's forearm.

2. Then, he brings the other hand over the crook of the opponent's elbow and clasps hands, keeping his hands close to his body as he moves his entire body around the opponent.

3. He positions his body so that the opponent's upper arm is aligned with the opponent's shoulders. The opponent's arm should be bent at a 90-degree angle.

4. By pulling up on the opponent's elbow and down on the wrist, the opponent's balance is taken, and his shoulder is easily dislocated. The defender must use his body movement to properly position the opponent—upper body strength will not work.

5. He drops his body weight by bending his knees to help get the proper bend in the opponent's elbow. The defender must also keep his own hands and elbows close to his body to prevent the opponent's escape.

STEP 1

STEP 2

STEP 3

STEP 4

STEP 5

Shoulder dislocation

Knee strike to face

The defender controls his opponent by grabbing behind his head with both hands and forcefully pushing his head down. At the same time, the defender brings his knee up and smashes the opponent in the face. When properly executed the knee strike to the face is a devastating technique that can cause serious injury to the opponent.

Knee strike to face

Improvised Weapons

To survive in any sort of combat, you must be able to deal with any situation that develops. Your ability to adapt any nearby object for use as a weapon in a win-or-die situation is limited only by your ingenuity and resourcefulness. An improvised weapon is a device that was not designed to be used as a weapon, but can be put to that use. It is generally used for self-defense or where the person is otherwise unarmed. In some cases, improvised weapons are commonly used by attackers in street fights, muggings, murders, or during riots, usually when conventional weapons, such as firearms, are unavailable or inappropriate.

Improvised weapons represent common, everyday objects that can be used in a variety of defensive applications. These objects are not physically altered in any way, in an effort to make them more functional as weapons. They are generally utilized in their normal state. Other than items designed as weapons, any object that can be used to cause bodily harm can be considered an improvised weapon.

Examples of Improvised Weapons

- Sports equipment, such as baseball bats, golf clubs, cricket bats, dumbbells, and helmets.
- Objects made of glass, such as beer bottles.
- Tools, such as sledgehammers, tire irons, shovels, and fire extinguishers.
- Construction materials, such as 2×4s, pipes, and bricks.
- Natural materials, such as rocks, sand, and liquids thrown into the enemy's eyes.
- Desk supplies, such as pens, pencils, scissors, and letter openers.

15
TERRORIST HAZARDS

Throughout human history there have been many threats to the security of nations. These threats have brought about large-scale losses of life, the destruction of property, widespread illness and injury, the displacement of large numbers of people, and devastating economic loss.

Recent technological advances and ongoing political unrest are components of the increased risk to national security. Learn what actions to include in your family disaster plan to prepare for and respond to terrorist threats.

Biological Threats
Biological agents are organisms or toxins that can kill or incapacitate people, livestock, and crops. A biological attack is the deliberate release of germs or other biological substances that can make you sick.

The three basic groups of biological agents that would likely be used as weapons are bacteria, viruses, and toxins. Most biological agents are difficult to grow and maintain. Many break down quickly when exposed to sunlight and other environmental factors, while others, such as anthrax spores, are very long lived. Biological agents can be dispersed by spraying them into the air, by infecting animals that carry the disease to humans, by contaminating food and water, and by person-to-person contact.

- **Aerosols**: Biological agents are dispersed into the air, forming a fine mist that may drift for miles. Inhaling the agent may cause disease in people or animals.
- **Animals**: Some diseases are spread by insects and animals, such as fleas, mice, flies, mosquitoes, and livestock.
- **Food and water contamination**: Some pathogenic organisms and toxins may persist in food and water supplies. Most microbes can be killed, and toxins deactivated, by cooking food and boiling water. Most microbes are killed by boiling water for one minute, but some require longer. Follow official instructions.
- **Person-to-person**: Humans have been the source of infection for smallpox, plague, and the Lassa viruses.

Before a Biological Threat
Unlike an explosion, a biological attack may or may not be immediately obvious. While it is possible that you will see signs of a biological attack, as was sometimes the case with the anthrax mailings, it is perhaps more likely that local health-care workers will report a pattern of unusual illnesses or there will be a wave of sick people seeking emergency medical attention. You will probably learn of the danger through an emergency radio or TV broadcast, some other signal used in your community, a telephone call, or emergency-response workers coming to your door.

How to Protect Against Biological Attack

- Plan places where your family will meet, both within and outside of your immediate neighborhood.
- It may be easier to make a long-distance phone call than to call across town, so an out-of-town contact may be in a better position to communicate among separated family members.
- You may also want to inquire about emergency plans at places where your family spends time: work, daycare, school, etc. If no plans exist, consider volunteering to help create one.
- Notify caregivers and babysitters about your plan.
- Consider installing a high-efficiency particulate air (HEPA) filter in your furnace return duct. These filters remove particles in the 0.3 to 10 micron range and will filter out most biological agents that may enter your house. If you do not have a central heating or cooling system, a stand-alone portable HEPA filter can be used.

During a Biological Threat

The first evidence of an attack may be when you notice symptoms of the disease caused by exposure to an agent. The following are guidelines to follow during a biological threat:

- If you become aware of an unusual and suspicious substance, quickly get away.
- Protect yourself. Cover your mouth and nose with layers of fabric that can filter the air, but still allow breathing. Examples include two to three layers of cotton such as a t-shirt, handkerchief, or towel. Otherwise, several layers of tissue or paper towels may help.
- There may be times when you would want to consider wearing a face mask to reduce spreading germs if you yourself are sick or to avoid coming in contact with contagious germs if others around you are sick.

- If you have been exposed to a biological agent, remove and bag your clothes and personal items. Follow official instructions for disposal of contaminated items.
- Wash yourself with soap and water and put on clean clothes.
- If a family member becomes sick, it is important to be suspicious.
- Do not assume, however, that you should go to a hospital emergency room or that any illness is the result of the biological attack. Symptoms of many common illnesses may overlap.
- Use common sense and practice good hygiene and cleanliness to avoid spreading germs.
- If the disease is contagious, expect to receive medical evaluation and treatment. You may be advised to stay away from others or even deliberately quarantined.
- In a declared biological emergency or developing epidemic, there may be reason to stay away from crowds where others may be infected.

Cover Your Nose and Mouth

Be prepared to improvise with what you have on hand to protect your nose, mouth, eyes, and cuts in your skin. Anything that fits snugly over your nose and mouth, including any dense-weave cotton material, can help filter contaminants in an emergency. It is crucial that most of the air you breathe comes through the mask or cloth, not around it.

Do whatever you can to make the best fit possible for children. There are also a variety of face masks readily available in hardware stores that are rated based on how small a particle they can filter in an industrial setting. Simple cloth face masks can filter some of the airborne "junk" or germs you might breathe into your body, but will probably not protect you from chemical gases.

Symptoms and Hygiene

If a family member develops any of the symptoms listed below, keep them separated from others, if possible, and practice good hygiene and cleanliness to avoid spreading germs. Seek medical advice as well.

- A temperature of more than 100 degree
- Nausea and vomiting
- Stomachache
- Diarrhea
- Pale or flushed face
- Headache
- Cough
- Earache
- Thick discharge from nose
- Sore throat
- Rash or infection of the skin
- Red or pink eyes
- Loss of appetite
- Loss of energy or decreases in activity

Hygiene

If someone is sick, you should practice good hygiene and cleanliness to avoid spreading germs.

- Wash your hands with soap and water frequently.
- Do not share food or utensils.
- Cover your mouth and nose when coughing or sneezing.
- Consider having the sick person wear a face mask to avoid spreading germs.
- Plan to share health-related information with others, especially those who may need help understanding the situation and what specific actions to take.

After a Biological Threat
In some situations, as with the case of the anthrax letters sent in 2001, people may be alerted to potential exposure. If this is the case, pay close attention to all official warnings and instructions on how to proceed. The delivery of medical services for a biological event may be handled differently to respond to increased demand. The basic public-health procedures and medical protocols for handling exposure to biological agents are the same as for any infectious disease. It is important for you to pay attention to official instructions via radio, television, and emergency-alert systems.

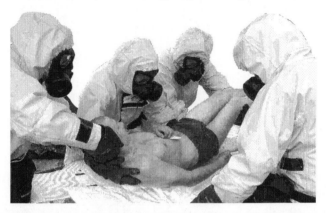

Chemical Threats
Chemical agents are poisonous vapors, aerosols, liquids, and solids that have toxic effects on people, animals, or plants. They can be released by bombs or sprayed from aircraft, boats, and vehicles. They can be used as a liquid to create a hazard to people and the environment. Some chemical agents may be odorless and tasteless. They can have an immediate effect (a few seconds to a few minutes) or a delayed effect (2–48 hours). While potentially lethal, chemical agents are difficult to deliver in lethal concentrations. Outdoors, the agents often dissipate rapidly. Chemical agents are difficult to produce as well.

A chemical attack could come without warning. Signs of a chemical release include people having difficulty breathing, experiencing eye irritation, losing coordination, becoming nauseated, or having a burning sensation in the nose, throat and lungs. Also, the presence of many dead insects or birds may indicate a chemical agent has been released.

Before a Chemical Threat

What you should do to prepare for a chemical threat:

- A roll of duct tape and scissors.
- Plastic for doors, windows, and vents for the room in which you will shelter in place. To save critical time during an emergency, pre-measure and cut the plastic sheeting for each opening.
- Choose an internal room to use as shelter, preferably one without windows and on the highest floor.

During a Chemical Threat

What you should do in a chemical attack:

- Quickly try to define the impacted area or where the chemical is coming from.
- Take immediate action to get away.
- If the chemical is inside a building where you are, get out of the building without passing through the contaminated area, if possible.
- If you can't get out of the building or find clean air without passing through the area where you see signs of a chemical attack, it may be better to move as far away as possible and shelter-in-place.

If you are instructed to remain in your home or office building:

- Close doors and windows and turn off all ventilation, including furnaces, air conditioners, vents, and fans.
- Seek shelter in an internal room and take your disaster-supplies kit.

- Seal the room with duct tape and plastic sheeting.
- Listen to your radio for instructions.

If you are caught in or near a contaminated area:

- Move away immediately in a direction upwind of the source.
- Find shelter as quickly as possible
- If you are outside, quickly decide what the fastest way to find clean air is. Consider if you can get out of the area or if you should go inside the closest building and shelter-in-place.

After a Chemical Threat
Decontamination is needed within minutes of exposure to minimize health consequences. Do not leave the safety of a shelter to go outdoors to help others until authorities announce it is safe to do so.

A person affected by a chemical agent requires immediate medical attention from a professional. If medical help is not readily available, decontaminate yourself and assist in decontaminating others.

Decontamination guidelines:

- Use extreme caution when helping others who have been exposed to chemical agents.
- Remove all clothing and other items in contact with the body. Contaminated clothing normally removed over the head should be cut off to avoid contact with the eyes, nose, and mouth. Put contaminated clothing and items into a plastic bag and seal it.
- Decontaminate hands using soap and water. Remove eyeglasses or contact lenses. Put glasses in a pan of household bleach to decontaminate them and then rinse and dry.
- Flush eyes with water.

- Gently wash face and hair with soap and water before thoroughly rinsing with water.
- Decontaminate other body parts likely to have been contaminated. Blot (do not swab or scrape) with a cloth soaked in soapy water and rinse with clear water.
- Change into uncontaminated clothes. Clothing stored in drawers or closets is likely to be uncontaminated.

Explosions

Terrorists have frequently used explosive devices as one of their most common weapons. Terrorists do not have to look far to find out how to make explosive devices; the information is readily available in books and other information sources. Explosive devices can be highly portable, using vehicles and humans as a means of transport. They are easily detonated from remote locations or by suicide bombers.

Conventional bombs have been used to damage and destroy financial, political, social, and religious institutions. Attacks have occurred in public places and on city streets with thousands of people around the world injured and killed.

Devastating acts, such as the terrorist attacks in Oklahoma City and on September 11, have left many concerned about the possibility of future incidents in the United States. Nevertheless, there are things you can do to prepare for the unexpected. Preparing for such events will reduce the stress that you may feel now and later, should another emergency arise. Taking preparatory action can reassure you and your children that you can exert a measure of control even in the face of such events.

Before an Explosion

- Build an emergency-supply kit, which includes items like non-perishable food, water, a battery-powered or hand-crank radio, extra flashlights, and batteries. You may want to prepare a kit for your workplace and a portable kit to keep in your car in case you are told to evacuate. This kit should include:
- Extra prescription medications and medical supplies.
- Bedding and clothing, including sleeping bags and pillows.

Bomb Threats

- Get as much information from the caller as possible. Try to ask the following questions:
- When is the bomb going to explode?
- Where is it right now?
- What does it look like?
- What kind of bomb is it?
- What will cause it to explode?
- Who placed the bomb?
- Keep the caller on the line and record everything that is said.
- Notify the police and building management immediately.

During an Explosion

- Get under a sturdy table or desk if things are falling around you. When they stop falling, leave quickly, watching for obviously weakened floors and stairways. As you exit from the building, be especially watchful of falling debris.
- During the evacuation, stay low if there is smoke. Do not stop to retrieve personal possessions or make phone calls.
- Do not use elevators.
- Check for fire and other hazards.
- Once you are out, do not stand in front of windows, glass doors, or other potentially hazardous areas.
- If you are trapped in debris, use a flashlight, if possible, to signal your location to rescuers.
- Tap on a pipe or wall so rescuers can hear where you are.
- Shout only as a last resort. Shouting can cause a person to inhale dangerous amounts of dust.
- Avoid unnecessary movement so that you don't kick up dust.
- Cover your nose and mouth with anything you have on hand. (Dense-weave cotton material can act as a good filter. Try to breathe through the material.)

After an Explosion

As we learned from the events on September 11, 2001, the following things can happen after a terrorist attack:

- There can be significant numbers of casualties and/or damage to buildings and infrastructure. Employers need up-to-date information about any medical needs you may have and on how to contact your designated beneficiaries.
- Heavy law enforcement involvement at local, state, and federal levels follows a terrorist attack due to the event's criminal nature.

- Health and mental-health resources in the affected communities can be strained to their limits, maybe even overwhelmed.
- Extensive media coverage, strong public fear, and international implications and consequences can continue for a prolonged period.
- Workplaces and schools may be closed, and there may be restrictions on domestic and international travel.
- You and your family or household may have to evacuate an area, avoiding roads blocked for your safety.
- Clean-up may take many months.

Nuclear Blast

A nuclear blast is an explosion with intense light and heat, a damaging pressure wave, and widespread radioactive material that can contaminate the air, water, and ground surfaces for miles around. A nuclear device can range from a weapon carried by an intercontinental missile launched by a hostile nation or terrorist organization, to a small portable nuclear devise transported by an individual. All nuclear devices cause deadly effects when detonated, including blinding light, intense heat (thermal radiation), initial nuclear radiation, blast, fires started by the heat pulse, and secondary fires caused by the destruction.

The nuclear threat present during the Cold War has diminished; however, the possibility remains that a terrorist could obtain access to a nuclear weapon. Generally referred to as improvised nuclear devices (IND), these are generally smaller, less powerful weapons than we traditionally envision. While experts may predict that a nuclear attack is less likely than other types, it is still important to know the simple steps that can save your life and the life of your family.

Hazards of Nuclear Devices
If an impending attack is on the horizon, people living near potential targets may be advised to evacuate or on their own decide to evacuate to an area not considered a likely target. Protection from radioactive fallout would require taking shelter in an underground area or in the middle of a large building.

In general, potential targets include:

- Strategic missile sites and military bases.
- Centers of government, such as Washington, DC, and state capitals.
- Important transportation and communication centers.
- Manufacturing, industrial, technological, and financial centers.
- Petroleum refineries, electrical power plants, and chemical plants.
- Major ports and airfields.

The three ways to protect oneself from radiation and fallout are distance, shielding, and time.

- **Distance**: The more distance between you and the fallout particles, the better. An underground area, such as a home or office building basement offers more protection than the first floor of a building. A floor near the middle of a high-rise may be better, depending on what is nearby at that level on which significant fallout particles would collect. Flat roofs collect fallout particles, so the top floor is not a good choice, nor is a floor adjacent to a neighboring flat roof.

- **Shielding**: The heavier and denser the materials (thick walls, concrete, bricks, books, earth, etc.) between you and the fallout particles, the better.
- **Time**: Fallout radiation loses its intensity fairly rapidly. In time you will be able to leave the fallout shelter. Radioactive fallout poses the greatest threat to people during the first two weeks, by which time it has declined to about 1 percent of its initial radiation level.

Before a Nuclear Blast
The following are things you can do to protect yourself, your family, and your property in the event of a nuclear blast.

- Know your community's warning systems and disaster plans, including evacuation routes.
- Find out from officials if any public buildings in your community have been designated as fallout shelters. Make your own list of potential shelters near your home, workplace, and school. These potential evacuation sites could include basements or the windowless, center area of middle floors in high-rise buildings, as well as subways and tunnels.
- During periods of heightened threat, increase your disaster supplies to be adequate for up to six weeks.

Taking shelter during a nuclear blast is absolutely necessary. There are two kinds of shelters—blast and fallout. The following describes the two kinds of shelters:

- Blast shelters are specifically constructed to offer some protection against blast pressure, initial radiation, heat, and fire. But even a blast shelter cannot withstand a direct hit from a nuclear explosion.

- Fallout shelters do not need to be specially constructed for protecting against fallout. They can be any protected space, provided that the walls and roof are thick and dense enough to absorb the radiation given off by fallout particles.

During a Nuclear Blast
The following are guidelines for what to do in the event of a nuclear explosion.

- If an attack warning is issued, take cover as quickly as you can, below ground if possible, and stay there until instructed to do otherwise.
- Find the nearest building, preferably built of brick or concrete, and go inside to avoid any radioactive material outside.
- Go as far below ground as possible or in the center of a tall building. The goal is to put as many walls and as much concrete, brick, and soil between you and the radioactive material outside.
- Stay where you are, even if you are separated from your family. Inside is the safest place for all people in the impacted area. It can save your life.
- Radiation levels are extremely dangerous after a nuclear detonation, but the levels reduce rapidly.
- People in the path of the radioactive material—downwind from the detonation—may also be asked to take protective measures.

If you are caught outside and unable to get inside immediately:

- Do not look at the flash or fireball. It can blind you.
- Take cover behind anything that might offer protection.
- Lie flat on the ground and cover your head. If the explosion is some distance away, it could take 30 seconds or more for the blast wave to hit.

- Take shelter as soon as you can, even if you are many miles from ground zero, where the attack occurred, as radioactive fallout can be carried by the winds for hundreds of miles. Remember the three protective factors: distance, shielding, and time.
- If you were outside during or after the blast, clean yourself as soon as possible, to remove radioactive material that may have settled on your body.
- Remove your clothing to keep radioactive material from spreading. Removing the outer layer of clothing can remove up to 90% of radioactive material.
- If practical, place your contaminated clothing in a plastic bag and seal or tie the bag. Place the bag as far away from humans and animals as possible, so that the radiation it gives off does not affect others.
- When feasible, take a shower with lots of soap and water to help remove radioactive contamination. Do not scrub or scratch the skin.
- Wash your hair with shampoo or soap and water. Do not use conditioner in your hair, because it will bind radioactive material to your hair, keeping it from rinsing out easily.
- Gently blow your nose and wipe your eyelids and eyelashes with a clean, wet cloth. Gently wipe your ears.
- If you cannot shower, use a wipe or clean, wet cloth to wipe your skin that was not covered by clothing.

After a Nuclear Blast

Decay rates of the radioactive fallout are the same for any nuclear device, no matter the size. However, the amount of fallout will vary, based on the size of the device and its proximity to the ground. Therefore, it might be necessary for those in the areas with highest radiation levels to shelter-in-place for up to 1 month.

The heaviest fallout would be limited to the area at or downwind from the explosion and 80 percent of the fallout would occur during the first 24 hours.

People in most of the areas that would be affected could be allowed to come out of shelter within a few days and, if necessary, evacuate to unaffected areas

Radiological Dispersion Device (RDD)

Terrorist use of an RDD—often called a "dirty nuke" or a "dirty bomb"—is considered far more likely than use of a nuclear, explosive device. An RDD combines a conventional, explosive device—such as a bomb—with radioactive material. It is designed to scatter dangerous and sub-lethal amounts of radioactive material over a general area. Such RDDs appeal to terrorists, because they require limited technical knowledge to build and deploy compared to a nuclear device. Also, the radioactive materials in RDDs are widely used in medicine, agriculture, industry, and research, that's why they are easier to obtain than weapons-grade uranium or plutonium.

The primary purpose of terrorist use of an RDD is to cause psychological fear and economic disruption. Some devices could cause fatalities from exposure to radioactive materials. Depending on the speed at which the area of the RDD detonation was evacuated, or how successful people were at sheltering-in-place, the number of deaths and injuries from an RDD might not be substantially greater than from a conventional-bomb explosion.

The size of the affected area and the level of destruction caused by an RDD would depend on the sophistication and size of the conventional bomb, the type of radioactive material used, the quality and quantity of the radioactive material, and the local meteorological conditions, primarily wind and precipitation. The area affected could be placed off-limits to the public for several months during cleanup efforts.

Before an RDD Event
There is no way to determine how much warning there will be before an attack by terrorists using an RDD, so being prepared in advance and knowing what to do and when to do it is important. To prepare for an RDD event, you should do the following:

- Have a roll of duct tape and scissors on hand.
- Choose an internal room for shelter, preferably one without windows.
- Find out from officials if any public buildings in your community have been designated as fallout shelters. Make your own list of potential shelters near your home, workplace, and school. These places could include basements or the windowless, center area of middle floors in high-rise buildings, as well as subways and tunnels.
- If you live in an apartment building or high-rise, talk to the manager about the safest place in the building for sheltering and about provisions for building occupants until it is safe to go out.

Taking shelter during an RDD attack is absolutely necessary. Remember, there are two kinds of shelters—blast and fallout. The following describes the two kinds of shelters:

- Blast shelters are specifically constructed to offer some protection against blast pressure, initial radiation, heat, and fire. But even a blast shelter cannot withstand a direct hit from a nuclear explosion.

- Fallout shelters do not need to be specially constructed for protecting against fallout. They can be any protected space, provided that the walls and roof are thick and dense enough to absorb the radiation given off by fallout particles.

During an RDD Event
While the explosive blast will be immediately obvious, the presence of radiation will not be known until trained personnel with specialized equipment are on the scene. Whether you are indoors or outdoors, home or at work, be extra cautious. It would be safer to assume radiological contamination has occurred, particularly in an urban setting or near other likely terrorist targets, and take the proper precautions. As with any radiation, you want to avoid or limit exposure. This is especially true of inhaling radioactive dust that results from the explosion. As you seek shelter from any location (indoors or outdoors) and there is visual dust or other contaminants in the air, breathe though the cloth of your shirt or coat to limit your exposure. If you manage to avoid breathing radioactive dust, your proximity to the radioactive particles may still result in some radiation exposure.

If the explosion or radiological release occurs inside, get out immediately and seek safe shelter.

Outdoors: Seek shelter indoors immediately in the nearest undamaged building. If appropriate shelter is not available, cover your nose and mouth; move as rapidly and safely upwind, away from the location of the explosive blast. Then, seek appropriate shelter as soon as possible.

Indoors: If you have time, turn off ventilation and heating systems, close windows, vents, fireplace dampers, exhaust fans, and clothes-dryer vents. Retrieve your disaster-supplies kit and battery-powered radio, and take them to your shelter room. Seek shelter immediately, preferably underground or in an interior room of a building, placing as much distance and dense shielding as possible between you and the outdoors, where the radioactive material may be.

Seal windows and external doors that do not fit snugly with duct tape to reduce infiltration of radioactive particles. Plastic sheeting will not provide shielding from radioactivity or from blast effects of a nearby explosion.

After an RDD Event
After finding safe shelter, those who may have been exposed to radioactive material should decontaminate themselves. To do this, remove and bag your clothing, isolate the bag away from you and others, and shower thoroughly with soap and water.

Contamination from an RDD event could affect a wide area, depending on the amount of conventional explosives used, the quantity, type of radioactive material released, and meteorological conditions. Thus, radiation dissipation rates vary, but radiation from an RDD will likely take longer to dissipate due to a potentially larger, localized concentration of radioactive material.

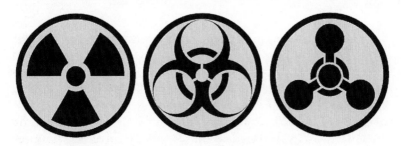

Personal Protection Equipment

Gas Masks
The best protection against a nuclear, biological, or chemical weapon is a gas mask. There are several important factors to

consider when looking for a gas mask. Shatter-proof lenses are important. For convenience, look for a mask that uses standard NATO filters. Try it on to check for limited visibility, comfort, ease of use, etc., and be sure to practice with it before you're in the streets fumbling with unfamiliar straps.

When proper shelter is not immediately available, a gas mask is the only way one can be protected from the release of certain chemical and biological agents, and from nuclear fallout. The levels of protection vary with types of agents used and concentration. The misuse of a gas mask in a toxic environment will turn a gas mask into a death mask.

Israeli gas masks are a great choice for many reasons; they are inexpensive, reliable, and readily available. The M-15 used by the Israeli Defense Forces (IDF) can be picked up for $65, with an included drinking tube and canteen. The civilian style is a good choice as well and even available in a child-sized version.

Another option is the US Army M-40 that has been used by our armed forces since the mid-1990s. A voicecom adapter may be placed over the front voicemitter to amplify the user's voice. The mask can be adjusted in the field to accept the filtering canister on either side, so that a weapon may be shouldered. This gasmask is my first choice, but may be unrealistic for some due to the $300+ price tag. If you cannot verify that the mask is new, don't buy it! Most of the filters that are included are expired, so you will need to purchase new, sealed 40mm NATO filters. I recommend a CBRN (chemical, biological, radiological, and nuclear) filter that is NIOSH-certified.

The truth about surplus is that many models of masks and filters are available in nearly unlimited quantities at low prices. In most cases, these prices are low because the mask is obsolete, recalled, or replaced due to design flaws or defective components. Before buying a surplus mask, do your homework, take time to review recalled gas mask models. Here are a few of the most widely-advertised surplus masks that should be AVOIDED.

- Russian gas masks (most are 30+ years old).
- EVAC-U-8 Hood: Advertised by some unscrupulous vendors for protection against NBC agents, this mask is actually intended for smoke/fire protection. 27,400+ have been recalled.
- Canadian M69 C-3 & C-4: The entire Canadian military has removed the C3 from service (replaced by a completely different model, the C4 is also defective). The C3 60mm filter port does not accept NATO threaded filters without a plastic adapter.

Individuals with respiratory problems should know that the filters in gas masks produce resistance that requires the user to breathe three to four times harder than normal.

The lifespan of any gas mask filter depends on the users breathing rate, the type of agent the filter must scrub, air temperature, and moisture content. A standard NATO filter can effectively perform from three hours to a few days, depending on conditions during use. They can filter out many different harmful gases and aerosol mists, including chemical and biological warfare agents, such as sarin and other nerve gases, mustard gas, cyanogen, arsine, radioactive fallout, bacteria, and some viruses.

Gas Mask Basic Procedures

1. Quickly take a deep breath, break the protective seal on the filter canister, and screw the filter onto the mask.
2. Place the mask over your face.
3. Exhale, blowing out all the air inside the mask through the exhalation valve.
4. A mask must fit snugly to your face to work properly. To achieve the right fit and suction, the correct mask size must be chosen.

MOPP Suit

MOPP (mission oriented protective posture—acronym pronounced as "mop") is a military term used to describe protective gear to be used in a toxic environment, i.e., during a chemical, biological, radiological, and nuclear (CBRN) strike. You can purchase new US-military-surplus MOPP suits inexpensively off the Internet, predominantly eBay. The suit consists of a smock with hood and trousers, which is worn over the uniform with the webbing on the outside. Try to stick to ones that have a date no later than the early 1990's and are still sealed in the original, military-issue packaging.

The MOPP suit was designed to allow the trapped air to move around, unlike most NBC suits of various other nations. It has a charcoal, impregnated inner layer, with the outer material being waterproof for up to 24 hours. Don't forget to add military spec rubber gloves and overboots.

When you put the suit on, slide the sleeves over the ends of the gloves and wrap your wrists with duct tape, creating a seal. Repeat the procedure at your ankles. Cover your head with the hood and pull the strings for a tight fit around your face and the gasmask.

Once you put the suit on, do not remove it until you leave the contaminated zone. When you arrive at your destination, you will need assistance to remove your improvised suit to avoid contact with the toxic agent. Carefully cut off and discard.

Cover any gear you will be carrying through a contaminated area. Industrial-strength trash bags work well if you seal tightly with duct tape; do your best to avoid punctures that could cause contamination of your contents.

Civil-Defense Geiger Counter

The Civil Defense CDV-700
The CDV-700 is the only Civil Defense meter that is actually a Geiger counter and will detect very low levels of radiation. This is probably one of the more common and affordable Geigers that can be found on Ebay, because there were over 450,000 made. It uses a Geiger tube in the probe that can detect beta and measure gamma radiation from .01mr/Hr to 50mr/Hr. This range is more than suitable for your average,

modern consumer. It will detect radiation in water, food, can be used to decontaminate things or people, and is great for demonstrating radioactivity. It is probably the best overall meter on the market. They are 100% waterproof, shockproof, EMP proof, and there are a TON of good and bad tips on how to use them correctly. It is best to avoid ones that say: "untested," or even, "it works." They may seem to work, but can actually have serious problems. If you do choose to buy a non-calibrated model, expect to have about $30-$50 in repairs to get it functioning or for a new Geiger tube.

If it isn't a CDV-700, it isn't a Geiger counter. Almost every seller on Ebay is now listing their CDV-715's as Geiger counters and fooling people into buying them. The CDV-715, 710, 720, and all others that ARE NOT the 700 are survey meters for VERY high levels of radiation produced from a nuclear bomb, that would be lethal within hours. Buy these as cool collectables or as a pre-emptive measure in case we get nuked.

RADSticker

RADSticker, a stockpileable personal casualty dosimeter, provides wearers timely, personal radiation-exposure information in the event of an accident at a nuclear power plant or a nuclear or dirty-bomb explosion. The RADSticker is a peel & stick, postage-stamp size, instant-color-developing dosimeter. It is ALWAYS on, with no need for a battery, ready and with you 24/7. Place on the back of your driver's license or on whatever you keep close at hand, for any future radiation emergency. The objective is to quickly determine the need for medical treatment and minimize panic. RADSticker has a sensor (a rectangle strip between the color bars) with 25, 50, and 100 rad bars on its bottom and 200, 400, and 1,000 rad bars on its top for triaging information and medical treatment in emergencies.

When exposed to radiation, the sensor develops color instantly. The color changes are permanent, cumulative, and proportionate to the dose. The technology was developed with multi-million dollar funding from several US agencies, such as DHS, DOD, DOJ, DOS, DHHS, and TSWG and was field tested by the DHS with 800 first responders in the states of NJ, NY, and IL.

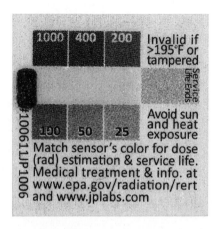

Potassium Iodide

In 1982, the FDA approved IOSAT potassium-iodide tablets for blocking the thyroid's absorption of cancer-causing radioactive iodine (only the thyroid absorbs iodine). By saturating the thyroid with potassium iodide's stable iodine, absorption of radioactive iodine, the predominate radioisotope released from a nuclear reactor release or nuclear bomb fallout, is not allowed

How Potassium Iodide Works
Certain forms of iodine help your thyroid gland work correctly. Most people get the minimal requirements of iodine from foods like iodized salt or fish. The thyroid can "store" only a certain amount of iodine.

In a radiation emergency, radioactive iodine may be released into the air. This material may be breathed or swallowed. It may enter the thyroid gland and damage it. The damage would probably not show itself for years. Fetuses, infants, and young children are the most susceptible, making KI pre-treatment critical.

Potassium iodide is a salt that stops the body from taking in radioactive iodine that can be emitted during a nuclear emergency.

It fills up the thyroid gland, preventing it from collecting the radioactive material and reducing the risk of cancer, among other things.

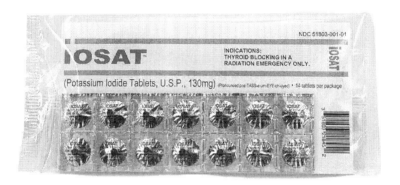

What KI cannot do
Knowing what KI cannot do is also important. KI cannot prevent radioactive iodine from entering the body. KI can protect only the thyroid from radioactive iodine, not other parts of the body. KI cannot reverse the health effects caused by radioactive iodine once damage to the thyroid has occurred. KI cannot protect the body from radioactive elements other than radioactive iodine—if radioactive iodine is not present, taking KI is not protective.

Who Should Not Take Potassium Iodide
The only people who should not take potassium iodide are those who know they are allergic to iodine. (A seafood or shellfish allergy does not necessarily mean that you are allergic to iodine.) Also, if you have certain skin disorders, such as dermatitis herpetiformis or urticaria vasculitis,

you should not take KI.

You may take potassium iodide even if you are taking medicines for a thyroid problem (i.e., a thyroid hormone or anti-thyroid drug). Pregnant and nursing women, children, and even babies may also take this drug.

How and When To Take Potassium Iodide
Potassium iodide (KI) should be taken as soon after a radioactive event, but before actual exposure, if at all possible. You should take one dose every 24 hours during the radiation threat. More will not help you because the thyroid can "hold" only limited amounts of iodine. Larger doses will increase the risk of side effects. Potassium Iodide comes in both tablet (65 mg and 130 mg) and liquid (65 mg per mL) forms. You will probably be told not to take the drug for more than 10 days.

The FDA has approved two different forms of KI—tablets and liquid—that people can take by mouth after a nuclear radiation emergency. Tablets come in two strengths, 130 mg and 65 mg. The tablets are scored so they may be cut into smaller pieces for lower doses. Each milliliter (mL) of the oral liquid solution contains 65 mg of KI.

According to the FDA, the following doses are appropriate to take after internal contamination with (or likely internal contamination with) radioactive iodine:

- Adults should take 130 mg (one 130 mg tablet OR two 65 mg tablets OR 2 mL of solution).
- Women who are breastfeeding should take the adult dose of 130 mg.
- Children between 3 and 18 years of age should take 65 mg (one 65 mg tablet OR 1 mL of solution). Children who are adult size (greater than or equal to 150 pounds) should take the full adult dose, regardless of their age.

- Infants and children between 1 month and 3 years of age should take 32 mg (½ of a 65 mg tablet OR ½ mL of solution). This dose is for both nursing and non-nursing infants and children.
- Newborns from birth to 1 month of age should be given 16 mg (¼ of a 65 mg tablet or ¼ mL of solution). This dose is for both nursing and non-nursing newborn infants.

Side Effects
Side effects are unlikely because of the low dose and the short time you will be taking the drug. Usually side effects of potassium iodide only occur when people are taking higher doses than necessary for a long period of time. You should be careful not to take more, or for longer, than recommended.

Possible side effects include skin rashes, swelling of the salivary glands, and "iodism" (metallic taste, burning mouth and throat, sore teeth and gums, symptoms of a head cold, and sometimes stomach upset and diarrhea).

Few people develop allergic reactions with more serious symptoms. These could be fever and joint pains, swelling of parts of the face or body, and at times severe shortness of breath requiring immediate medical attention.

Rarely, taking iodide causes overactivity of the thyroid gland, underactivity of the thyroid gland, or enlargement of the thyroid gland (goiter).

Unfortunately, the Federal Government only has enough potassium iodide for people living within 10 miles of nuclear reactors in the United States, according to the U.S.N.R.C. (United States Nuclear Regulatory Commission). Therefore we must prepare ourselves and our loved ones.

16
LIFE AFTER AN EMP ATTACK

Most Americans are oblivious to the fact that a single electromagnetic pulse (EMP) attack could potentially wipe out most of the electronics in the United States and instantly send this nation back to the nineteenth century. If a nuclear bomb was detonated high enough into the atmosphere, over the middle part of the country, the EMP would fry electronic devices from coast to coast. The damage would be millions of times worse than 9/11. Just imagine a world where nobody has power, most cars will not start, the Internet has been fried, the financial system is offline indefinitely, nobody can make any phone calls, and virtually all commerce across the entire country is brought to a complete stop. A nation that does not know how to live without technology would be almost entirely stripped of it at that point. Yes, this could really happen. An EMP attack is America's "Achilles' heel," and everyone around the world knows it. It is only a matter of time before someone uses an EMP weapon against us, and we are completely unprepared.

An EMP attack occurs when a nuclear bomb explodes in the atmosphere. "If a nuclear device designed to emit EMP were exploded 250 to 300 miles up over the middle of the country, it would disable the electronics in the entire United States," says Nordling, president and CEO of Minneapolis-based Emprimus. With 25 employees and associates, Emprimus claims to be the only company that designs and tests shielding against EMP for the private sector. That includes protection against devices that use high-power microwaves (HPM) to target particular facilities.

Russia or China have the capability of exploding an EMP device over the U.S., and countries like Iran or North Korea are believed to be working on acquiring one. Those countries could also launch a more limited EMP or HPM attack against selected targets, like power plants, oil refineries, or Wall Street. Terrorists could appropriate such weapons from rogue states. In the event of an EMP attack, the electrical power grid would be destroyed because its computers would be inoperative and transformers critical to it would take years to replace. Only a few countries build the transformers, and they take more than a year to make.

What would you and your neighbors do if the power went out and it did not ever come back on? What would you do if an EMP attack happened in the middle of the winter and you suddenly were not able to heat your home any longer? What would you do if all the electronics in your car got fried and you simply could not drive anywhere? What would you do if all the supermarkets in your area shut down because food could not be transported across the country anymore? What would you do if your debit cards and credit cards simply did not work any longer and you could not get any of your money out of the bank?

Cell phones and personal or business computers would stop working. Gas stations would be unable to pump gas, and there would be no natural gas, electricity, or water service. Cold storage would be down; food processing plants would be off-line. There would be no trucking, no railroads, no airplanes, no ATMs, and no inter-bank transfers. Americans would revert to eating whatever food they could hunt, fish, or forage within walking distance of their homes. City dwellers would flee en masse or face starvation.

The US military discovered the EMP effect in 1962 during the Starfish Prime nuclear explosion in the atmosphere over the Pacific.

Within instants, the street lamps, television sets, and telephone communications went out 900 miles away in Hawaii, without any visible signs of an attack. The military designated a young Air Force 2nd Lieutenant named William Graham to investigate. He determined that EMP was a bi-product of a nuclear blast, and that it had the effect of frying everything made of silicon hundreds—and possibly thousands—of miles away from the place of the blast.

A single EMP attack would be the worst disaster that the United States has ever seen by far. An EMP could potentially devastate the vast majority of all the microchips in the United States. In an instant, nearly all of our electronic devices would be rendered useless.

Yes, the federal government knows all about this. The following excerpt is from an April 2008 report by the Commission to Assess the Threat to the United States from Electromagnetic Pulse (EMP) Attack: "The consequences of lack of food, heat (or air conditioning), water, waste disposal, medical, police, fire fighting support, and effective civil authority would threaten society itself."

Most of us have become completely and totally dependent on electricity and technology. Without it, most of us would be in huge trouble.

The following is how an article in the Wall Street Journal described the potential consequences of an EMP attack:

> No American would necessarily die in the initial attack, but what comes next is potentially catastrophic. The pulse would wipe out most electronics and telecommunications, including the power grid. Millions could die for want of modern medical care or even of starvation since farms wouldn't be able to harvest crops and distributors wouldn't be able to get food to supermarkets. Commissioner Lowell Wood calls EMP attack a "giant continental time machine" that would move us back more than a century in technology to the late 1800s.

It wouldn't be so bad if we had the knowledge and the infrastructure to live the way that folks did back then, but today that simply is not the case.

Dr. William Graham was Ronald Reagan's science adviser and the chairman of the Commission to Assess the Threat to the United States from Electromagnetic Pulse (EMP) Attack. Dr. Graham believes that in the event of a large-scale EMP attack, the vast majority of Americans would either freeze, starve, or die from disease.

According to Graham, in the aftermath of an EMP attack life in America "would probably be something that you might imagine life to be like around the late 1800s but with several times the population we had in those days, and without the ability of the country to support and sustain all those people."

Would you be able to survive?

All of those big bank accounts may never be able to be recovered after an EMP attack. Your money might invisibly disappear into nonexistence.

The following is what Graham believes would happen to the financial system in the event of an EMP attack:

> Most financial records are stored electronically. ATMs, which depend upon both power and telecommunications, would not be available; banks, which try to back up records but in general aren't strongly aware of the EMP problem, would face the problem of unprotected storage and computer systems.

This is the danger of having a financial system that is so dependent on technology. We may wake up one day and find that all the money is gone. If an EMP attack actually happened, the biggest concern for most of us would be trying to figure out how to survive. The president of the Center for Security Policy, Frank Gaffney, is convinced that a single EMP attack could result in the deaths of the vast majority of the population of the United States. "Within a year of that attack, 9 out of 10 Americans would be dead, because we can't support a population of the present size in urban centers and the like without electricity."

Are you starting to get a feel for the scope of the problem? The sad thing is that so much could be done to protect this country from an EMP attack. Right now, most vital U.S. military infrastructure has at least some protection from an EMP attack, however, the general population has been left totally vulnerable. It has been estimated that the entire power grid could potentially be protected for about $20 billion. Remember, all it would take is one strategically placed EMP attack to wipe out this nation.

An EMP weapon is not the only danger that can produce this type of effect. The truth is that a really bad geomagnetic storm could also potentially produce just as much damage. In the past 152 years, Earth has been struck by roughly 100 solar storms causing significant geomagnetic disturbances (GMD), two of which were powerful enough to rank as "extreme GMDs." If an extreme GMD of such magnitude were to occur today, in all likelihood it would initiate a chain of events leading to catastrophic failures at the vast majority of our world's nuclear reactors, quite similar to the disasters at both Chernobyl and Fukushima, but multiplied over 100 times. (There are nearly 450 nuclear reactors in the world, with hundreds more either under construction or in the planning stages. There are 104 of these reactors in the USA and 195 in Europe.) When massive solar flares launch a huge mass of highly-charged plasma (a coronal mass ejection, or CME) directly towards Earth, colliding with our planet's outer atmosphere and magnetosphere, the result is a significant geomagnetic disturbance.

The first recorded evidence of space weather effects on technology was in 1847 when currents were registered in electric telegraph wires. Later, in 1859, a major failure of telegraph systems in New England and Europe coincided with a large solar flare called the "Carrington Event", after astronomer Richard Carrington who witnessed the instigating flare. However, the real modern-era wakeup call to geomagnetic susceptibility of our infrastructure was the (moderate intensity) geomagnetic storm that shut down the entire Hydro Quebec grid in March 1989. There were also reports of computer failures in August of that year in Toronto, Canada.

It is virtually guaranteed that a powerful geomagnetic storm, capable of knocking out a significant section of the US electrical grid, will occur within the next few decades. In fact, this may well happen even within the next few years as we approach the next period of elevated solar activity, known as "solar maximum," which is forecast to peak in 2013.

General Eugene Habiger, the former head of U. S. Strategic Command, had this to say about the possibility of an EMP attack. "It is not a matter of if, it is a matter of when."

Faraday Cages

We've established that an EMP incident will fry all electronics. This occurs whether or not they are plugged in or turned on. This also affects automobiles, batteries, computers, medical equipment, etc. Needless to say, in such an instance, life as we know it will change dramatically. Even more distressing is the fact that the strike of an EMP is not likely to give any warning. You don't see it. You don't feel it. You are simply left with the sudden consequences and whatever preparedness you have on hand. So, your new best friend may be a Faraday cage. In fact, with the knowledge of the protection that a Faraday cage can provide you, you may be able to enjoy nearly as comfortable a lifestyle as you did prior to any electromagnetic pulse.

While being mentally prepared to live in the Stone Age may be helpful, it's not necessary. Aren't you glad?

Common Myths Regarding Faraday Cages

- It doesn't matter if your electronics aren't plugged in, how long the antenna is, what the voltage is, or whether or not it operates with batteries—all non-protected electronics will be affected by an EMP.
- Batteries will short out.
- Electronic phone systems will be fried.
- Surge protectors are useless in the event of an EMP exposure.
- Just because your car has rubber tires, it will not be impervious to the effects of an EMP. Rubber containers are insufficient protection.
- Faraday cages DO need to be grounded. If not, then the Faraday cage merely becomes a reflector or an amplifier.
- Yes, a microwave can act as a Faraday cage, but why in the world would you want to use it for that? That's just silly when they are easily made.

- Faraday cages do not have to be solid, thus the name "cage" instead of the often misused term "box." In fact, many will resemble a bird cage or a very finely meshed chicken-coop wire.

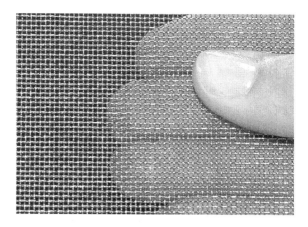

- Contrary to what you may have seen on the Internet, a sheet of foil on a box isn't protective either. It's not thick enough to withstand the pulse. However, you CAN protect your items if they are buried a couple of feet underground.
- The cages do not have to be solid, but they do have to be constructed continuously, without gaps between the protective materials.
- Lastly, a car is NOT a Faraday cage sufficient to withstand an EMP incident. It has some similar components, yes, but most cars made today consist of fiberglass and disjointed parts, not a continuous metal material. In addition to that, they are on tires. Tires on a car do NOT serve as grounding. Folks are simply getting an EMP strike confused with a lightning strike.

Michael Faraday invented the Faraday cage in 1836. This clever device will block out external electrostatic fields and electromagnetic radiation. One mistake many people make when it comes to an EMP is to compare it to a lightning bolt. The effects of an EMP and a direct lightning bolt are very similar, but not in regard to their visibility and effect on the body. An EMP is more like a radio wave, not a visible bolt of lightning or electric current.

This point needs to be reiterated again. It's important that any Faraday cage that you plan to use is grounded. It has to be grounded in order to disperse the energy.

What you should know is that a Faraday cage is not fool proof. The higher the frequency of the magnetic pulse, the faster it is. This is what causes the burn out. The cages must be grounded, continuously connecting, and the openings of them cannot be too large. Chicken-coop wire would work, but only if you double or even triple layer it, as the openings are too large. As a reference, look at the front of your microwave door. It's a small mesh. Just like a snake can slither its way through the right-sized hole, so can an electronic wave.

You can have an instant Faraday cage with a galvanized trash can or a large stock pot, like what is used in a restaurant. (Be sure to clamp the lid down. Remember— continuous connection is the key. Again, since Faraday cages are not fool proof, depending on the strength of the pulse, it is recommended that you bury your electronics and extra batteries in the containers at least 2 feet underground.

An easy way to make a Faraday cage would be to acquire some 2 x 4 feet, brass-mesh sheets. (Mythbusters, as aired on the Discovery Channel, did a couple of experiments using this successfully.) Make a box frame with the 2x4s and staple the brass mesh to the outside. Create a securely attached access entry within the frame. Solder a ground wire to one of the corners and ground the cage. Scrap metal and mesh wires can easily be obtained in junk yards, on E-bay, the clay modeling section of a craft store, or at your local hardware or "farm and feed" store. The important aspect of this is that mesh or sheet metal only shields magnetic fields if the frequency is up in the RF range. To properly stop the wave, you need some iron, steel, or some slabs of thick copper. Most electronics are useful in the VHF/UHF/SHF range today and will need more substantial protection.

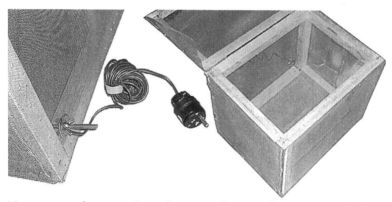

You can make your "cage" as small or as large as you'd like. It wouldn't be out of the question to continuously line a basement or hole in the ground with copper- mesh wire and a grounding rod.

The bottom line is, with a properly constructed Faraday cage, you can likely protect your electronics and batteries from an electromagnetic attack of an EMP incident or solar flare, thus preserving the function of all that is contained therein.

17
THOSE WHO DON'T HAVE TO DIE

There are five categories of people that are going to have a difficult time surviving an SHTF scenario. If you fit into one or more of these categories, I would suggest that you reevaluate your survival plans and change them accordingly.

The first of these categories are the physically disabled. Do you remember the aftermath of hurricane Katrina? Who were the first to die? They were the brittle diabetics who couldn't get any insulin, the little old grannies stuck in the nursing homes that suffered from heatstroke because of lack of air conditioning, and the obese, diabetic amputees who were stranded on their rooftops and couldn't exert enough energy to swim. Also in the mix were people with respiratory problems; people who were dependent on oxygen and positive pressure ventilation. This is what happens when the grid goes down.

If you fall into this category, now is the time to increase your chances for survival. For those that require medication to stay alive, try to store extra medication; for those that need oxygen, try to keep extra oxygen tanks on hand; and for those on hemodialysis, switch to continuous ambulatory peritoneal dialysis (CAPD) if possible, which doesn't require a machine. Better yet, visit an integrative medicine physician. You are more than the sum of your illnesses. You need to be treated as a whole person, and conventional medicine is woefully lacking in this respect. While stocking up on prescription medications can be challenging, herbs, spices, vitamins, minerals, and homeopathies are readily available. Take the time to check-out your local health-food store, where the sales associates are often well trained regarding supplements. If you do try an item that works well for your condition or is a logical prophylactic, yet find it too expensive to continue to purchase at the store, attempt to buy online, as I have found that you can often buy the exact same product for sometimes half the cost, especially when you buy in bulk. Attempt to treat the cause, not the effect, or symptom, of your disease. For the sex crazed, become monogamous and marry, but if too stubborn, then at least keep extra condoms about to prevent STDs. Keep face masks, gloves, and gowns on hand to help prevent communicable diseases.

Around 80 percent of new cases of cancers, diabetes, and cardiovascular diseases are now being recorded, not in the rich West, but in poorer parts of the globe, according to the World Health Organization (WHO) figures. The explosion is a "consequence of importing lifestyles from Western countries," Francis Collins, head of the US-based National Institutes of Health, told the World Health Summit at Berlin's Charite hospital. Currently, there are around 300 million people around the world classified as obese, with a body mass index (BMI)—a measure computing body weight and height—of over 30, according to the International Obesity Task Force (IOTF). The rise in the developing world is all the more surprising because these countries are also ravaged by hunger, but the increase in obesity does not necessarily mean that people there are becoming better fed. Obesity often masks underlying deficiencies in vitamins and minerals, the IOTF says.

As these countries develop economically, people's diets change as more and more of them move to cities and eat high-fat and high-sugar foods, often in Western-style fast food eateries. Urban life also tends to be more sedentary.

As a result, people put on weight, making them more susceptible to chronic illnesses including diabetes, heart disease and cancer, adding to the strain on already overstretched health-care systems. Diabetes sufferers are expected to number 300 million in 2025, up from 135 million in 1995, the WHO predicts. Deaths will double between 2005 and 2030. In 2005, an estimated 1.1 million people died from diabetes, with almost 80 percent of deaths occurring in low- and middle-income countries, the WHO said. Instead, particularly in Africa, efforts are focused on fighting contagious diseases like malaria, tuberculosis and AIDS, which are also mass killers. "From a medical point of view, they are preventable," said Pekka Puska, director general of the National Institute for Health and Welfare in Finland (THL).

For those with lifestyle-related illnesses, change your diet, lose weight, exercise, sleep, drink enough purified water, rest your mind and body, enjoy sunlight and fresh air, and stop smoking, drinking, and doing drugs. In a review of the scientific literature on the relationship between stress and disease, Carnegie Mellon University psychologist Sheldon Cohen has found that stress is a contributing factor in human disease, and in particular, depression, cardiovascular disease, and HIV/AIDS, as published in a JAMA (Journal of the American Medical Association) article. Depend on God and his divine power to give you the peace that only He can give. Read your Bible and pray every day, so that your spirituality and emotionality, along with your immune system, will be adequately equipped to resist disease. Restore your health now, so that in a crisis, you will no longer suffer from the non-communicable diseases that impair you today.

The second category includes the vast majority of the entitlement generation. They have the "take care of me from the cradle to the grave" mentality, and exactly like what happened during Hurricane Katrina, the same thing is only going to happen again, just under a different set of circumstances. Like him or not, Rush Limbaugh had it right when he put the Hurricane Katrina mess into context: "What we've seen in New Orleans is first and foremost the utter failure of generation after generation after generation of the entitlement mentality." Flood victims had been victimized twice, once by nature and again by the perception that government would somehow save them from nature's rage, he said. "They had no idea what to do because they've been told somebody else was going to fix it." After fostering dependency among the citizens of New Orleans, Limbaugh said state and local officials failed to respond to the dependency they helped to create, and not just local and state, but federal as well.

If you are the type of person that has a chip on your shoulder and believes the world owes you something, think again. Although at this present time your entitlement dreams may be coming true in part, in an SHTF scenario, they won't. Don't wait until it's too late to change your way of thinking.

Recently, I read a story about a man who sat down with a friend, who was waitress, and discussed the issue of tipping. She, being a single mother, depended on her tips to help provide for her family. She started talking about how much she hated how little people have tipped in this recession. She continued on about how she is barely making it in the world because of other people's lack of tipping.

Amazed by her attitude and her entitlement mentality, the man asked her what she has done in this recession to call for higher tips in a down economy. He asked her what she was doing daily to make her a better waitress or to make her patrons experience an above-average experience. Or was she doing the same things over and over again expecting a different outcome?

She stared at him blindly after he asked her these questions. She had never thought about making the experience of her patrons better. She had never thought that her tips might be in direct relation to her attitude. She had been so caught up in the entitlement mentality that she believed that she was entitled to the tips—that for doing her basic job she would be tipped at a higher rate.

By adopting an entitlement mentality, Americans are sowing the seeds of their own destruction. Because of an ever-growing list of social programs, subsidies, and entitlements, more than half of all Americans now look to the government for at least a portion of their sustenance. As a result, many Americans have come to view government as the solution to their problems, rather than the cause of them. The principles of limited government that undergirded our constitution and bill of rights are being steadily undermined by the seductive allure of government handouts. This dangerously misguided trend promotes an entitlement mentality in a country that has long been known for its positive work ethic. The entitlement mentality, in turn, encourages the growth of government and the cycle continues, creating a downward spiral toward disaster.

How, then, can we overcome this degenerative disease plaguing our society? We must change our mentality from one of entitlement, to one of ownership. We must see that everything we do has value and meaning. We need to *want* to make a difference in this world. A good work ethic is a product of these thought processes. Being industrious doesn't just happen by accident. As President John F. Kennedy said in his inaugural address, "Ask not what your country can do for you, but what you can do for your country." Have you been asking yourself that question lately?

The third category includes the alcoholics and drug users. Which withdrawals can actually kill?

1. **Alcohol**: Yes, after long-term use, withdrawal from alcohol can kill. Alcohol withdrawal syndrome can take on mild, moderate, or severe forms. If while withdrawing from alcohol a person develops a fever, extreme nausea, diarrhea, or DT (delirium tremens), they need to be rushed to see a doctor as soon as possible. In fact, alcohol withdrawal after heavy, chronic use is best managed under the care of a doctor or a professional medical detox unit. By using

medications that relieve withdrawal symptoms, these professionals can essentially eliminate any of these risks.

2. **Benzodiazepines:** Benzos were introduced as a replacement to barbiturates that were causing common overdose cases, many of which resulted in death. Nevertheless, withdrawal from extended use of benzodiazepines can kill. Whether Xanax (alprazolam), Ativan (lorazepam), Valium (diazepam) or other variations, long-term use of Benzodiazepines requires medical supervision to be completed successfully with minimal side-effects and risk to the patient. Normally, the withdrawal process is managed by slowly reducing the dose and transferring the patient from a slow acting, to a long acting, form of the drug. Still, full resolution of benzodiazepine withdrawal syndrome can take up to 6 months (or even longer).

3. **Opiates**: Many people are surprised to learn that in most cases, withdrawal from many opiates is not deadly. Still there are some very important exceptions. Methadone, a long-acting opiate often prescribed as a replacement for heroin, can cause death during withdrawal if it's consumed in high enough doses for a long enough period. The debate of whether the state should be prescribing something like this should be saved for a later date.

It is one of the better ways of getting people off of heroin, though obviously, it does replace dependence on one substance with another, more manageable one. Also, some of the recently popular methods of rapid detox from heroin addiction can themselves cause death, and many other negative side effects. Overall, check-in with a physician and conduct opiate withdrawal in a controlled setting. Withdrawal under Suboxone or Subutex can be far less horrific.

Much of the danger in withdrawal from all of these drugs has to do with the body's response to the extreme changes in the chemical processes going on in the brain and the rest of the body. Alcohol, benzos, and opiates interfere with the GABA system, the body's most common downregulator.

That's pretty much it. Cold turkey withdrawal from cocaine, marijuana, crystal meth, ecstasy, GHB (never mix GHB with alcohol though!), and many other recreationally used drugs will not lead to death in the vast majority of cases. While it may make you uncomfortable, and you may feel moody, constipated, dehydrated, hungry or nauseous, and a whole slew of other symptoms, the chances of someone actually dying from withdrawal are very small.

Are you addicted to alcohol? Are you addicted to drugs? If your answer to either of these questions is a yes, then don't hesitate to seek professional help. Don't wait until a SHTF situation that forces you to quit, because to quit then may mean to die.

The fourth category of people is classified in two ways: the neo-hippies and the yuppies. Another name we can give this category is the urban and suburban city dwellers. They both have complementary but equally deficient skill sets.

The neo-hippies are your typical barefooted, mother earth worshiping, vegan, "lower-your-carbon-foot-print" mantra chanters.

Even though they have good survival skills, such as small-scale agriculture and raising micro-livestock, what they are deficient in is firearms! These people typically do not like weapons or believe in self-defense, and because of this, they are the perfect targets; there will be little difference with the yuppies.

The yuppies have accrued so much debt that they have been unable to prepare. They don't have food stored away because they are too busy paying for the mortgage to their suburban "mansion." Rather than making provisions for a crisis, they spent their hard-earned money on new cars, TVs, fashion, and dinners out. These people are mainly deficient is supplies and will react when it's too late because they are so caught up in the "Republican-Democrat cheer for your team gang" that when the grid is down long-term it will be too late. While these people may go to the shooting range every now and then and have some level of self-defense capability, they will not be able to mentally cope, since they have been in denial for so long and because of that, they will probably not recognize the warning signs.

Luckily, there is still time for the neo-hippies and yuppies. This is why these people need to be warned so that they, too, can prepare at present, before they no longer can.

The fifth, and last, category in this section includes the criminals. Criminals may have no conscience and be ready to take advantage of their "prey" WROL, however, armed citizens will rightfully fight back. This even happens today: According to the National Institute of Justice's report, "Guns in America: National Survey on Private Ownership and Use of Firearms," guns are used over 1.5 million times a year in self-defense. A story in US News and World Report, by G. Witkin, found that 95% of 911 calls are dispatched too late to stop a crime. Armed citizens shoot and kill twice as many criminals as police do. However, less than 1% of defensive gun uses result in a kill (see Gary Kleck's book Point Blank: Guns and Violence in America). Although this may be the case, in a world without proper medical care, even minor flesh wounds could lead to death without antibiotics and proper wound care. Remember, we are talking about recent statistics, in a "civilized" country, but what will happen when the civil turn uncivil? Based on production data from firearm manufacturers, there are roughly 300 million firearms owned by civilians in the United States as of 2010. Of these, about 100 million are handguns.

Based upon surveys, the following are estimates of private firearm ownership in the U.S. as of 2012:

Households with a Gun

- Percentage: 40–47%
- Number: 47–55 million

Adults Owning a Gun

- Percentage: 30–35%
- Number: 70–80 million

Adults Owning a Handgun

- Percentage: 17–20%
- Number: 40–47 million

These numbers are staggering. Just imagine the number of injuries and deaths that will occur when the SHTF, as criminals will go on even more of a rampage than they already do now. Actually, of the thousands of gun deaths annually, most of these people are criminals killed by criminals, according to the FBI "Crime in the United States" report. A nice, little old granny may think twice about killing a criminal in self-defense, but a fellow criminal definitely will not.

He who lives by the sword dies by the sword. You can expect to become a victim of whatever means you use to get what you want. As you can see, it just isn't worth being a big bully or thug, especially in the end of time. If your own don't take you out first, then the good guys are a good back-up plan!

There are, of course, other categories and subcategories, but this section covers the majority of the populace. Again, I hope that you will take an honest look at yourself, your family, and your friends. Please asses if you or those you love fall into any one of these classifications, and if so, then please do what you must now, in order to change the trajectory of the future.

18
LESSONS LEARNED FROM HURRICANE KATRINA

This chapter includes one person's observations, stories, and recommendations post-Hurricane Katrina, as repeated on various survivalist blogs and described by the person's friend in the first paragraph below.

"The following information was provided via several emails by a friend heavily involved in the New Orleans disaster of hurricane Katrina, during the course of the disaster itself. Many of the comments were LIVE to that moment in time...."

I've had over 30 people staying with me since Sunday, evacuating from New Orleans and points south in anticipation of Hurricane Katrina. Only two families were my friends. They told other friends of theirs that they knew a place where they could hole-up, and so a whole bunch arrived here! I didn't mind, because there were six RV's and travel trailers, so we had enough accommodation. However, I've had the opportunity to see what worked—and what didn't—in their evacuation plans and bug-out kits, and I thought a few "lessons learned" might be appropriate to share here.

Have a bug-out kit ready at all times. Many of these folks packed at the last minute, grabbing whatever they thought they'd need. Needless to say, they forgot some important things (prescription medications, important documents, baby formula, diapers, etc.). Some of these things (e.g. prescriptions) obviously can't be stocked up against possible emergency need, but you can at least have a list in your bug-out kit of what to grab at the last minute.

Renew supplies in your bug-out kit on a regular basis. Batteries lose their charge. Foods have an expiration date. So do common medications. Clothes can get moldy or dirty unless properly stored. All of these problems were found with the folks who kept backup or bug-out supplies on hand and caused difficulties for them.

Plan on needing a LOT more supplies than you think. I found myself with over 30 people on hand, many of whom were not well supplied and the stores were swamped with literally thousands of refugees, buying up everything in sight. I had enough supplies to keep myself going for 30 days. Guess what? Those supplies ended up keeping 30-odd people going for two days. I now know that I must plan on providing for not just myself, but others in need. I could have been selfish and said, "No, these are mine," but what good would that do? Someone would just try to take them, and then we'd have all the resulting unpleasantness. Far better to have extra supplies to share with others, whilst keeping your own core reserve intact (and, preferably, hidden from prying eyes!).

In a real emergency, forget about last-minute purchases. As I said earlier, the stores were swamped by thousands of refugees, as well as locals buying up last-minute supplies. If I hadn't had my emergency supplies already in store, I would never have been able to buy them at the last minute. If I'd had to hit the road, the situation would have been even worse, as I'd be part of a stream of thousands of refugees, most of whom would be buying (or stealing) what they needed before I got to the store.

Make sure your vehicle will carry your essential supplies. Some of the folks who arrived at my place had tried to load up their cars with a humongous amount of stuff, only to find that they didn't have space for themselves! Pets are a particular problem here, as they have to have air and light, and can't be crammed into odd corners. If you have to carry a lot of supplies and a number of people, invest in a small luggage trailer or something similar (or a small travel trailer with space for your goodies), it'll pay dividends if the S really does HTF.

A big bug-out vehicle can be a handicap. Some of the folks arrived here with big pick-ups or SUV's, towing equally large travel trailers. Guess what? On some evacuation routes, these huge combinations could not navigate corners very well, and/or were so difficult to turn that they ran into things (including other vehicles, which were NOT about to make way in the stress of an evacuation). This led to hard feelings, harsh words, and at least one fist-fight. It's not a bad idea to have smaller, more maneuverable vehicles, and a smaller travel trailer, so that one can "squeeze through" in a tight traffic situation. Another point to be made is that a big SUV or pickup burns a lot of fuel. This is bad news when there's no fuel available!

Make sure you have a bug-out place handy. I was fortunate in having enough ground (about 1.8 acres) to provide parking for all these RV's and trailers and to accommodate 11 small children in my living room so that the adults could get some sleep on Sunday night after many hours on the road in very heavy, slow-moving traffic. However, if I hadn't had space, I would have unhesitatingly told the extra families to find somewhere else—and there wasn't anywhere else here that night. Even shops like Wal-Mart and K-Mart had trailers and RV's backed up in their parking lots (which annoyed the heck out of shoppers trying to make last-minute purchases). Even on my property, I had no trailer sewage connections, so I had to tell the occupants that if they used their onboard toilets and showers, they had to drive their RV's and trailers somewhere else to empty their waste tanks. If they hadn't left this morning, they would have joined long, long lines to do this at local trailer parks (some of which were so overloaded by   visiting trailers and RV's that they refused to allow passers-by to use their dumping facilities).

Provide entertainment for younger children. Some of these families had young children (ranging from 3 months to 11 years). They had DVD's, video games, etc., but no power available in their trailers to show them! They had no coloring books, toys, etc., to keep the kids occupied. This was a bad mistake.

Pack essentials first, then luxuries. Many of these folks had packed mattresses off beds, comforters, cushions, bathrobes, etc. As a result, their vehicles were grossly overloaded, but often lacked real essentials like candles, non-perishable foods, etc. One family (both parents are gourmet cooks) packed eighteen (yes, EIGHTEEN!!!) special pots and pans, which they were going to use on a two-burner camp stove. They were horrified by my suggestion that under the circumstances, a nested stainless-steel camping cookware set would be more practical. "What? No omelet pan?" Sheesh...

Don't plan on fuel being available en route. A number of my visitors had real problems finding gas to fill up on. With thousands of vehicles jammed nose-to-tail on four lanes of interstate, an awful lot of vehicles needed gas. By the time you got to a gas station, you were highly likely to find it sold out or charging exorbitant prices, because the owners knew you didn't have any choice but to pay what they asked. Much better to leave with a full tank of gas, and enough in spare containers to fill up on the road, if you have to, in order to reach your destination.

Have enough money with you for at least two weeks. Many of those who arrived here had very little in cash, relying on check-books and credit cards to fund their purchases. Guess what? Their small banks down in South Louisiana were all off-line, and their balances, credit authorizations, etc. could not be checked—so many shops refused to accept their checks and insisted on electronic verification before accepting their credit cards. Local banks also refused (initially) to cash checks for them, since they couldn't check the status of their accounts on-line. Eventually (and very grudgingly) local banks began allowing them to cash checks for not more than $50-$100, depending on the bank. Fortunately, I have a reasonable amount of cash available at all times, so I was able to help some of them. I'm now going to increase my cash on hand, I think... Another thing—don't bring only large bills. Many gas stations, convenience stores, etc., won't accept anything larger than a $20 bill. Some of my guests had plenty of $100 bills, but couldn't buy anything.

Don't be sure that a disaster will be short-term. My friends have left now, heading south to Baton Rouge. They want to be closer to home for whenever they're allowed to return. Unfortunately for them, the Governor has just announced the mandatory, complete evacuation of New Orleans, and there's no word on when they will be allowed back. It will certainly be several weeks, and it might be several months. During that period, what they have with them—essential documents, clothing, etc.—is all they have. They'll have to find new doctors to renew prescriptions, find a place to live (a FEMA trailer if they're lucky—thousands of families will be lining up for these trailers), some way to earn a living (their jobs are gone with New Orleans, and I don't see their employers paying them for not working when the employers aren't making money either), and so on.

Don't rely on government-run shelters if at all possible. Your weapons WILL be confiscated (yes, including pocket-knives, kitchen knives, and Leatherman-type tools). You will be crowded into close proximity with anyone and everyone (including some nice folks, but also including drug addicts, released convicts, gang types, and so on). You will be under the authority of the people running the shelter, who WILL call on law enforcement and military personnel to keep order (including stopping you leaving if you want to), and so on. It's much, much better to have a place to go to, a plan to get there, and the supplies you need.

Warn your friends not to bring others with them!!! I had told two friends to bring themselves and their families to my home. They, unknown to me, told half-a-dozen other families to come too: "He's a good guy, I'm sure he won't mind!" Well, I did mind... but since the circumstances weren't personally dangerous, I allowed them all to hang around. However, if things had been worse, I would have been very nasty indeed to their friends (and even nastier to them, for inviting others without clearing it with me first!).

If you are a place of refuge for your friends, make sure they know that this applies to them ONLY, not their other friends. Similarly, if you have someone willing to offer you refuge, don't presume on his or her hospitality by arriving with others unforewarned.

Have account numbers, contact addresses, and telephone numbers for all important persons and institutions. My friends will now have to get new postal addresses and will have to notify others of this: their doctors, insurance companies (medical, personal, vehicle, and property), bank(s), credit card issuer(s), utility supplier(s), telephone supplier(s), etc. Basically, this pertains to anyone who sends you bills, to whom you owe money, or who might owe you money. None of my friends brought all this information with them. Now, when they need to change postal addresses for correspondence, insurance claims, etc., how can they do this when they don't know their account numbers, what telephone numbers to call, who and where to write, etc.?

Have portable weapons and ammo ready. Only two of my friends were armed, and one of them had only a handgun. The other had a handgun for himself, another for his wife, a shotgun, and an "evil" black rifle—MUCH better! I was asked by some of the other families, who'd seen TV reports of looting back in New Orleans, to lend them firearms. I refused, as they'd never handled guns before and thus would have been more of a danger to themselves and other innocent persons than to looters. If they'd stayed a couple of days, so that I could teach them the basics, that would have been different, but they wouldn't, so I didn't. Another thing, you don't have to take your entire arsenal along. Firearms for personal defense come first, and then firearms for life support through hunting (and don't forget the skinning knife!). A fishing outfit might not be a bad idea either (you can shoot bait!). Other than that, leave the rest of your guns in the safe (you do have a gun safe, securely bolted to the floor, don't you?), and the bulk ammo supplies too. Bring enough ammo to keep you secure, but no more. If you really need bulk supplies of guns and ammo, they should be waiting for you at your bug-out location, not occupying space (and taking up a heck of a lot of weight!) in your vehicle. (For those bugging out in my direction, ammo supply will NOT be a problem...)

Route selection is very, very important. My friends (and their friends) basically looked at the map, found the shortest route to me (I-10 to Baton Rouge and Lafayette, then up I-49 to Alexandria), and followed it slavishly. This was a VERY bad idea, as something over half-a-million other folks had the same route in mind. Some of them took over twelve hours for what is usually a four-hour journey. If they'd used their heads, they would have seen (and heard, from radio reports) that going North up I-55 to Mississippi would have been much faster. There was less traffic on this route. They could have turned left and hit Natchez, MS, and then cut across LA on Route 84. This would have taken them no more than five or six hours, even with the heavier evacuation traffic. Lesson: think outside the box, and don't assume that the shortest route on the map in terms of distance will also be the shortest route in terms of time.

The social implications of a disaster situation: Feedback from my contacts in the LSP and other agencies is very worrying. They keep harping on the fact that the "underclass" that's doing all the looting is almost exclusively Black and inner-city in composition. The remarks they're reporting include such statements as "I'm ENTITLED to this stuff!", "This is payback time for all Whitey's done to us", and "This is reparations for slavery!" Also, they're blaming the present, confused disaster-relief situation on racism "Fo sho, if Whitey wuz sittin' here in tha Dome waitin' for help, no way would he be waitin' like we is!" No, I'm not making up these comments. They are as reported by my buddies. This worries me very much. If we have such a divide in consciousness among our city residents, then when we hit a SHTF situation, we're likely to be accused of racism, paternalism, oppression, and all sorts of other crimes just because we want to preserve law and order. If we, as lawful individuals and families, provide for our own needs in emergency, and won't share with others (whether they're of another race or not) because we don't have enough to go around, we're likely to be accused of racism rather than pragmatism, and taking things from us can (and probably will) be justified as "Whitey getting his just desserts." I'm absolutely not a racist, but the racial implications of the present situation are of great concern to me. The likes of Jesse Jackson, Al Sharpton, and the "reparations-for-slavery" brigade appear to have so polarized inner-city opinion that these folks are (IMHO) no longer capable of rational thought concerning such issues as looting, disaster relief, etc.

Implications for security: If one has successfully negotiated the danger zone, one will be in an environment filled, to a greater or lesser extent, with other evacuees. How many of them will have provided for their needs? How many of them will rely on obtaining from others the things they need? In the absence of immediate state or relief-agency assistance, how many of them will feel "entitled" to obtain these necessities any way they have to, up to and including looting, murder, and mayhem? Large gathering places for refugees suddenly look less desirable than being on one's own, or in an isolated spot with one's family, also looks less secure. One has to sleep sometime, and while one sleeps, one is vulnerable. Even one's spouse and children might not be enough; there are always going to be vulnerabilities. One can hardly remain consciously in Condition Yellow while bathing children or making love! A team approach might be a viable solution here.

"Too many chiefs and not enough Indians" in New Orleans at the moment: The mayor has already blown his top about the levee breach: he claims that he had a plan in place to fix it by yesterday evening, but was overruled by Baton Rouge, who sent in others to do something different. This may or may not be true. My LSP buddies tell me that they're getting conflicting assignments and/or requests from different organizations and individuals. One will send out a group to check a particular area for survivors, but when they get there, they find no one and later learn that another group has already checked and cleared the area. Unfortunately, in the absence of centralized command and control, the information is not being shared amongst all recovery teams. Also, there's alleged to be conflict between city officials and state functionaries, with both sides claiming to be "running things," and some individuals in the Red Cross, FEMA, and other groups appear to be refusing to take instructions from either side, instead (it's claimed) wanting to run their own shows. This is allegedly producing catastrophic confusion and duplication of efforts and may even be making the loss of life worse, in that some areas in need of rescuers aren't getting them. (I don't know if the same problems are occurring in Mississippi and/or Alabama, but I wouldn't be surprised if they were.) All of this is unofficial and off-the-record, but it doesn't surprise me to hear it. Moral of the story if you want to survive: don't rely on the government or any government agency (or private relief organization, for that matter) to save you. Your survival is in your own hands—don't drop it!

Long-term vision: This appears to be sadly lacking at present. Everyone is focused on the immediate, short-term objective of rescuing survivors. However, there are monumental problems looming that need immediate attention, but don't seem to be getting it right now. For example, the Port of Louisiana is the fifth-largest in the world, and vital to the economy, but the Coast Guard is saying (on TV) that they won't be able to get it up and running for three to six months, because their primary focus is on search and rescue, and thereafter, disaster relief. Why isn't the Coast Guard pulled off that job now and put to work right away on something this critical? There are enough Navy, Marine, and Air Force units available now to take over rescue missions.

Another example includes the over million refugees from the Greater New Orleans area floating around. They need accommodation and food, but most of them are now unemployed and won't have any income at all for the next six to twelve months. There aren't nearly enough jobs available in this area to absorb this workforce. What is being done to find work for them, even in states remote from the problem areas? The government for sure won't provide enough for them in emergency aid to be able to pay their bills. What about mortgages on properties that are now underwater? The occupants both can't and won't pay, the mortgage holders will demand payment, and we could end up with massive foreclosures on property that is worthless, leaving a lot of folks neck-deep in debt and without homes (even damaged ones). What is being done to plan for this and alleviate the problem as much as possible? I would have thought that the state government would have had at least the skeleton of an emergency plan for these sorts of things, and that FEMA would have too, but this doesn't seem to be the case. Why weren't these things considered in the leisurely days pre-disaster, instead of erupting as immediate and unanswered needs post-disaster?

Personal emergency planning: This leads me to consider my own emergency planning. I've planned to cover an evacuation need and could probably survive with relative ease for between two weeks and one month, but what if I had been caught up in this mess? What would I do about earning a living, paying my mortgage, etc.? If I can't rely on the state,

I for darn sure had better be able to rely on myself! I certainly need to re-examine my insurance policies, to ensure that if disaster strikes, my mortgage, major loans, etc., will be paid off (or that I will receive enough money to do this myself). I also need to provide for my physical security and must ensure that I have supplies, skills, and knowledge that will be "marketable" in exchange for hard currency in a post-disaster situation. The idea of a "team" of friends with whom to bug out and survive with is looking better and better. Some of the team could take on the task of keeping a home maintained (even a camp-type facility), looking after kids, providing base security, etc. Others could be designated as foragers for supplies and as traders or barterers. Still others could be earning a living for the whole team with their skills. In this way, we'd all contribute to our mutual survival and security in the medium to long-term. Life might be a lot less comfortable than prior to the disaster, but hey, we'd still have a life! This bears thinking about, and I might just have to start building "team relationships" with nearby people of like mind!

The "bank problem": I was at my bank this morning, depositing checks I'd been given by my visitors in exchange for cash. The teller warned me bluntly that it might be weeks before these checks could be credited to my account, as there was no way to clear them with their issuing banks, which were now under water and/or without communications facilities. He also told me that there had been an endless stream of folks trying to cash checks on South Louisiana banks without success. He warned me that some of these local banks will almost certainly fail, as they don't have a single branch above water, and the customers and businesses they served are also gone, so checks drawn on them will eventually prove worthless. Even some major regional banks had run their Louisiana "hub" out of New Orleans and now couldn't access their records. I think it might be a good idea to have a "bug-out bank account" with a national bank, so that funds should be available anywhere they have a branch, rather than keeping all of one's money in a single bank (particularly a local one) or credit union. This is, of course, over and above one's "bug-out stash" of ready cash.

Helping one's friends is likely to prove expensive. I estimate that I'm out over $1,000 at the moment, partly from having all my supplies consumed and partly from making cash available to friends who couldn't cash their checks. I may or may not get some of this back in due course. I don't mind it. If I were in a similar fix I hope I could lean on my friends for help in the same way; but I hadn't made allowances for it. I shall have to do so in the future, as well as planning to contribute to costs incurred by those who offer me hospitality under similar circumstances.

People who were prepared were frequently mobbed and threatened by those who weren't. This was reported in at least seven incidents, five in Mississippi and two in Louisiana (I suspect that the relative lack of Louisianan incidents was because most of those with any sense got out of Dodge before the storm hit). In each case, the person/family concerned had made preparations for disaster with supplies, shelter, etc., in good order. Several had generators ready and waiting. However, their neighbors who had not prepared all came running over after the disaster, wanting food, water, and shelter. When the prepared families refused, on the grounds that they had very little and only enough for themselves, there were many incidents of aggression, attempted assault, and theft of their supplies. Some had to use weapons to deter attack, and in some cases, shots were fired. I understand that in two incidents, attackers/would-be thieves were shot. It's also reported that in all of these cases the prepared families now face threats of retribution from their neighbors, who regarded their refusal to share as an act of selfishness and/or aggression and are now threatening retaliation. It's reportedly so bad that most of the prepared families are considering moving to other neighborhoods so as to start afresh with different neighbors.

Similar incidents are reported by families who got out in time, prepared to spend several days on their own. When they stopped to eat a picnic meal at a rest stop, or an isolated spot along the highway, they described being approached rather aggressively by others wanting food, fuel, or other essentials. Sometimes they had to be rather aggressive in turn in order to deter these insistent requests. Two families recounted attempts being made to steal their belongings (in one case, their vehicle) while overnighting in camp stops on their way out of the area. They both instituted armed patrols, with one or more family members patrolling while the others slept, to prevent this. This seems to me to be a good argument to form a "bug-out team" with likeminded, security-conscious friends in your area, so that all concerned can provide mutual security and back-up.

I can understand these families being unwilling to share the little they had, particularly in light of not knowing when supplies would once again be available. However, this reinforces the point I made in my "lessons learned" post last week about needing much more in the way of supplies than initially thought of! If these families had stored some extra food and water and hidden their main reserve where it would not be seen, they could have given out some help to their neighbors and preserved good relations. Also, a generator under such circumstances is a noisy and bright, if powering your interior lights, invitation saying, "This house has supplies, come and get them." I suspect that kerosene lanterns, candles, and flashlights might be a more "community-safe" option if one is surrounded by survivors.

When help gets there, you may get it whether you like it or not. There are numerous reports of aggressive, overbearing behavior by those rescuers who first arrived at disaster scenes. It's perhaps best described as, "I'm here to rescue you, I'm in charge, so do as I say and if you don't, I'll shoot you". It appears that mid-level state functionaries and Red Cross personnel (the latter without the "shoot you" aspect, of course) were complained about most often. In one incident, a family who had prepared and survived quite well was ordered, not invited, to get onto a truck, with only the clothes on their backs. When they objected, they were threatened. They had pets and wanted to know what would happen to them; they report that a uniformed man (agency unknown) began pointing his rifle at the pets with the words "I'll fix that." The husband then trained his own shotgun on the man and explained to him, in words of approximately one syllable, what was going to happen to him if he fired a shot. The whole "rescuer" group then left, threatening dire consequences for the family (including threats to come back once they'd evacuated and torch their home). The family was able to make contact with a state police patrol and report the incident and are now determined that no matter how much pressure is applied, they will not evacuate. They've set-up a "shuttle run" so that every few days two of them go upstate to collect supplies for the rest of the family who defend the homestead in the meantime.

Another aspect of this is that self-sufficient, responsible families were often regarded almost with suspicion by rescuers. The latter seemed to believe that if you'd come through the disaster better than your neighbors, it could only have been because you stole what you needed, or somehow gained some sort of unfair advantage over the "average victims" in your area. I'm at a loss to explain this, but it's probably worth keeping in mind.

There seems to be a cumulative psychological effect upon survivors. This is even clear (or perhaps particularly) in those who were prepared for a disaster. During and immediately after the disaster, these folks were at their best dealing with damage, setting up alternative accommodation, light, food sources, etc. However, after a few days in the heat and debris (perhaps worst of all being the smell of dead bodies nearby), many found their ability to remain positive and "upbeat" being strained to the limit. There are numerous reports of individuals becoming depressed, morose, and withdrawn. This seemed to happen to even the strongest personalities. The arrival of rescuers provided a temporary boost, but once evacuated, a sort of "after-action shell-shock" seemed to be a common experience. I don't know enough about this to comment further, but I suspect that staying in place has a lot to do with it. There is no challenge to keep moving, find one's survival needs, care for the group, and one is surrounded by vivid reminders of the devastation. By staying among the ruins of one's former life, one may be exposing oneself to a greater risk of psychological deterioration.

There is widespread frustration over the lack of communication and empathy by rescuers and local/state government. This is partly due to the absence of electricity, so that TV's were not available to follow events as they unfolded, but it's also due to an almost deliberate policy of non-communication by rescuers. There are many accounts of evacuees wanting to know where the bus or plane was going that they were about to board only to be told, "We don't know" or "to a better place than this." Some have found themselves many states away from their homes. Other families were arbitrarily separated upon rescue and/or evacuation and are still scattered across two or three states. Their efforts to locate each other are very difficult, and when they request to be reunited at a common location, all of those with whom I have contact report a blanket refusal by the Red Cross and state officials to even consider the matter at this time. They're being informed that it will be "looked into" at some future date and that they may have to pay the costs involved if they want to join up again—this, to families who are now destitute! I'm very angry, but it's so widespread a problem that I don't know what can be done about it. I hope that in the future some means will be implemented to prevent it from happening again. Lesson learned: never EVER allow yourselves to be separated as a family, even if it means waiting for later rescue and/or evacuation. Insist on this at all costs!

Expect rescuers (including law enforcement) to enforce a distinctly unconstitutional authority in a disaster situation. This is very widely reported and is very troubling. I hear repeated stories from numerous states that as evacuees arrive at refugee centers they and their belongings are searched without Constitutional authority, and any personal belongings seen as potentially suspicious (including firearms, prescription medication, etc.), are confiscated without recourse to the owner. I can understand the point of view of the receiving authorities, but they are acting illegally, and I suspect there will be lawsuits coming from this practice. Another common practice reported on the ground in the disaster areas is for people to be ordered to evacuate, irrespective of their needs and wishes, even those folks who were well-prepared and have survived in good shape. If they demur, they are often threatened and bullied in an attempt to make them abandon their homes, pets, etc. Another lesson learned in a disaster: Don't expect legal and constitutional norms to be followed. If you can make it on your own do so, without relying on an unsympathetic and occasionally overbearing rescue system to control you and your destiny.

Don't believe that rescuers are all knights in shining armor who will respect your property. There have been numerous reports of rescuers casually appropriating small items that took their fancy in houses they were searching. Sometimes this was blatant, right in front of onlookers, and when protests were made the response was either threatening or a casual, "Who's going to miss it now?" Some of our field agents report that this happened right in front of their eyes. Another aspect of this is damage caused to buildings by rescuers. I've had reports of them kicking in the front door to a house, or a window, instead of trying to obtain access with as little damage as possible. Rescuers are said to have climbing on clean, highly polished tables with hobnailed boots in order to get at an attic hatch to check for survivors, etc. When they left the house, often the door or window was left open, almost a standing invitation to looters, instead of being closed and/or secured. When the families concerned get home, they won't know who caused this damage, but they will certainly be angered by it. I think that if one evacuates one's home, it might be a good idea to leave a clearly-visible notice that all residents have evacuated, so as to let would-be rescuers know that the house is empty. On the other hand, this might make it easier for looters, so what you gain on the swings, you lose on the roundabouts.

If you choose to help, you may be sucked into a bureaucratic and legal nightmare. Example: A local church in the beginning stages of the crisis offered its hall to house evacuees. Local and state officials promptly filled it up with over 100 people. Their "social skills" proved extremely difficult to live with—toilets were blocked, restrooms left filthy, graffiti was scrawled and/or carved on the walls, arguments were frequent (often escalating to screaming matches and sometimes to physical violence), and evacuees roamed the neighborhood (leading to all sorts of reports of petty theft, vandalism, etc.). Church workers were subject to aggressive begging and demands. Requests to the authorities to provide better security, administrative assistance, etc., apparently fell on deaf ears; the crisis was so widespread and overwhelming that a small facility such as this one seemed to have been very low on the priority checklist. After two days of this, with complaints from the neighbors becoming more and more insistent, the church informed local officials that it wanted the evacuees removed at once. They were promptly subject to bureaucratic, heavy-handedness (including threats to withhold previously-promised reimbursement for their expenses), threats of lawsuits for daring to insinuate that the evacuees were somehow "lower-class" in their conduct, for alleged racism, slander, general political incorrectness, and threats of negative publicity, in that officials threatened to put out a press release denouncing the church for its "elitist" and "uncooperative" attitude in a time of crisis. The church initially caved in to this pressure and allowed the evacuees to stay, but within a couple more days the pressure from neighbors and from its own members became impossible to bear, and they insisted on the evacuees being removed to a Red Cross shelter. I'm informed that repairs to their hall will cost over $10,000. This is only one example among many I could cite, but it makes the point clear—if you offer your facilities to authorities you place yourself (to a certain extent) under their control, and you're potentially liable to a great deal of coercive, insensitive bureaucratic bullying. Those of you in the same position as this church (i.e., with facilities you could make available) might wish to take note.

Law enforcement problems will often be "glossed over" and/or ignored by authorities. In many cities housing evacuees, there have been private reports of a significant increase in crime caused by their presence, but you'll find that virtually all law-enforcement authorities publicly deny this and/or gloss over it as a "temporary problem". This is all very well for publicity, but it ignores the increased risk to local residents. I've been tracking crime reports in about a dozen cities through my contacts with local law enforcement and the Louisiana State Police. All the LEO's I speak with, without exception, tell me of greatly increased crime, including rape, assault, robbery, shoplifting, vandalism, gang activity, etc. However, you won't see these reports in the news media and will often see senior LE figures actively denying it. The officers with whom I speak are angry and bitter about this, but they dare not "go public," as their jobs would be on the line if they did so. They tell me that often they're instructed not to report certain categories of "incidents" at all, so as not to "skew" or "inflate" the "official" crime figures. I've also heard reports from Texas, Alabama, and Tennessee of brand-new, high-end motor vehicles (e.g., Cadillac's, Lincolns, BMW's, etc.) with New Orleans dealer tags being driven through various towns, on their way North and West. The drivers were described as "gang-bangers" (and sundry, less complimentary terms). However, there have been no reports of stolen vehicles from New Orleans, because there are no workers to check out dealer lots, or report thefts, and no working computers to enter VIN's, etc., into the NICS database of stolen vehicles, so officers have had no choice but to let these vehicles proceed. Draw your own conclusions.

Your personal and/or corporate supplies and facilities may be commandeered without warning, receipt, or compensation. I've had numerous reports from in and near the disaster zone of individuals (i.e., boat-owners, farmers with barns and tractors, etc.) and corporate groups (e.g., companies with heavy equipment, churches with halls, etc.) finding an official on their doorstep demanding the use of their facilities or equipment. If they demurred, they were told that this was an "emergency situation" and that their assistance was being required, not requested. Some of them have lost track of the heavy equipment "borrowed" in this way, don't know where it is, whether or not it's still in good condition, and when (if ever) it will be returned (and in the meantime, they can't continue their normal operations without this equipment). Others have had their land and facilities effectively confiscated for use by rescue and relief workers, for storage of supplies, etc. In some cases, in the absence of their owners, the property of the individuals and groups concerned (e.g., farm gasoline and diesel supplies, the inventory of motor vehicle dealers, suppliers of foodstuffs, tarpaulins, etc.) have been commandeered and used by law enforcement and relief workers, without permission, receipts, reimbursement, etc. Protests have been met with denials, threats of arrest, insinuations of being "uncaring" and "uncooperative," etc. Lesson learned: If you've got what officials need in a time of crisis, forget about constitutional protections of your property! Sure, you can sue after the fact, but if you need your goods and facilities for your own survival, you're basically SOL. Those of us who stockpile necessities for potential crises like this might want to consider concealing our stockpiles to prevent confiscation. If you need certain equipment for your own day-to-day use (e.g., tractors for farmers, generators, etc.) you might have a hard time retaining possession of these things. This problem applies to relief workers as well. I've had several reports of private relief workers (e.g., those sent in by churches or other private organizations) having their vehicles and supplies commandeered by "official" relief workers, without compensation or receipt, and being kicked out of the disaster area with warnings not to return. The fact that the "private" workers were accomplishing rather more than the "official" workers was apparently of no importance.

If you look like you know what you're doing you may be a target of those less prepared. There have been many, many reports of individuals who were more or less prepared for a disaster being preyed upon by those who were not prepared. Incidents range from theft of supplies, attempts to bug out with these persons (uninvited), to actual violence. It's genuinely frightening to hear about these incidents, particularly the attitude of those trying to prey on the prepared. They seemed to feel that because you'd taken steps to protect yourself and your loved ones, you had somehow done so at their expense, and they were therefore "entitled" to take from you what they needed. There's no logical explanation for this attitude, unless it's bred by the utter dependence of many such people on the government for welfare, Social Security, Medicare/Medicaid, etc. Since they've always been dependent on others and regarded this as an "entitlement," in a disaster situation, they seem to automatically assume that they're "entitled" to what you've got! In one case, the family's pet dog was held hostage, with a knife at its throat, until the family handed over money and supplies. In two cases, families were threatened with the rape of their women unless they cooperated with the aggressors. In four cases that I know of, children were held hostage to ensure assistance. There have also been reports of crimes during the bug-out process. Families sleeping in their cars at highway rest areas were a favorite target, including siphoning of gas from their tanks, assaults, etc. The morals from the stories are obvious. One family can't secure itself against these threats without great hardship. It's best to be "teamed up" with neighbors to secure your neighborhood as a whole, rather than be the one house with facilities in an area filled with those less prepared. If you're in the latter situation, staying put may not be a safe option; instead, a bug-out plan may be vital. When bugging out, you're still not safe from harm and must maintain constant vigilance.

Those who thought themselves safe from the disaster were often not safe from refugees. There have been many reports of smaller towns, farms, etc., on the fringe of the disaster area being overrun with those seeking aid. In many cases help was demanded rather than requested, and theft, looting, and vandalism have been reported. So, even if you think you're safe from the disaster, you may not be safe from its aftermath.

Self-reliance seems to draw suspicion upon you from the authorities. For reasons unknown and unfathomable, rescue authorities seem to regard with suspicion those who've made provision for their safety and have survived (or bugged out) in good shape. It seems to be a combination of, "How could you cope when so many others haven't?" to "You must have taken advantage of others to be so well off", and "We've come all this way to help, so how dare you not need our assistance?" I have no idea why this should be the case, but there have been enough reports of it that it seems to be a widespread problem.

Relief workers from other regions and states often don't know local laws. This is a particular problem when it comes to firearms. I've had many reports of law enforcement sent to assist in Louisiana from states such as New Jersey, California, etc., trying to confiscate firearms on the streets, when in fact the armed citizens were legally armed under local law. One can't reason with these officers in the heat of the moment, of course, and as a result a number of people lost their firearms and still have not recovered them. In the chaos of the immediate post-disaster situation, they may never do so, because I'm not sure that normal procedures such as logging these guns into a property office were followed. I understand that in due course, steps were taken to include at least one local law-enforcement officer in patrols, so that he could advise officers from other areas as to what was legal and what wasn't. Also, in Louisiana law enforcement is conducted differently than in some other states, and officers from other states who came to assist were sometimes found to be domineering and aggressive in enforcing laws that don't normally apply here. So, if you're in a disaster area and help arrives from elsewhere, you may find that the help doesn't know (or care) about local laws, norms, etc. Use caution!

Relief organizations have their own bureaucratic requirements that may conflict with your needs. A good example of this is the Red Cross. In many cases, across three states, I've had reports that locals who needed assistance were told that they had to register at a particular Red Cross shelter or facility. The help would not come to them; they had to go to it. If they wished to stay on their own property they were sometimes denied assistance and told that if they wanted help, they had to move into the shelter to get it. Also, assistance was often provided only to those who came in person. If you left your family at home and went to get food aid, you might be denied aid for your whole family because there was no evidence that they existed: only the number that could be physically counted by relief workers (who would not come to you, but insisted you come to them) would be provided with food. Needless to say, this caused much anger and resentment.

I hope that these "lessons learned" are of use to you. I'm more and more convinced that in the event of a disaster I must rely on myself (and a few friends) and never count on government or relief organizations for the help I'll need. Also, I'm determined to bug out a fairly long distance from a disaster, in my home area, so as to be clear of the post-disaster complications that may arise.

Martial Law: The Pretext Is Now Set

The bottom line on Hurricane Katrina is that whether you believe it was all incompetence or part incompetence and part malevolence, the lasting pretext is the same. When a disaster takes place, you have no rights and the federal government can arrest you if you don't follow their every order. FEMA is clearly using this human catastrophe as a means of executing its decade's-long plans and providing the pretext for future-takeover scenarios of all major American cities.

FEMA is not an elected body; it does not involve itself in public disclosures, and it even has a quasi-secret budget in the billions of dollars. It has more power than the President of the United States or the Congress; it has the power to suspend laws, move entire populations, arrest and detain citizens without a warrant, and hold them without trial; it can seize property, food supplies, transportation systems, and can suspend the Constitution.

Not only is it the most powerful entity in the United States, but it was not even created under constitutional law by the Congress. We cannot go any further down the line toward a martial-law police state in America without actually being in one. How much more has to happen before people realize there is a constitutional crisis in effect now.

A series of Executive Orders dating from the 1960s onward underlines the history of FEMA. The plan for total control of every aspect of our lives has been under construction for quite some time. Listed are just some of the Executive Orders relating to FEMA. As you read them, bear in mind that they mean nothing by themselves. They are not law, nor can they become law by and of themselves.

- **Executive Order Number 12148** created the Federal Emergency Management Agency to interface with the Department of Defense for civil-defense planning and funding. In 1980, with the advent of the Reagan administration, FEMA was used as the vehicle for the creation of a quasi-secret, centralized "national emergency" entity headed by a federal "emergency czar." FEMA has only spent about 6 percent of its budget on national emergencies. The bulk of their funding has been used for the construction of secret, underground facilities to assure continuity of government in case of a major emergency, foreign or domestic.
- **Executive Order Number 12656** appointed the National Security Council as the principal body with the authority to exercise emergency powers. This allows the government to increase domestic intelligence and surveillance of U.S. citizens and would restrict the freedom of movement within the United States, as well as grant the government the right to isolate large groups of civilians. The National Guard could be federalized to seal all borders and take control of U.S. air space and all ports of entry.

- **Executive Order 10990** allows the government to take over all modes of transportation and control of highways and seaports.
- **Executive Order 10995** allows seizure of all communications media in the United States.
- **Executive Order 10997** allows seizure of all electric power fuels and minerals, public and private.
- **Executive Order 10998** allows the government to take over all food resources and farms.
- **Executive Order 10999** allows seizure of all means of transportation, including personal cars, trucks, or vehicles of any kind, and total control of highways, seaports, and waterways.
- **Executive Order 11000** allows seizure of all American people for work forces under federal supervision, including the splitting up of families if the government finds it "necessary."
- **Executive Order 11001** allows seizure of all health, education, and welfare facilities, public and private.
- **Executive Order 11002** empowered the Postmaster General to register all men, women, and children in the U.S.
- **Executive Order 11003** allows seizure of all airports and aircraft.
- **Executive Order 11004** allows seizure of all housing, finances, and the authority to establish forced relocation. Authority to designate areas to be abandoned as "unsafe," establish new locations for populations, relocate communities, and build new housing with public funds.
- **Executive Order 11005** allows seizure of all railroads, inland waterways, and storage facilities, public and private.
- **Executive Order 11051** specifies the responsibility of the Office of Emergency Planning and gives authorization to put all Executive Orders into effect in times of increased international tensions and economic or financial crisis.

- **Executive Order 11921** allows the Federal Emergency Preparedness Agency to develop plans to establish control over the mechanisms of production and distribution, of energy sources, wages, salaries, credit, and the flow of money in U.S. financial institutions in any undefined national emergency. It also provides that when a state of emergency is declared by the President, Congress cannot review the action for 6 months.

As you can see, The Federal Emergency Management Agency has broad powers in every aspect of the nation. Should it so wish, it can completely wipe out the Constitution, yet this would be completely unlawful, as it was not created under Constitutional law by the Congress. The power of the Federal Government is now greater than at any time in history. The Posse Comitatus Act has been eroding ever since it was passed.

For years people have refuted the evidence, passed it off as being intended for something else, or simply refused to believe it. Now everything that we were warned about is happening. In the wake of the recent natural disasters on American soil, dangerous precedents have been set. We have been forced to watch how in times of crisis we must submit and follow the orders of Federal Commanders, no matter if they deny us of our basic human rights. Whether it be a state attack, a terrorist attack, an accident, or a natural disaster matters not anymore; the outcome will be the same. We are just one event, ANY event, away from martial law.

Even with all the power bestowed upon FEMA, they are still unorganized and inept, again, as observed with the handling of Hurricane Katrina. We must know the warning signs before we become trapped and vulnerable after a state of martial law has been declared. We needn't be scared, but prepared.

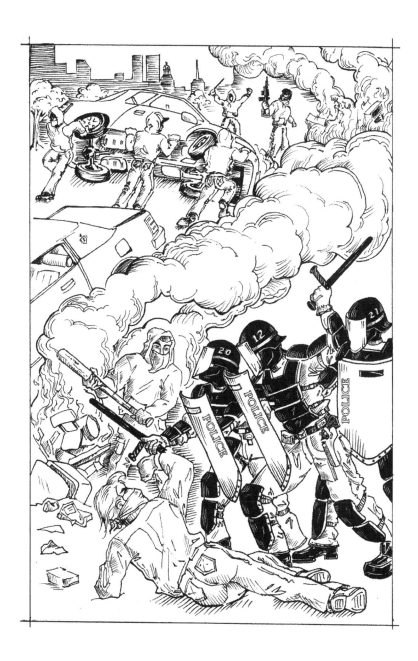

19
ECONOMIC RIOTS AND
CIVIL UNREST

You should let the video footage of the wild violence that took place in London burn into your memory, because the same thing is going to be happening all over the United States as the economy continues to crumble. We have raised an entire generation of young people with an entitlement mentality, but now the economy is producing very few good jobs that will actually enable our young people to work for what they feel they are "entitled" to. If you are under 30 in America today, things look really bleak. The vast majority of the good jobs are held by people that are older, and they aren't about to give them up if they can help it. It is easy for the rest of us to tell young Americans to take whatever they can, but the reality is that there is intense competition for even the most basic jobs. For instance, McDonald's recently held a "National Hiring Day" during which a million Americans applied for jobs. Only 6.2% of the applicants were hired. In the good old days you could just walk down to your local McDonald's and get a job whenever you felt like it, but now any job is precious. The frustration among our young people is palpable. Most of them feel entitled to the American Dream; they feel like the system has failed them. Unfortunately, many of them are already turning to violence. The economic riots and the civil unrest that we have already seen are nothing compared to what is coming. Americans are angry, and as the economy continues to collapse, that anger is going to reach unprecedented heights.

Recently, even many in the mainstream media have been openly speculating if the riots that happened in London could happen here in the U.S. as well. There is a growing acknowledgement that this country is headed down a very dark path.

The sad thing is that these riots accomplish absolutely nothing. The recent London riots did not create any jobs, and they certainly did not solve any economic problems. Instead, they actually hurt the economy even more so, because a huge amount of property was destroyed and people are even more afraid to continue with business as usual.

All over the United States we are already seeing some very troubling signs of the violence that is coming. The following are signs that economic riots and civil unrest inside the United States are now more likely than ever.

1. Going to the state fair used to be such fun for American families, but now no place is safe. The following is how one local ABC News affiliate described the "flash mob" attacks that took place at the Wisconsin state fair recently:

    > Milwaukee police said that around 11:10 p.m., squads were sent to the area for reports of battery, fighting, and property damage being caused by an unruly crowd of "hundreds" of people. One officer described it as a "mob beating."

    > Police said the group of young people attacked fair goers who were leaving the fair grounds. Police said that some victims were attacked while walking. They said others were pulled out of cars and off of motorcycles before being beaten.

    One eyewitness said that the flash mob attacks at the Wisconsin state fair absolutely overwhelmed the limited police presence that was there:

    > When I saw the amount of kids coming down the road, all I kept thinking was, 'There's not

enough cops to handle this.' There's no way. It would have taken the National Guard to control the number of kids that were coming off the road. They were knocking people off their motorcycles.

2. U.S. consumer confidence is now at its lowest level in 30 years.

3. Joblessness among young Americans is at an epidemic level, and when rioting does break out, it is usually young people that are leading the way. That is why the following statistics from an article in The Atlantic are so troubling:

> One in five Americans are between 15 and 29-years old. And one in five of those Americans are unemployed. For minorities and the under-educated, the picture is much worse. Black teenagers have an unemployment rate of 44 percent, twice the rate for white teens.

4. "Flash mobs" have become such a problem in Philadelphia that the mayor has imposed a strict curfew on young people. Now all teens between the ages of 13 and 18 must be indoors by 9 o'clock at night. The mayor also says that teens need to start pulling up their pants:

> "Pull your pants up and buy a belt 'cause no one wants to see your underwear or the crack of your butt."

5. Desperate people do desperate things. Many of America's forgotten poor are trying to survive any way they can. For instance, a group of vagrants recently set up a makeshift camp near Prospect Park Lake in Brooklyn. According to the New York Post, many nearby residents have been disturbed by what these drifters are doing to survive:

The drifters have been illegally trapping and cooking up the critters that call the park home, including squirrels, ducks and swan-like cygnets.

They used crude tactics to hunt their prey, including barbed fishing hooks that ripped off the top half of one poor gosling's beak. They then cooked the meat over illegal fires. Some of the animals were eaten raw.

6. Over the past 100 years, the American population has moved steadily into our big cities and the surrounding suburbs. This has created virtual ghost towns in our rural areas from coast to coast. Back in 1910, 72 percent of Americans lived in rural areas. Today, only 16 percent of Americans live in rural areas. When you crowd huge masses of people close together that makes riots and civil unrest much more likely.

Most Americans are already fed up, and the economy is not even that bad yet. One recent survey found that 73 percent of Americans believe that the nation is "on the wrong track." Another recent poll found that only 17 percent of Americans now believe that the U.S. government has the consent of the governed.

Sadly, instead of coming together and trying to do something productive, many Americans will resort to rioting, looting, and civil unrest. We have already seen this during local emergencies such as Hurricane Katrina.

The thin veneer of civilization that we all take for granted is starting to disappear. Hatred and anger are growing by the day. The United States is becoming a very frightening place, so get ready.

Be Prepared

1. If you know an area is ripe for a riot, but you can't avoid traveling there, take some simple precautions to help protect yourself. First, be prepared for the worst; the unexpected can happen at any moment. Crowds are dangerous when they're in an ugly mood, and normally placid people can turn frenzied just by being in the presence of other frenzied people.

    -   There's a very good chance you will not hear of rioting in your city on the news. There will be a news blackout.
    -   Wear dark clothes that minimize the amount of exposed skin (long pants and long-sleeved shirts and good work boots) when going out. Try to blend in with everyone.
    -   Carry toothpaste with you. Smear it under your eyes if tear gas is released and you have nothing else available to protect you.

- Take a motorcycle helmet with you. If bricks or other large items are being thrown about, at least you can protect your vulnerable head. If need be, it can be used as a striking weapon to get away if you are cornered.
- Think about your possible escape routes and safe havens before anything actually happens. Crossroads are the best, because you've got at least one road to race off down if rioters go crazy or the police start charging.
- Carry small amounts of cash with you in case you need to quickly arrange transportation, throw a few bills to create a diversion to get away, or bribe police at a checkpoint.
- If you're traveling abroad, register with your country's consulate, and carry your passport and/or visa with you at all times. Even domestically, have ID and emergency contact information on you in case you are arrested or become unconscious.
- Take two telephones, if possible (one in your pocket and one in a bag). If one is lost or stolen, you still have the other one.
- Look for homes that can serve as "safe houses". If you can, talk to the owners first.
- Carry pepper spray, so you can fight fire with fire.
- Military-grade smoke bombs make a great diversion for your get away.

Remain Calm

2. Riots bring intense emotions boiling to the surface, but if you want to survive one, you'd be better off keeping your own emotions in check. Your adrenaline and survival instincts will kick in, but strive to think rationally and pursue safety methodically.

- Have sugar candies on hand. Adrenaline will drain you of energy quickly, and a sugar hit will help you move out faster.
- Avoid confrontation by keeping your head down, but if someone pushes you or catches you by surprise in a riot, your reaction should be to push back rather aggressively and turn toward that person ready to fight.
- Walk at all times. If you run or move too quickly, you might attract unwanted attention.

Get Inside and Stay Inside

3. Typically, riots occur in the streets or elsewhere outside. Being inside, especially in a large, sturdy structure can be your best protection to weather the storm, such as a basement, sub-basement, sub-sub-basement, or an interior doorway to hide from the mob.

- Keep doors and windows locked. Avoid watching the riot from windows or balconies, and try to move to inside rooms, where the danger of being hit by stones or bullets is minimized.
- Try to find at least two possible exits in case you need to evacuate the building in a hurry.
- Buy an ABC fire extinguisher. The ABC type is useful for all types of fires. In the riots to come, fire will be a big danger. This may prevent you from being burned out of your home.
- If rioters are targeting your building or home and gain entry, try to sneak out or hide.

Stay on the Sidelines

4. If you're caught up in a riot, don't take sides. Try to look as inconspicuous as possible, and slowly and carefully move to the outside of the mob.

Stay close to walls or other protective barriers when available, but try to avoid bottlenecks. These are areas where the crowd can be squashed into a tight place, such as tunnels, pillars, high fences, and walls that go on for a long way.

If You are Stuck in a Car, Stay Calm

5. Remain inside the car unless your car becomes a focus for the riot, in which case it risks being torched, smashed, or rolled over. Calmly and swiftly leave it behind, and get to safety if that happens.

   - If you have no alternative but to drive, keep to streets away from the rioting. Avoid all main routes, and keep alert for news of where people are.
   - Don't stop your car. If you're lucky enough to have a car that you can drive away from the riot, drive quickly, and don't stop for anything or anyone until you've reached someplace that you know is safe. If people seem to block your escape route, honk your horn, and don't slow down even if they throw something through your windshield. They will understand and move or be run over.
   - Driving toward police lines can be interpreted as preparation to use your car as a ramming device. Police are trained and prepared to protect themselves against deadly threat, meaning that you may be shot at if they think you are going to run them down with a car.
   - Activists' fear of cars can be a reality, as there have been numerous cases of irate non-participants running down protesters. Any pushing through the crowd should be done with the demeanor of patience; aggression may lead to an attempt to disable your car before it is used as a weapon.

Use the Social Media to Alert You

6. Just as the rioters have started using social media and texting to alert one another where to go, you can flip this on its head and ask people to help you know where to stay away from. Messages informing you of what streets and areas are currently being targeted provide you with instantaneous warnings of where to avoid.

Avoid Being Hit by Riot Control Chemicals or Weapons

7. Police may deploy riot control agents (tear gas, water cannons, rubber bullets, etc.) to disperse a crowd. These weapons and chemicals can cause severe pain, respiratory distress, and blindness. Try to stay away from the front lines of a riot, and learn to recognize the signs that a riot-control agent has been used and how to handle exposure.

    -   Avoid wearing an oil-based moisturizer or sunscreen, as chemicals cling to these and onto your skin. Remove with detergent-free soap before going near the riot.
    -   Wear glasses rather than contact lenses; tear gas behind contact lenses is unimaginably painful. Swimming goggles can protect eyes (or a gas mask).
    -   Put wet bandannas in a plastic bag, and carry around in case they are needed. Wrap them around your mouth if tear gas is released. They need constant replacement, as they will keep soaking up the gas.
    -   Wear vinyl or latex gloves to protect your hands from pepper spray; the nerve endings will make them feel like agony if sprayed.

- Carry spare clothes to change into if you're hit by chemicals or a water cannon. Keep them in a plastic bag for protection.
- Avoid rubbing your hands or fingers into eyes, nose, or mouth after a chemical attack. Stay calm.
- Never hang around when bullets, gas, and cannons are being deployed. These riot-control agents can kill if they hit you in the wrong way, and even if they don't, they can maim and hurt you. If you're so injured that you fall down and cannot get up again, you also risk being trampled by the fleeing and terrified crowd.

Move Away from the Riot

8. The more time you spend in the midst of a riot, the greater your chance of being injured or killed. With that said, in most circumstances, it's better to move out of a riot slowly.

- If you run, you will draw attention to yourself, so it's usually best to walk.
- It can also be dangerous to move against a crowd, so go with the flow until you are able to escape into a doorway or up a side street or alley.
- It may be advantageous to stay with the crowd until you are certain you can safely escape, because it will help you remain inconspicuous and improve your odds of survival if shots are fired.
- Think of crowd movement like currents in the ocean. In a large riot, the crowd in the middle will be moving faster than the people on the perimeters. As such, if you find yourself in the middle, you should not try to move in a different direction, but follow the flow, and slowly make your way to the outside. This requires patience in order to work properly.

- Avoid major roads. Major roads, squares, and other high-traffic areas are likely to be crowded with rioters. If possible, stick to less-traveled side streets to avoid mobs.
- Avoid public transportation. Buses, subways, and trains will likely be out of service, and stations and depots will probably be jam-packed with people. Even if you succeed in getting on a train or bus, rioters may stop it or be taking rides on it themselves. Subway stations are particularly bad places to be at, both because they are generally difficult to escape from and because riot-control agents are generally heavier than air and may drift down into subway stations and accumulate there.

Get to a Safe Place, and Stay Put

9. Choose a safe haven carefully. Sometimes it can be as close as your hotel room, but other times you'll need to get out of the country entirely. If you're abroad, you will generally want to head to your country's embassy or to the airport. Try to contact the embassy before going there to let them know you're coming and to find out if it is safe to go there. If a mob is gathered outside, embassy staff may be able to direct you to a safer location. In any case, just try to put as much distance as possible between yourself and the riot.

Homemade Decontamination Spray

1. If you know you have to go out into the rioting crowd try to make this spray before leaving.
2. Find some antacid. Tums, Pepto-Bismol, Gaviscon, Eno, Milk of Magnesia, Alka-Seltzer, or even bicarbonate of soda (baking soda) are suitable.
3. Dilute with water.
4. Add to a spray bottle that you can easily carry.

5. Spray on eyes, nose, and skin if you are attacked by chemicals. The spray will help neutralize the attack.

Tips

- Try to figure out why the riot is occurring. Knowing the cause of a riot can help you determine an appropriate response. However, don't waste too much time trying to investigate the cause, and don't venture into a riot just to find out why the rioters are rioting.
- Get a video camera. Try to get one that looks like a camera used by a TV station. They are really cheap nowadays, since people are buying flat-screen camcorders. They are also small and lightweight. You can tape people destroying things. That can be a perfect disguise. You can pretend you're part of the press. Rioters and the police will attack anybody or anything, but they won't attack the press.
- Dress appropriately. If the anger of the rioters is directed toward foreigners, try to look like a local. Choose clothing that will help you blend in.

If the rioters are divided into factions, though, try to appear neutral. Don't wear clothing or carry accessories that might mark you as belonging to one faction or another. In either case, try to avoid looking conspicuously wealthy, as you are likely to draw the unwanted attention of opportunistic thieves.

- If a riot breaks out in a stadium, your response should be different depending on where you are in relation to the rioters. If you are in the midst of a riot, try to quickly move to an exit. Don't run and try not to jostle others. If you are at some distance from the action, stay where you are unless instructed to move by police or security personnel. Don't rush for the exits unless you're in imminent danger. People are frequently trampled by stampeding crowds near exits.
- When in the middle of a tear-gas attack, stay out of the fire line of police. Gas canisters fired from launchers will cause significant injury upon impact.
- Some gas is not very heavy, and some is, so it's best to avoid clouds and gas at all. Never touch your eyes or try to clean your tears; you will only smear them in your face causing yourself more pain.
- Riots don't drop out of thin air. Generally, there may be signs of public anger and violence at least one day (in some cases even three to four days) before the actual riot. Reading the newspapers and following the news may give you a warning about impending protests, rallies, marches, etc. Being informed and avoiding troubled areas may be your best defense.
- Riots may start as fun, but later on become more dangerous. You may not be able to flee the city at that point; stake out a hideout for cash, food, and bartering items that is apart from what you have at home, so that if it's destroyed by fire (a real danger), you have a back-up plan.

Warnings

- Watch your footing in a mob situation. If you stumble and fall to the ground, you're likely to be trampled. This is especially dangerous in stadiums and other enclosed areas, where many unfortunate victims have been crushed to death.
- If you fall down, pull yourself up into a ball. Protect your face, ears, and internal organs. In this position you are a smaller object that can be avoided. You will receive less damage if you are stepped on. If others trip on you, they will help create a larger "pile" that rioters will avoid.
- Never touch a tear-gas canister with bare hands; once discharged, they're very hot. If necessary, just kick it back to where it came from.
- The use of riot-control measures, including rubber bullets, tear gas, and water cannons originate from the police line, and the likelihood of injury, and even death, is greatest there.

20
DEFENSIVE DRIVING FOR ESCAPE AND EVASION

Surveillance

One off the keys to avoiding a confrontation in your car is recognizing when you are under surveillance. In a planned carjacking, you are under surveillance for a period of time prior to the confrontation. The observation period may range from one day to even several months. In order to stop the confrontation before it takes place, you must develop surveillance awareness. In order to develop this ability, you must constantly be alert to suspicious people in the vicinity of your home and work. This especially goes for those who live in an area where houses are spread greatly apart. Don't become a raving paranoid, constantly on red alert against everyone and everything, but it should be in the back of your mind that someone's eyes may be watching you.

The Single Tail

The easiest type of surveillance to detect is when you are being followed by a single surveillant. The loner must stay close enough to keep you in sight, yet far enough away to avoid detection—no easy feat. In residential areas, he can remain a few cars back because of the density of traffic. He also has the option of following the victim on a parallel street. In rural areas, about all he can do is remain in the distance and hope for the best. The single tail may employ certain tricks of the trade to make his job easier. At night, he may break a taillight or place a small luminous sticker on the rear of the victim's vehicle to make it more distinguishable. To decrease the possibility of detection, he may change his seating position or use various types of disguises. If you suspect you are being followed by a single tail, try things like speeding through some areas and going slow through others. The signal lights can be used to your advantage if you come up to an intersection. Try signaling and wait until your suspect's signal comes on—just drive straight through with your signal on and see what happens.

Eluding a Tail

1. After running a red light or driving the wrong way on a one way street, watch to see if anyone follows.
2. While travelling on a freeway at high speed, suddenly cut across four lanes of traffic and make an exit.
3. After rounding a blind curve, make a bootlegger's turn and take off in the opposite direction.
4. After turning a corner, pull over and park. Take note of all vehicles passing by.
5. Go through alleys, dirt roads, or even cut across people's lawns.
6. While driving over a long, undivided bridge, suddenly make a bootlegger's turn.
7. Have a friend follow you to detect any surveillance.

Cornering
It is a commonly-held belief that the best way to handle corners is to blast through them as quickly as possible. This is completely wrong. The speed at which you exit a corner is much more important than the speed at which you take the corner itself. The car which exits the corner at the greater speed will be going faster on any straight stretch of road that follows.

Proper Apex
The apex of any turn is that point in which your wheels are closest to the inside edge of the corner. By choosing a relatively late apex, the driver can exit a corner at a greater speed than if he had chosen an early one.

The Bootlegger's Turn
Legend has it that the bootlegger's turn was invented by hillbilly moonshiners for the purpose of eluding revenue agents. The maneuver enables you to change your direction 180 degrees, without stopping, within the width of a two lane road. It has been used to get away from roadblocks and also to elude pursuers. The bootlegger's turn is easiest to perform in cars having an automatic transmission and a hand-emergency brake.

1. Get speed to around 25–30 mph.
2. Let off the gas and crank the steering wheel ¼–½ a turn. At the exact same time, pull the emergency break hard. Those of you with a manual transmission will have to depress the clutch as well.
3. When your vehicle is at approximately 90 degrees, release the emergency break, step on the gas, and straighten out the steering wheel. If you have a manual transmission, you will have to let the clutch out as you are hitting the gas.
4. Get out of Dodge.

The bootlegger's turn will cause incredible wear and tear on your front tires. For this reason, it is recommended that you learn how to do this maneuver on your ex-wife's car. Needless to say, don't tell her what you are planning on using her car for.

Movies, such as *The Transporter,* and TV programs, such as *The Dukes of Hazzard,* often show the bootlegger's turn during their chase scenes. The driving in these shows is done by professionals, but you too can learn a lot just by watching them. You can also learn a lot by watching auto races and demolition derbies, both live and on TV.

Moonshiner's Turn

The moonshiner's turn is another slick maneuver pioneered by the mountain people of the Southern United States. The moonshiner's turn looks like a bootlegger's turn in reverse, allowing you to change your direction 180 degrees within the confines of a two lane road, while going backward.

1. Accelerate in reverse 20–30 mph.
2. Let off the gas and crank the steering wheel all the way to the left as fast as possible.
3. When the car has turned 90 degrees, shift into low gear, hit the gas, and straighten out the steering wheel.
4. Now is your chance for escape.

This maneuver is particularly effective against roadblocks at night. Often the attackers manning the roadblock will use high-intensity lights to blind the victim as he approaches. By using the moonshiner's turn, the victim's vision is directed away from the lights.

Ramming

The most common type of vehicle ambush is the stationary roadblock. In this type of attack, one or two vehicles are lined up across the road. The attackers will usually be standing alongside the blockade vehicles with high-intensity lights and lots of firepower (automatic weapons and high-powered rifles). When the unwary and untrained victim sees the roadblock, he will stop, whereupon the attackers will rush the vehicle and drag him away. Faced with the above situation, you might decide to ram. To those of you who have experienced it only through television shows, ramming may seem like a suicidal stunt reserved for Evel Knievel types. Actually, as long as you wear a seat belt, ramming is almost completely safe. The true danger of ramming is that your vehicle may become inoperable after the collision. For this reason, ramming is usually a method of last resort. If at all possible, go around the roadblock rather than through it.

Single-Vehicle Blockades

1. Slow down almost to a complete stop and put the car in low gear. This will give your attackers the impression that you are going to stop.
2. Suddenly hit the gas hard and pick a ramming point.
3. Hit the target at an angle, and keep the accelerator fully depressed through the collision. Your speed at impact should be between 15–30 mph.
4. After breaking through, don't stop. Even if your car is badly damaged, keep going.

Double-Vehicle Blockade

Follow the procedure as described in ramming of a single-vehicle blockade, except the preferred ramming point is right in the middle of the two cars. If any of the attackers are so foolish as to get in front of you, run them over. To practice ramming, go to your local auto junkyard and buy three running wrecks. Move all three to an unused parking lot or abandoned area and practice per the directions listed. For safety's sake, wear a helmet and seatbelt. You might also want to smash out all the glass ahead of time. Work with the three cars until not one will even start.

Vehicle Attack

If you are fortunate enough to get behind your attacker's car, you can easily knock him off the road. The most effective means of doing so is to ram his bumper on the left-hand side, with the right-hand side of yours, as if you were going to pass but didn't pull left far enough. You should be going

10–20 mph faster than he is, as you must *hit*, not *push*. After impact, his vehicle will be facing slightly right and go sliding sideways down the road until his tires regain traction. When this happens, his car will go in the direction it is pointing— off the road.

An effective secondary method is one in which you would pull alongside the left rear of the enemy's vehicle, very quickly turn to the right, enough to turn a corner, and slam into his rear section. You will actually be facing the edge of the road. This will cause him to spin out and go off the road. Immediately after impact, hit the brakes and counter steer to break contact.

If you don't want to hit the other vehicle hard, or it is much larger and heavier than yours, follow this procedure.

1. Pull up alongside the enemy vehicle and position yourself so that the center of your vehicle is in line with the other vehicle's front tires.
2. Crank slightly to the left and press the center of your car against the front of his.
3. Now steer him off the road and keep going.

Assassinations
A very common method of assassination is for an attacking vehicle to pull alongside the victim's car and simply blast away at everyone inside. If the driver is hit, they're all as good as dead. The best defense against this type of attack is to slam on the brakes, causing the attacker to overshoot your vehicle. A bootlegger's turn could also be employed (if the shoulder of the road is wide enough), or you could make a quick turn off the road. Keep in mind that after you slam on the brakes, a moonshiner's turn may be the only escape; pray for no oncoming traffic. If you are faced with an attack from a motorcycle, ram him as hard as possible, thereby ending the threat.

Chase Situations
The most important thing to remember in any chase situation is not to crash. Even if you should somehow make it through an accident in one piece, you would be a sitting duck for any pursuer.

The probability of an accident is so great that high speeds are not recommended in chase situations. By keeping your speed relatively low, say under 60 mph, you will have greater vehicle control and evasive maneuvers will be easier to accomplish. Of course, if you have a superior car to that of your pursuer, you can just outrun him on open roads. If you absolutely can't get away from your pursuers, after attempting every maneuver possible, drive your car into a wooded area. When your car won't go any further, get out and get behind cover.

If your pursuers are still intent on coming after you, they are going to have to exit their vehicle. When they do, you can ambush them.

Vehicle Improvements

Tires
Buy the best radial tires you can afford. Radials offer increased durability, superior handling, and better gas mileage than old-fashioned, bias-ply tires. Also, to some degree, radials are bullet resistant. Be sure to slightly overinflate all four tires and to fill them with run-flat foam.

Radiator
Hard driving, hot weather, and rough terrain make for overheated engines. A heavy-duty radiator will help prevent rapid overheating.

Shocks and Springs
Other than good tires, nothing will improve your car's handling more than top-quality shocks and springs. As with tires, price is the indication of quality, so get the best you can afford.

Brake Lines
Rubber-brake lines have been known to swell and flex, causing the brakes to fade.
Stainless-steel brake lines are used in racing competition and are recommended, particularly for those living in mountainous areas.

Steering Pump
If your car has power steering, a series of quick turns might cause the steering fluid to foam, making steering extremely difficult. A hefty steering pump serves to prevent this.

Battery
Adding additional lights and communications' gear to a car is great cause for using a heavy-duty battery.

Lights
You should replace your old-fashioned, sealed-beam headlights with quartz-iodine lights. These give off twice the

light and enable you to drive much faster at night. Quartz-iodine headlights can be purchased for almost any vehicle. You might also consider mounting additional lights on your vehicle. Auxiliary lights should be mounted low and angled slightly outward.

Gas Cap
If you don't have a locking gas cap, get one; it's just a matter of time before your fuel is siphoned. Many pranksters and vandals are known for putting things like salt, sugar, iron filings, etc., into a car's fuel tank. Also, as told in *The Poor Man's James Bond*, a gas tank can be blown up by simply dropping a few specially-filled gelatin capsules into the tank.

Gun and Crowbar
Kidnappers and thugs have been known to throw their victim into the trunk of the victim's car. If this were to happen to you, a gun and prying instrument stored in the trunk could prove useful in your escape.

Thick Bolt through Tailpipe
A thick, heavy bolt put through the tail pipe and welded into place will certainly save you from pulling tomatoes from the exhaust, not to mention shotgun shells in the muffler.

Ram Bumpers
Bumpers can be reinforced by bolting or welding extra supports from the vehicle's frame to the bumper. Further reinforcement can be made by welding a two-inch metal pipe to the vehicle frame, right in back of the bumper. These extra reinforcements could prove useful in a ramming situation.

21
CARJACKING—DON'T BE A VICTIM

Carjacking
It's a crime of opportunity, a thief searching for the most vulnerable prey. Sometimes it's the first step in another crime. For some young people, carjacking may be a rite of passage, a status symbol, or just a thrill. Cars, especially luxury ones, provide quick cash for drug users and other criminals. Sophisticated alarms and improved locking devices make it harder for thieves to steal unoccupied cars, but it's easy to buy, steal, or barter for guns in this country, and a pointed gun makes a powerful threat toward the operator of a vehicle. More teens and adults commit crimes of violence than ever before, and this trend will only continue to climb, especially since intense media interest may have created "copycat" carjackers.

The crime is extremely hazardous, threatening the physical safety of both the carjacker and the victim. To secure the car, the carjacker may sometimes shoot the victim or physically push/pull the victim out of the driver's seat to force him or her out of the car.

Carjacking is a very violent crime, typically involving the use of a weapon, often leading to the victim being shot and killed. Then the public is put at risk not only by the speeding, reckless, and generally unsafe driving of the carjacker, but the carjacker often engages in drive-by shootings, or otherwise discharges his weapons from the vehicle. Even worse, the carjacker typically intends to use the stolen vehicle in another crime, and the public is again put at risk by the reckless driving of the carjacker, in the case of a police pursuit or shootout.

What do Carjackers Look For?
Intersections controlled by stop lights or signs, garages and parking lots for mass transit, shopping malls, and grocery stores, self-serve gas stations and car washes, ATMs, residential driveways and streets, as people get into and out of cars, highway exit and entry ramps, or anyplace else that drivers slow down or stop.

Avoidance
The first step to avoiding an attack is to stay alert at all times, and be aware of your environment. The most likely places for a carjacking to occur are in:

- High-crime areas.
- Lesser-traveled roads (rural areas).
- Intersections where you must stop.
- Isolated areas in parking lots.
- Residential driveways and gates.
- Traffic jams or congested areas.

Keep Savvy

- Vary the times and routes to and from work. Avoid fixed schedules and routines.
- Have thorough knowledge of the area you are driving in, this includes country roads and long detours.
- In traffic, look around for possible avenues of escape. Keep some distance between you and the vehicle in front, so you can maneuver easily if necessary, about one-half of your vehicle's length. You should always be able to see the rear tires of the vehicle in front of you.
- When stopped, use your rear and side-view mirrors to stay aware of your surroundings. Keep your doors locked and windows up. This increases your safety and makes it more difficult for an attacker to surprise you.

The Ambush
The following are common attack plans.

- The Bump—The attacker bumps the victim's vehicle from behind. The victim gets out to assess the damage and exchange information. The victim's vehicle is stolen.
- Good Samaritan—The attacker(s) stage what appears to be an accident. They may simulate an injury. The victim stops to assist, and the vehicle is taken.
- The Ruse—The vehicle behind the victim flashes its lights or the driver waves to get the victim's attention. The attacker tries to indicate that there is a problem with the victim's car. The victim pulls over and the vehicle is jacked.
- The Trap—Carjackers use surveillance to follow the victim home. When the victim pulls into his or her driveway waiting for the gate to open, the attacker pulls up behind and blocks the victim's car.
- The dare—The attacker walks out into the middle of the street as the victim approaches, daring the person to stop.

How to React

- If someone walks right out in front of you in a threatening manner, just accelerate and aim right for that person; I promise he will get out of the way!
- If you are bumped from behind or if someone tries to alert you to a problem with your vehicle, pull over only when you reach a safe public place.
- If you are driving into a gated community, call ahead to have the gate opened. Otherwise wait on the street until the gate is open before turning in and possibly getting trapped.
- Think before stopping to assist in an accident. It may be safer to call and report the location, number of cars involved, and any injuries you observed.
- In all cases keep your cell phone or radio with you and immediately alert someone regarding your situation.
- If your car has been left alone, check it thoroughly for tampering before driving it.
- If suspicious people are observed loitering around your vehicle and your alarm hasn't gone off, avoid it.
- Be suspicious of people approaching your car, asking for directions, or handing out flyers.
- A new carjacking scheme involves the placement of a sticker or flyer on the victim's rear window to fool them into exiting the vehicle with the engine running.

During A Carjacking

In most carjacking situations, the attackers are interested only in the vehicle. Try to stay calm. Do not stare at the attacker, as this may seem aggressive and cause them to harm you. There are two options during an attack: non-resistive, non-confrontational behavior and resistive or confrontational behavior. Your reaction should be based on certain factors:

- Type of attack
- Environment (isolated or public)

- Mental state of attacker (reasonable or nervous)
- Number of attackers
- Weapons
- Whether children are present

Non-Confrontational Response

- Give up the vehicle freely.
- Listen carefully to all directions.
- Make no quick or sudden movements that the attacker could construe as a counter attack.
- Make the attacker aware if children are present. The attacker may be focused only on the driver and not know children are in the car.

Resistive or Confrontational Response

- Make sure you have the skills to take the carjacker(s) out and survive.
- Consider the mental state of the attacker.
- Are you able to run them over?
- Are there any possible avenues of escape?
- How many attackers are you up against? There is usually more than one.
- Are there weapons involved? (Weapons are used in the majority of carjacking situations.)

After The Attack

- Put as much distance between yourself and the carjacker as quickly as possible, in case the thief attempts to pursue you.
- If you are in a populated area, immediately go to a safe place. After an attack or an attempted attack, you might not be focused on your safety. Get to a safe place before contacting someone to report the incident.

- If there is any rule of law left, describe the attacker(s) to law enforcement. Try to note height, weight, scars birth marks, tattoos, body piercings, hair and eye color, the presence of facial hair, build (slender, large), and complexion (dark, fair). Then they can write it in their book and tell you to have a nice day.
- If they were able to steal your vehicle, hopefully you already know your vehicle's license number, color, make, model, and year, as well as any marks (scratches, dents, damage) and personal decorations (stickers, colored wheels), that way the authorities are more likely to retrieve it.

My Experience with a Carjacker

Everything appeared normal while driving my Honda home one night after watching a zombie movie with my girlfriend's, now wife's, brother at their house. It was around 1:00 am. All of the streets were vacant, and the signal lights were stop and go before I approached the freeway onramp. As I was stopped at the last light, a rather-large, black male in an ankle-length trench coat stepped off the curb and walked toward my car. Placing his hand onto my front bumper, he shouted, "don't move." As he made his way from the passenger side to the driver's side, he slid his left hand across the hood with very direct eye contact, still shouting, "don't move." I knew his intentions. When he opened his coat and put his right hand on what I'm positive was a handgun tucked into his front waistband, I sort of panicked.

I grew up in a *Wonder Years* neighborhood, but on the outskirts were your typical thugs, so I knew this guy wasn't selling Kirby vacuum cleaners to passing cars. He wanted my Honda and was willing to possibly kill me for it. My dad has always taught me to be safe and aware of my surroundings. I could hear him saying his famous words: "Just get out of there; you have no business being around those people." So I did just that. I ducked down a little in case of some gun fire and floored it, catching the guy's leg as he was making his move, kind of sucking him under the car. It felt like taking a speed bump a little too fast. Did it kill him, no, but I saw him in my rear-view mirror lying in the street, belly down with his two legs together and up, like some kind of ghetto mermaid. I didn't stop or call 911; I was too scared. I thought, forget about checking on him, if he was willing to pull a gun on me before... now he is definitely willing to pull the trigger. Could I have done things differently? I don't think so, other than not being out at that time of night on vacant streets. Would I do things differently now as an adult with kids? No. I just wish I could have driven away without hurting him, but maybe that lesson saved his life in the long run.

After the collapse, carjacking is going to be rampant and much more violent WROL. Criminals will not think twice about taking your life, not so much for your vehicle, but for the fuel in the tank.

Run a red light if you must, and expect the unexpected during WROL. Even if a brick is thrown through your windshield, don't stop until you are in a safe, well-populated area. Sometimes carjackers will lay out improvised spike strips or put obstacles on the road to make you stop. Better to drive through and ruin your wheels than to stop and possibly lose your life.

Non-confrontation is often the best response if you are outgunned and have no street experience. The objective is not to take out the criminal, but to survive.

22
CASH WILL BE KING AND PRECIOUS METALS WILL BE QUEEN

In the US, three-quarters of all non-cash payments are done so electronically. Debit cards make up 35 percent of all non-cash payments and has surpassed all other forms of non-cash payments. The amount of consumers that own a debit card is at 80 percent.

Electronic money, like debit cards, is convenient and easy to use and is favored by most merchants (despite the small percentage paid to VISA, MasterCard, etc., for the convenience). Merchants save money while transacting with electronic money because it enables electronic book-keeping methods that eliminate most human intervention.

The first thing to understand is that nearly all of the current money supply is in the form of electronic data entries on computers rather than in cash. Most of the wealth of the world is in promises to pay (credit) rather than in cash. When a disaster hits and the computers in the banks or ATMs go down, or if there are bank runs, all that electronic wealth could evaporate overnight. Most people currently thought of as wealthy have their wealth tied up in credit-related investments of one kind or another—the stock market, bonds, CD's, real estate, etc. Almost no one keeps a big stash of cash around anymore, because there's been no need for large amounts of cash for a long, long time. All of these people that are currently rich could suddenly become poor if a financial crash were to hit. I don't mean metaphorically poor, I really mean freezing, starving poor, broke, and destitute. All their resources will be in the wrong form for the new conditions that lie ahead. Only those who have cash will be wealthy after a national disaster; survival requires cash.

Can't the government simply print enough paper money to replace all the electronic money? The answer is no, it's impossible. The presses at the Bureau of Engraving and Printing are already running at capacity 24 hours a day just to replace the paper money that wears out each year.

Without getting into the argument about the current "fiat" money system (paper money), and the definition of "real" money, the fact is that humans have been trained to work for either paper money or invisible, electronic money.

Implications of Electronic Versus Paper Money
Using electronic money will leave a definitive footprint, captured forever, of your purchase (where, when, and sometimes, even what). Spending habits are quickly profiled and updated each time electronic money is used.

Cash, or paper money, is obviously not tagged to you and your profile with your purchase date, place, and product (unless you provide a store-discount card or group-membership card). In a world of electronic money, how much actual cash should be kept on hand, and under what circumstances?

While Traveling

If you are close enough to home, a $100 minimum should be enough to get you out of a typical jam, should the need arise. A better recommendation may be to keep several hundred, enough to cover an automobile repair if stranded, or to get you back home.

At Home

In a scenario where "the system" goes down, for whatever reason, cash will be king during the first phase of the event. The more cash the better—period.

Since humans have been trained that paper money has value, cash will be demanded until such time that things get bad enough and one's value system begins to change.

Enough cash should be kept at home (don't assume that you'll get yours out of the bank) to at least pay the rent/mortgage until the situation gets back in order, perhaps from a job loss, outside circumstance, or even an economic collapse. Add in the other expenses that you could not live without, then add 20 percent more as a cushion, and you will have your minimum number.

Four Months Survival on Cash

- Rent $1,200 per month = $4,800
- Utilities $400 per month = $1,600
- Fuel $400 per month = $1,600
- Food (if you have food storage, then this is zero) $600 per month = $2,400
- Cushion $1,200

Do you see how fast this can add up? Not even including, insurances, other loans, etc., this already totals over $10,000. Of course, everyone's budget is different, but the point is that things can go downhill rapidly if the system gets disrupted.

Cash will be King

Start converting some of your credit investments and electronic forms of money into cash. If you have cash after the disaster, you will be one of the few wealthy people in the world. A word of warning: You must be very careful to keep a low profile both now and in the future. You want to attract as little attention as possible, now while you convert to cash and later when you use your cash, for two different but equally vital reasons.

First, although you have every right to convert all your investments and savings into cash, doing so might invite the attention of the government DEA agents who may think you're some kind of drug dealer. The drug laws are so powerful regarding the confiscation of suspected drug dealers' wealth that you could find yourself in a protracted legal battle to get back the money that belongs to you. You want to avoid attracting the attention of bank tellers or branch managers who might report to the DEA that you are withdrawing large sums of cash.

Secondly, when everyone around you is impoverished and hungry, it's very prudent to keep your own wealth out of sight. A desperate man will go to extremes to feed his family and keep them sheltered and warm; a hungry man will do what is necessary to procure food. Someone who flashes a lot of cash is courting danger.

Although most people do not believe that the current financial system could collapse, the fact is, it certainly could and will. In today's electronic world of money, there is only a minute amount of actual cash in circulation compared to the total number of transactions that occur daily.

There are various reasons why a bank run may occur in the U.S., but the overwhelming driving mechanism will be panic. Once the public realizes that a particular institution can't make good on its debt or the country's currency goes into a death spiral, depositors will be out in droves. ATMs will be limited on cash and generally allow withdrawals of about

$300 per day. Likewise, banks will simply not have enough money to pay out the entire account balance of every depositor, so they will more than likely implement withdrawal restrictions similar to what you might get from an ATM.

At that point, the future of your finances will fall into the hands of the federal government by way of the FDIC, which itself is wholly undercapitalized and unable to effectively cover the deposits of a single major U.S. bank, let alone the entire banking system. There will be very little, if any, warning before such an event occurs. That's why they call it a bank run. One morning depositors wake up and learn that their life savings are about to disappear. The inevitable emotional effect when faced with such losses is stress, anxiety, panic, and fear. This is what it looked like at Northern Rock bank in the UK as reported in *Bloomberg*, after the bank was declared insolvent on September 14, 2007:

> Hundreds of Northern Rock customers crowded into branches in London today to pull out their savings after the mortgage-loan provider sought emergency funding from the Bank of England.
>
> "It's scary," said Peter Pye, 60, a retired university lecturer standing in a line of about 30 people outside the Moorgate branch in the financial district. "I have my life's savings in Northern Rock." He said he would withdraw a "six-figure" sum and leave 5,000 pounds in the account.

Remember this: Cash will be king during the first phase of an economic collapse. The second phase will be more about tangible goods, rather than fiat money.

You often hear about stockpiling gold and silver, but for all practical purposes, I think cash will still be king during a SHTF situation, especially in the beginning. While I do think owning precious metals are a good long-term strategy, having some extra cash in your bags is probably going to do more for you in an emergency situation.

Here's Why Cash Will Still be King

1. Most emergencies are small-scale disasters. If you have to buy something during a natural disaster, most cashiers are not going to take your gold!

2. There are millions of vending machines scattered throughout the country. It may sound weird, but I've heard of a number of people who have vending machines routed out on their evacuation maps. Having some smaller bills in your bug out bag can help you stock up on supplies as you go. It's not the most nutritious food in the world, but in an emergency it's still food. If the situation is bad enough, you could just bust open the machine.

3. When going into hostile environments the Navy SEALs always carry cash as part of their survival supplies. They do this because in most parts of the world cash is king. If they find themselves in a sticky situation, having cash can help them buy weapons, a ride out of town, or even payoff the locals for a temporary hiding place. You can apply these same principles to a SHTF situation and see why cash is a necessity.

4. People are stupid! Even if the dollar collapses most of the country is completely clueless and will still see it as having value. People are conditioned to perceive paper currencies as having value and in the beginning most people will still believe that it has value.

What to Have on You
Get your cash in tens and twenties and a few fifties. If you receive any crisp new bills, stop off at a convenience store and buy a candy bar or something, hand the clerk a new bill and you will receive older, worn bills in change.

After the fall, anyone with brand new money may invite envy as a hoarder or may become a target for robbers. You want to avoid attracting attention to yourself both now and then. You will need ones and fives after a disaster, but it's too noticeable to cash a large check and ask for a lot of very small bills.

Coins

You will also need coins. Gold and silver will be useful during the rebuilding phase, several years after the crisis, but for the first couple of years, ordinary dimes and quarters, nickels, and pennies will be the most easily-traded form of money.

People are completely used to ordinary pocket change coins, so that's what they will most readily accept for local transactions—and I believe nearly all transactions will be local after a major national disaster. You need to start saving up a coin stash. Once a month or so, take a few $20 bills to a bank in which you do not have an account and trade them for rolls of quarters or dollar coins. Any bank will exchange paper for coins without question.

Gold And Silver

Gold and silver coins are real money, based on their standard precious metal content; they have always been a historical refuge in times of crisis and because of increased public awareness about possible disasters, gold and silver coins have become very sought after. You are not interested in collectible coins; you're only interested in gold and silver coins for their precious-metal content. The cheapest way to hold silver coins is to buy pre-1965, junk-silver dimes and quarters. No one knows the future value ratio of silver coins to copper-clad coins (our currently circulating ones) after a disaster, but there's no doubt that silver coins will be worth considerably more than clads once people get used to having them. You pay a higher premium for silver dollars than you do for silver dimes and quarters but it would be wise to have some silver dollars on hand as part of your survival plan.

They are bigger and more impressive looking than dimes and quarters; even though a silver dollar may have the same metal content as ten silver dimes or four silver quarters, it just looks more valuable. The alternative is to buy brand new American Silver Eagles. These are current, manufacture-pure silver coins from the US Mint. The American Silver Eagle is the official silver bullion coin of the States. Though not commonly seen in circulation, they are legal tender and worth far more than their face value.

Gold
Gold coins are the most desirable, most valuable, form of real, hard money. Gold is scarce, it does not rust or corrode, it's very beautiful to look at, it's highly desirable as jewelry, it has industrial uses, and a long, long monetary history in many cultures worldwide. It's the real deal. Right now the price of gold is going into uncharted territory, which should warn us that inflation is way up. Inflation or the threat of inflation causes an immediate rise in the price of gold. The best gold coins are American coins in 1 oz., 1/2 oz., 1/4 oz., and 1/10 oz. denominations. People have no experience with real gold money and they will probably more readily accept U.S. gold coins than foreign coins. Although the U.S., 1 oz. Liberty coin is slightly more expensive to buy than the South African Kruger Rand, for example, when you go to spend gold, you'll find it easier to move the American coins.

Get smaller denomination gold coins than larger ones. In other words, buy more 1/10 oz. coins than 1/4 oz. coins, and more 1/4 oz. coins than 1/2 oz. coins, etc. The reason for this is that gold is an immense store of value for its size and weight. You will not be able to go into a local flea market or general store with a one oz. gold coin and be able to buy a few loaves of bread and cheese. How will the store owner make change for such a high value coin? You will use the fraying paper money, followed by clad coins, and then silver coins before you'll place any gold on the counter. Gold is for large purchases, so a small gold coin will be of far greater use on most occasions than a larger one. Save your 1 oz. gold coins to purchase major items.

Storing Cash
Now you need to find a safe place to hide your cash. First, tell no one that you have a load of cash, except possibly your spouse, and don't tell your spouse unless you're absolutely certain of the strength of your marriage. I'm not kidding. Hard times drive people to do things they would not do ordinarily, and when the SHTF, these will be the hardest times in our country's history. If your spouse is completely trustworthy, consider yourself fortunate and keep no secrets; otherwise, be cautious.

If you plan to hide your cash somewhere in your house, you want to make sure to protect it from fire, so purchase a fireproof-storage box. You should be able to get one for under $50. It will protect your cash from burning for a half hour in direct flame.

Put your paper money and your gold and silver in the box. If you fill it up, buy another one and fill that one up too. As you begin changing some of your electronic-credit wealth into cash, gold and silver, your money is fully under your control. As long as you keep it safe, it will always be there for you.

Secret-Hiding Places
Hiding your money under a mattress or on top of a book

shelf is a joke. During a collapse and civil unrest, burglaries will be extremely common, and unless you're very creative with your hiding places, you will lose all that you prepped for. Take a good hard look around your place; there are limitless possibilities for hiding your money. Look for dead spaces in cabinets, large appliances, an unused water heater, furniture, unused pipes, electrical boxes, and cooling and heating ducts.

Everyone has something to hide; the only rule to a secret hiding place is that your stash be readily available. Sure you can hide your money in a fireproof box covered in 3 feet of cement, but no one would be able to get to it, and neither would you. Sometimes the most obvious place is also the least obvious.

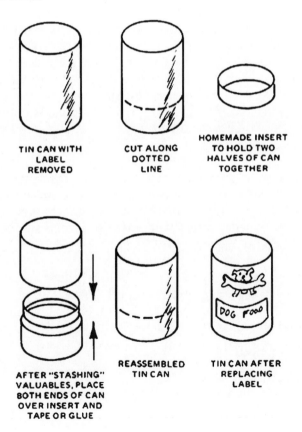

TIN CAN WITH
LABEL
REMOVED

CUT ALONG
DOTTED
LINE

HOMEMADE INSERT
TO HOLD TWO
HALVES OF CAN
TOGETHER

AFTER "STASHING"
VALUABLES, PLACE
BOTH ENDS OF CAN
OVER INSERT AND
TAPE OR GLUE

REASSEMBLED
TIN CAN

TIN CAN AFTER
REPLACING
LABEL

DOG FOOD

23
BLACK-MARKET TRADING

The black market is actually the free market. Currently, the black market's activity is limited mainly to illegal products and activities, such as drugs and prostitution. When TSHTF, the government will sanction control over everything, which will create shortages of, and restrictions on, even legitimate products and services. This will create a massive black market. You will not be able to get every day products and services in the legal, or so-called, white market; you will have to buy and sell in the black market. When the dollar collapses and becomes monopoly money, you are going to see an enormous increase in black markets. You may not want to partake in the black market, but you will not have a choice. It's the only way you will be able to achieve urban survival once your supplies have been depleted. The banks will be closed, so people will not be able to withdraw the money they had deposited to pay their bills. Sure there is a risk of markup, but that's what is associated with black markets.

You may already be familiar with the black market. Unfortunately, you may have scored some illegal drugs or picked up some company for the night. Those markets are particularly violent, but there is an unwritten law. You can snuff out your competitor or knock off other dealers, but the customer must be sheltered from any of the violence. If you hang out at a local coffee shop in the business district, around lunch time, you'll see yuppie, business wannabes buying drugs. These people want all the make-believe glamor that comes with drugs and are willing to pay big bucks for it, but they sure don't want the violence that comes with the drug trafficking.

They are so wimpy they could not deal with the behind-the-scenes drama mentally or physically. The hardcore violence is handled far out of view from the customers. Just like when I get my yummy In-N-Out burger, I never picture it as a bloody corpse hanging on a hook waiting to be processed.

What will this new, post-collapse black market entail? It will be comprised of everyday people bartering for food, potable water, medical supplies, and other daily needs. They will pop up immediately. Your local grocery store will simply be endless rows of empty shelves, so their parking lot will be a place where people will gather and barter for needed goods. Their customers are used to their local market, so they will naturally gravitate their make-shift black market there.

Italy, for example, has a massive black market. Actually, it may be up to 1/3 of their economy. Items you would expect to be factory-made in the white market, such as light manufacturing, gets completed by literally hundreds of thousands of individuals working out of their makeshift factory garages. If you have a kickass workshop, you can match the quality of any mass-made factory and achieve modest output. For example, the black market's labs can nearly match those of pharmaceutical companies. The black market has manufactured "roofies" (Rohypnol), also known as the "date rape" drug. No legitimate drug company would even try to produce such an appalling product. The government would never allow it; but a fiend can pick up those pretty little pills effortlessly off the black market.

Regardless of how much you prep, you will never think of everything you will ever need. Eventually, you will be forced to enter the black market one way or the other—maybe for medical supplies, canned food, ammo, or even a few solar panels that you thought were a waste of money before TSHTF. You may need something like a box of roofing nails or a roll of electrical tape.

The simple things like that you tend to forget about in your preparedness checklist, but if you have to have them, and the stores are being looted to the bone, better hop on over and see if a brother's got it at the black market.

Trading with someone is better than giving to charity, in the sense that it will benefit both of you. By trading, you will develop reliance on each other instead of it just being a one-sided relationship, where disloyalty may creep about. It's possible that neither you nor your neighbor has anything to trade amongst each other. The one thing you can always trade is shared protection. Covering each other's backs is a great place to start building trust.

What if you get ripped off? In the black market, you don't have the option of getting a refund, and I doubt there would be an exchange policy. For example, if you trade for some reloaded ammo and it turns out to be filled with fine-grain sand rather than real powder, well then, you've been played. The best thing you can do is take it as a learning experience and not deal with that "traitor" again. Otherwise, if you seek recourse or revenge, you may be filled with the ammo they've been saving. The black market is much more like the Wild West than Costco.

Despite the potential of desperation, it's morally imperative to be fair to the party that is most in need. Remember that one day, that person who is most in need may be you.

Pre-Crisis Exercise
Watch people shop and what type of advertising works in order to lure them in. Go to an auction and nonchalantly observe transactions. Listen in on sales pitches, closing offers, and body language. Practice bartering—exchanging your money for goods—at an auction. Watch how prices change from the start of the event to the close. Learn from vendors the art of presentation.

Short-Term Crisis

During a short-term crisis that isolates people from stores, bartering will include exchanging cash for goods or the exchanging of food items. If you are sure the crisis will be short-lived, you can consider providing goods at low-barter cost to assist those in greatest need.

Long-Term Crisis

An economic collapse will cause a long-term crisis that will end production, storage, and transportation of goods. Consider the various stages of a long-term crisis and decide what skills would benefit you and what you should stockpile in preparation. What will become scarce? What will people need during each phase? What goods should be held back for the next phase? What essential material can be refurbished and repaired using low-tech methods and tools?

Value of Goods

The value of your trade goods will be determined by essential need and observed shortage. Even if there is a large supply of a specific item, the price will be greater if there is an alleged low supply. The value of goods will also change over the duration of the crisis as needs, conditions, and availability changes.

Early Phases

Early on there will be some goods that will disappear quickly, some will be essential, while others will soon become the new luxury items. When was the last time you considered a bar of soap a luxury, or even a necessity, that you had to ration? As bartering becomes more prevalent after the SHTF, you will have to be able to decide where, what, and when to barter. Additionally, for economic survival, you need to be careful not to over-value or under-value goods and services you can provide, or the goods and services that others have available.

Alternate Options

When some goods become scarce or unavailable, there may

be possible alternatives to replace them. When toilet paper vanishes, newspaper will be sought after. Homemade soap will soon replace dwindling, mass-produced soap, and homemade disinfectant will be high on the list. With no electrical power, being able to make candles and lanterns may become your new job. As time passes, tools and other non-consumables will break and wear out, therefore, your future calling may include becoming a technician.

Danger of Inefficient Bartering
If you stock barter items for trade during an economic crisis, be careful not to barter yourself into the poor house. Inefficient bartering can result in you running out of barter goods, having exchanged them for consumables that you cannot replace.

Use of Sympathy Technique
As a buyer, you may be able to elicit some sympathy from a seller, by providing a sad story of need and be able to pull off a lower barter price or exchange. If you adopt this practice, be truthful, or you will get a reputation for being a crook.

Beware Bait & Switch
Don't assume the goods you receive from behind the curtain or from under the table will be the same quality as the goods that are seen on display. Provide payment only after you have examined the exact goods you will receive. Check expiration dates on canned and other packaged perishables. Check for wear and damage on all items.

Have a List
When out bartering, you may not be able to have all of your barter items on hand, so keep a list of them instead, but don't give away any information related to the quantity or location, except for making offers.

Poker-Face Buying
Don't drool over or have a big, dumb smile on your face when you see something you really want. It's a sure way to have the price go up. Too much negative or positive emotion

displayed during a barter transaction can hurt you both. A good buyer-seller relationship will be established only if both parties think they got a fair deal.

No Impulse or Panic Buying
Don't get caught up in the "rarity" of a specific trade good simply based on what is on display. Stick to your list and only get what you need, or what you think will increase in value for selling at a later date.

First and Last Offers
Let the buyer be the first to set the price. He or she may be willing to give more than you expected. If you don't like the price, tell them how scarce and necessary the item is. This will psychologically reinforce the buyer's initial interest in the item. A poker face is helpful. If you have to make a first offer, make it higher than what you expect you can get, but not unreasonable high. A counter-offer will probably be made by the potential buyer. There are options: add more goods for a sweetener, or remove some to meet the needs of the buyer. When a potential buyer exhibits an "I can do without it" attitude, you need to decide if you can live with a lower offer or just need to let him or her walk away. Never leave a bartering situation with less than you arrived with.

Competition
Your goods must be cheaper, more attractive, or in better condition than the goods of your competitors. The crucial key is "visually" better. If there is no outward cue that it is better made and/or works better, then the perception of it being more valuable is lost.

Location
If you arrive late, you will end up with a back lot area for your goods. Be early and get a prime location about twenty yards from the entrance for a large trade day. Better yet, see if you can reserve a good location before trade day. For smaller trade days, pick a location about five spots in, on the left, of the main thoroughfare.

Right-handed people will generally look to their left first. It takes a minute or two for people to adjust to the idea of buying, even though they came for that very reason, so you want to be close to the left side of the front entrance, but not too close.

Security
Make sure you leave adequate security back home when your group goes out for a day of bartering, or you may return to find all your precious things gone for good.

Assess Trade-Day Threats
Remember, we are talking about a total collapse, so depraved and/or desperate people will be looking for any advantage they can get. If trade-day organizers do not provide perimeter and internal security, you need to evaluate how many of your group members need to be visibly carrying a firearm to discourage theft and assault; however, don't act as a perceived threat to others. Practice situational awareness, and refrain from going off with someone alone so they can "show you something."

After Making a Deal
Once a bargain is made, be sure to quickly close the deal by making the actual exchange. Take your new purchases and keep them undercover and under guard. Trade days will attract thieves.

Prevent Post-Trade Theft
Be on guard for people loitering around your barter area. They may be casing the joint. Keep all your trade goods inside your roped-off trade area, and establish a "no goods" zone of more than an arm's length inside your rope barrier. Don't be talkative about where you live, the number of people there, or conditions at your living area. Don't wear your best clothes to trade days, but be clean, neat, and polite. Strike a balance between appearing not too needy and not too well-off.

Make your Defense Visible
Keep your firearms very visible during travel to and from a trade day. Thieves on foot and modern highwaymen will prey upon the unaware and unarmed.

Beware "Security" Services
Rogue groups may materialize in your area with muscles and weapons, offering security for your refuge or protection during your passage to and from trade days. These same people may also be engaged in shake-downs, extortion, and intimidation tactics, as well as sizing-up you and your supplies for the taking.

Top 100 Black-Market-Trading Items
Post Collapse

1. Generators
2. Water filters/purifiers
3. Portable toilets
4. Seasoned firewood
5. Lamps, oil, and wicks
6. Coleman fuel
7. Guns, ammo, pepper spray, knives, bats, and slingshots
8. Manual can openers, rotary egg beaters, and whisks.
9. Honey, syrups, white and brown sugar

10. Rice, beans , and wheat
11. Vegetable oil
12. Charcoal and lighter fluid
13. Water containers
14. Mini heater head (propane)
15. Grain grinder (non-electric)
16. Propane cylinders
17. Survival-guide books
18. Mantles: Aladdin, Coleman, etc.
19. Baby supplies: baby wipes, diapers, formula, ointments, Tylenol/Motrin, etc.
20. Washboards, mop bucket w/wringer (for laundry)
21. Cook stoves (Propane, Coleman, and Kerosene)
22. Vitamin and mineral tablets
23. Propane cylinder handle-holder
24. Feminine hygiene, hair care, skin products
25. Thermal underwear (tops & bottoms)
26. Bow saws, axes, hatchets, wedges (also, honing oil)
27. Aluminum foil (regular and heavy duty—great cooking and barter item)
28. Gasoline containers (plastic and metal)
29. Garbage bags (impossible to have too many)
30. Toilet paper, Kleenex, and paper towels
31. Milk (powdered and condensed—shake liquid every three to four months)
32. Garden seeds (non-hybrid)
33. Clothes pins, line, and hangers
34. Coleman pump-repair kit
35. Tuna fish (in oil)
36. Fire extinguishers (or large box of baking soda in every room)
37. First-aid kits
38. Batteries (all sizes—buy farthest-out expiration dates)
39. Garlic, spices, vinegar, and baking supplies
40. Big dogs (and plenty of dog food)
41. Flour, yeast, and salt
42. Matches (strike anywhere is preferred—boxed, wooden matches will go first)
43. Writing paper, pads, pencils, and solar calculators

44. Insulated ice chests (good for keeping items from freezing in wintertime)
45. Work boots, belts, Levis, and durable shirts
46. Flashlights, light sticks, and LED lanterns
47. Journals, diaries, scrapbooks (jot down ideas, feelings, experiences, and historic times)
48. Garbage cans (plastic is great for storage, water, and transporting—if they have wheels)
49. Men's hygiene, shampoo, toothbrush, toothpaste, mouthwash, floss, nail clippers, etc.
50. Cast-iron cookware
51. Fishing supplies
52. Mosquito coils, repellent, and sprays/creams
53. Duct tape
54. Tarps, stakes, twine, nails, rope, and 550 cord
55. Candles
56. Laundry detergent
57. Backpacks and duffel bags
58. Garden tools and supplies
59. Scissors, fabrics, and sewing supplies
60. Canned fruits, veggies, soups, stews, etc.
61. Bleach (plain, NOT scented: 5–6% sodium hypochlorite)
62. Canning supplies (jars, lids, and wax)
63. Knives and sharpening tools (files, stones, and steel)
64. Bicycles (tires, tubes, pumps, chains, etc.)
65. Sleeping bags, blankets, pillows, and mats
66. Carbon monoxide alarm (battery powered)
67. Board games, cards, and dice
68. Rat, mouse, and roach killer
69. Mousetraps, ant traps, and cockroach magnets
70. Paper plates, cups, and utensils
71. Baby wipes, oils, waterless, and anti-bacterial soap (saves a lot of water)
72. Rain gear, rubberized boots, etc.
73. Shaving supplies (razors, creams, talc, and aftershave)
74. Hand pumps & siphons (for water and for fuels)
75. Soy sauce, vinegar, bouillons, gravy, and soup bases

76. Reading glasses
77. Chocolate, cocoa, Tang, Emergen-C, and punch (water enhancers)
78. Survival Kit in a Sardine Can
79. Woolen clothing, scarves, earmuffs, and mittens
80. Boy Scout handbook, as well as Leader handbook
81. Window-insulation kit
82. Graham crackers, saltines, pretzels, trail mix, and jerky
83. Popcorn, peanut butter, and nuts
84. Socks, underwear, T-shirts, etc.
85. Lumber (all types)
86. Wagons and carts (for transport to and from)
87. Cots and inflatable mattresses
88. Gloves (work, warming, gardening, and latex)
89. Lantern hangers
90. Screen patches, glue, nails, screws, nuts, and bolts
91. Teas
92. Coffee
93. Cigarettes
94. Wine and liquors (for bribes and medicinal uses)
95. Paraffin wax
96. Condoms
97. Chewing gum and candies
98. Atomizers (for cooling/bathing)
99. Hats and cotton handkerchiefs
100. Goats and chickens

This list is not all encompassing, so think of anything that may be important to YOU and store it. Even if some of these things don't interest you, they are superb to use for bartering, so stock-up anyway. Make sure that you have multiples of each item, because as the old adage goes, "two is one, and one is none."

Top-Priority Trades/Skills for Barter

Right now, if something breaks, the replacement is only as far away as the closest Wal-Mart. However, in the event of an economic collapse or a disaster that causes the trucks to stop running, it won't be easy to replace broken items. The ability to repair broken items will be in very-high demand. It will be a rare skill, because we live in a world of planned obsolescence. Few people actually know how to repair an item in a sturdy and long-lasting way.

Brandon Smith of Alt-Market calls this, "bringing back the American Tradesman:"

> If you wish to survive after the destruction of the mainstream system that has babied us for so long, you must be able to either make a necessary product, repair a necessary product, or teach a necessary skill. A limited few have the capital required to stockpile enough barter goods or gold and silver to live indefinitely. The American Tradesman must return in full force, not only for the sake of self-preservation, but also for the sake of our heritage at large.

There is no limit to the skills that could be used in a barter situation. Provided below is a brief list of skills which have served people well in various economic downturns and will do the same for you in this country. Keep in mind that almost any skill that other people can't perform well has potential for trade, but some skills are more sought after than others. It is those people who are able to produce their own goods, as well as effectively repair existing goods, that have the greatest potential for survival in a barter market. Next are those people who have specific abilities that are difficult to learn and who have the knack for teaching those abilities to others. If you do not have any of these skills, or perhaps only one, then it would be wise to begin learning at least one or more now.

Keep in mind that extreme competition will exist in a barter economy, so knowing as many skills as possible increases your chances for success.

- Mechanic
- Welder
- Blacksmith
- Gunsmith/ammo reloading
- Construction
- Architect
- Boatwright/nautical
- Agriculturalist/gardening/seed saving
- Animal husbandry
- Veterinarian
- Bee Keeping
- Doctor/nurse/medical assistant/first aid
- Midwife
- Dentistry
- Herbalist/natural medicine
- Chemist
- Well construction/water-table expert/water purification
- Engineer
- Community planning
- Manufacturing
- Electrician
- Martial-arts expert
- Botany/wild-foods expert
- Hunting/animal trapping/fishing/gathering
- Home economist/food processing and preservation
- Textiles/sewing
- Soap making/candle making/hygiene products
- Small-appliance repair
- Electronics repair
- HAM-radio expert
- School teacher/homeschooling/tutoring

- Firearms proficiency/security services/self-defense planning
- Preacher/theologian
- Alternative energy and fuels expert
- Winemaking/brewing/alcohol distillation (ONLY RECOMMENDED for medicinal/topical purposes)
- UNFORTUNATELY prostitution (NOT RECOMMENDED, but inevitable, as can be seen throughout human history)

Again, there are definitely many more trades of value that could be learned. This list is only to help you on your way to self-sufficiency and entrepreneurship in an alternative market. Unfortunately, too many Americans have absolutely no skills worth bartering in a post-collapse world.

24
COPING WITH DISASTER

Disasters are upsetting experiences for everyone involved. The emotional toll that disaster brings can sometimes be even more devastating than the financial strains of damage and loss of home, business, or personal property.

Children, senior citizens, people with access or functional needs, and people for whom English is not their first language are especially at risk. Children may become afraid, and some elderly people may seem disoriented at first. People with access or functional needs may require additional assistance. Seek crisis counseling if you or someone in your family is experiencing issues with disaster-related stress.

Understand the Individual Effects of a Disaster

- Everyone who sees or experiences a disaster is affected by it in some way.
- It is normal to feel anxious about your own safety and that of your family and close friends.
- Profound sadness, grief, and anger are normal reactions to an abnormal event.
- Acknowledging your feelings will help you to recover.
- Focusing on your strengths and abilities will help you to heal.
- Everyone has different needs and different ways of coping.
- It is common to want to strike back at people who have caused great pain.

Children and older adults are of special concern in the aftermath of disasters. Even individuals who experience a disaster "second hand" through exposure to extensive media coverage can also be affected.

As you recover, it is a good idea to make sure that you have updated your family-disaster plan and replenished essential disaster supplies just in case a disaster happens again. You will always feel better knowing that you are prepared and ready for anything.

Recognize Signs of Disaster-Related Stress
When adults have the following signs, they might need crisis counseling or stress management assistance:

- Difficulty communicating thoughts
- Trouble sleeping
- Effort maintaining balance in their lives
- Low threshold of frustration
- Increased use of drugs/alcohol
- Limited attention span
- Headaches/stomach problems
- Tunnel vision/muffled hearing
- Colds or flu-like symptoms
- Disorientation or confusion
- Reluctance to leave home
- Depression/sadness
- Feelings of hopelessness
- Mood-swings and easy bouts of crying
- Overwhelming guilt and self-doubt
- Fear of crowds, strangers, or being alone

Easing Stress
The following are ways to ease disaster-related stress:

- Talk with someone about your feelings—anger, sorrow, and other emotions—even though it may be difficult.

- Do not hold yourself responsible for the disastrous event or be frustrated because you feel you cannot help directly in the rescue work.
- Take steps to promote your own physical and emotional healing by healthy eating, rest, exercise, relaxation, and meditation.
- Maintain a normal family and daily routine, limiting demanding responsibilities on yourself and your family.
- Spend time with family and friends.
- Participate in memorials.
- Ensure you are ready for future events by restocking your disaster-supplies kits and updating your family-disaster plan. Doing these positive actions can be comforting.

Helping Kids Cope with Disaster

Disasters can leave children feeling frightened, confused, and insecure. Whether a child has personally experienced trauma, has merely seen the event on television, or has heard it discussed by adults, it is important for parents and teachers to be informed and ready to help if reactions to stress begin to occur.

Children may respond to disaster by demonstrating fears, sadness, or behavioral problems. Younger children may return to earlier behavior patterns, such as bedwetting, sleep problems, and separation anxiety. Older children may also display anger, aggression, school problems, or withdrawal. Some children who have only indirect contact with the disaster, but witness it on television, may develop distress.

Recognize Risk Factors

For many children, reactions to disasters are brief and represent normal reactions to "abnormal events." A smaller number of children can be at risk for more enduring psychological distress as a function of three major risk factors:

- **Direct exposure to the disaster** includes being evacuated, observing injuries or death of others, or experiencing injury along with fearing one's life is in danger.
- **Loss/grief** relates to the death or serious injury of family or friends.
- **Ongoing stress from the secondary effects of disaster** would include temporarily living elsewhere, loss of friends and social networks, loss of personal property, parental unemployment, and costs incurred during recovery to return the family to pre-disaster life and living conditions.

Vulnerabilities in Children
In most cases, depending on the risk factors above, distressing responses are temporary. In the absence of severe threat to life, injury, loss of loved ones, or secondary problems such as loss of home, moves, etc., symptoms usually diminish over time. For those that were directly exposed to the disaster, reminders of the disaster, such as high winds, smoke, cloudy skies, sirens, or other reminders of the disaster, may cause upsetting feelings to return. Having a prior history of some type of traumatic event or severe stress may contribute to these feelings.

The way a child copes with a disaster or an emergency is often tied to the way their parents cope. They can detect adults' fears and sadness. Parents and adults can make disasters less traumatic for children by taking steps to manage their own feelings and by making plans for coping. Parents are almost always the best source of support for children in disasters. One way to establish a sense of control and to build confidence in children before a disaster is to engage and involve them in preparing a family-disaster plan. After a disaster, children can contribute to a family-recovery plan.

Meeting the Child's Emotional Needs

Children's reactions are influenced by the behavior, thoughts, and feelings of adults. Adults should encourage children and adolescents to share their thoughts and feelings about the incident. Clarify misunderstandings about risk and danger by listening to children's concerns and answering their questions. Maintain a sense of calm by validating children's concerns and perceptions and with discussion of concrete plans for safety.

Listen to what the child is saying. If a young child is asking questions about the event, answer them simply, without the elaboration needed for an older child or adult. Some children are comforted by knowing more or less information than others; decide what level of information your particular child needs. If a child has difficulty expressing feelings, allow the child to draw a picture or tell a story of what happened.

Try to understand what is causing anxieties and fears. Be aware that following a disaster, children are most afraid that:

- The event will happen again.
- Someone close to them will be killed or injured.
- They will be left alone or separated from their family.

Reassuring Children after a Disaster

- Personal contact is reassuring. Hug and touch your children.
- Calmly provide factual information about the recent disaster and current plans for insuring their safety, along with recovery plans.
- Encourage your children to talk about their feelings.
- Spend extra time with your children, such as at bedtime.
- Re-establish your daily routine for work, school, play, meals, and rest.
- Praise and recognize responsible behavior.

- Understand that your children will have a range of reactions to disasters.

Monitor and Limit Exposure to the Media
News coverage related to a disaster may elicit fear, confusion, and arouse anxiety in children. This is particularly true for large-scale disasters or a terrorist event, where significant property damage and loss of life has occurred. Particularly for younger children, repeated images of an event may cause them to believe the event is recurring over and over again.

Use Support Networks
Parents help their children when they take steps to understand and manage their own feelings and ways of coping. They can do this by building and using social-support systems of family, friends, community organizations and agencies, faith-based institutions, or other resources that work for that family. Parents can build their own unique social-support systems, so that in an emergency situation or when a disaster strikes, they can be supported and helped to manage their reactions. As a result, parents will be more available to their children and better able to care for them. Parents are almost always the best source of encouragement for their children in difficult times. But to support their children, parents need to attend to their own needs and have a plan for their own support.

Preparing for disaster helps everyone in the family accept the fact that disasters do happen and provides an opportunity to identify and collect the resources needed to meet basic needs after disaster. Preparation helps; when adults feel prepared, they cope better, and so do children.

A Child's Reaction to Disaster by Age

Below are common reactions in children after a disaster or traumatic event.

Birth through 2 years: When children are pre-verbal and experience a trauma, they do not have the words to describe the event or their feelings. However, they can retain memories of particular sights, sounds, or smells. Infants may react to trauma by being irritable, crying more than usual, or wanting to be held and cuddled. The biggest influence on children of this age is how their parents cope. As children get older, their play may involve acting out elements of the traumatic event that occurred several years in the past and was seemingly forgotten.

Preschool (3 through 6 years): Preschool children often feel helpless and powerless in the face of an overwhelming event. Because of their age and small size, they lack the ability to protect themselves or others. As a result, they feel intense fear and insecurity about being separated from caregivers. Preschoolers cannot grasp the concept of permanent loss. They can see consequences as being reversible or permanent. In the weeks following a traumatic event, preschoolers' play activities may reenact the incident or the disaster over and over again.

School age (7 through 10 years): The school-age child has the ability to understand the permanence of loss. Some children become intensely preoccupied with the details of a traumatic event and want to talk about it continually. This preoccupation can interfere with the child's concentration at school and their academic performance may decline. At school, children may hear inaccurate information from peers. They may display a wide range of reactions—sadness, generalized fear, or specific fears of the disaster happening again, guilt over action or inaction during the disaster, anger that the event was not prevented, or fantasies of playing rescuer.

Pre-adolescence to adolescence (11 through 18 years): As children grow older, they develop a more sophisticated understanding of the disaster event. Their responses are more similar to adults. Teenagers may become involved in dangerous, risk-taking behaviors, such as reckless driving, alcohol use, or drug use. Others can become fearful of leaving home and avoid previous levels of activities. Much of adolescence is focused on moving out into the world. After a trauma, the view of the world can seem more dangerous and unsafe. A teenager may feel overwhelmed by intense emotions, yet feel unable to discuss them with others.

25
CONCLUSION

America Is Dependent On Survivalists
The title "survivalist" would have seemed redundant a couple of generations ago. When the Greatest Generation was growing up, preparedness was simply a way of life. Before the Federal Emergency Management Agency (FEMA), Social Security, Medicare, Medicaid, and other federal-aid programs were around, people knew that they had to be able to take care of themselves in the event of natural and man-made disasters.

At the core, that's what survivalists are. They are people who are aware that life is full of uncertainty and who have decided to put things into place for when bad times occur.

FEMA (Foolishly Expecting Meaningful Aide)
The cost for local, state, and federal agencies to plan, equip, and staff for every disaster that might happen is cost-prohibitive. When disaster strikes, the government is quick to talk and "ramp-up," but government help is slow in coming and inefficient when it arrives. The irony is how often highly qualified and motivated front-line first responders are prevented from doing as much as they could by top-heavy bureaucracies.

Survivalists, on the other hand, are able to act fast and efficiently to take care of their own households and provide stability, structure, and assistance for their streets, neighborhoods, and beyond. Because they know the terrain and the players in the areas where they live and operate, they can quickly establish stable micro-environments for recovery to grow from.

Stable Base

An organization (or nation) of people with narrowly focused, specialized skills may accomplish great things when everything is going smoothly, but it quickly falls apart when trouble comes, and key people are knocked-out.

The survivalist mind-set of jack-of-all-trades makes for a stable organization (or nation). If the specialist falls or needs help, others can help pick up the slack—even if it means they're doing it at a slower speed or lower level of proficiency.

Noah and Joseph in the Bible

Survivalists have been around saving the day since the beginning of time. In Genesis 6–9, Noah and his family prepare for a worldwide flood over the course of 125 years. "You are to take every kind of food that is to be eaten and store it away as food for you and for them [the animals]." (Genesis 6:21) That's A LOT of prepping! God tells Noah to build an ark, giving him exact dimensions and instructions for its construction. Noah follows His guidance faithfully. Noah warned the people of his day to repent and go on board before it was too late. While the rest of humanity drowned, only he, his wife, his three sons, and their three wives survived. They survived for a year in that boat—370 days to be exact, if using the Hebrew calendar. That is some serious prepping, especially when you consider all of the animals onboard—one pair of each kind of unclean animal and seven pairs of each kind of clean animal and bird. We should thank Noah for his obedience to God; otherwise, none of us would be here today.

Also, in Genesis 37–50, the story of Joseph is told. Joseph is asked to interpret Pharaoh's enigmatic dreams. Through God's inspiration, he is the only one who can do so, and because of this and his recommendations on "prepping," he is placed in charge of Egypt, only second to Pharaoh. As foretold in the dreams, there are seven years of surplus, followed by seven years of famine. He makes ample preparations during the seven years of bounty. At the end of the seven years, as predicted, a severe drought and famine hit that lasted for the next seven years. Because of Joseph's preparations, Egypt survived and was able to help the surrounding nations survive as well.

In both instances, Noah and Joseph were not just selfishly trying to save their own hides, but instead, thought of others and did whatever they could to bring them to the truth and save them from destruction. Please take the time to read each of these stories as written in the Bible. You won't regret it!

Founding Fathers
With the Constitution and Bill of Rights, our Founding Fathers shifted responsibility from the Federal government to the individual citizen, promoting a survivalist mentality. They did it with the 2nd and 4th Amendments, they did it by example (Washington leading a mostly barefoot army across the Delaware), and they did it throughout their writings.

Siege Warfare
Many of the things that happened after Hurricane Katrina are textbook examples of why siege warfare is so effective. The normal city has a three-day supply of food. The normal survivalist has a six- to 24-month supply of food.

Which do you think is more stable in the event of a siege, whether from disasters or warfare? If you focus only on food and water supplies, a city, county, region, or country with many survivalists will be much more resilient to being cut off from outside help than one with few survivalists.

Criminals Fear the Aware and Prepared
Survivalists gradually become more aware and prepared than the average person. This will show itself in your walk, in your eyes, and how you carry yourself. In short, you stop looking like a wounded gazelle and more like a badger—cute and cuddly, but ready to do anything necessary to stop a threat to yourself or to your loved ones.

Tyrants Fear Survivalists

In addition to living a lifestyle that insulates them from siege, some taxes, and being babysat, survivalists are usually well-armed and seek advanced training. Good men have nothing to fear from an armed populace, but tyrants who seek to control the lives of others will always try to disarm them, first through confiscation, taxation, or pressure through media and the education system.

It worked for Adolf Hitler, Mao Zedong, and many more narcissistic, mass murders throughout the ages. It worked so far back, in fact, that Aristotle spoke extensively about how, in any society, those who control the arms control the state.

More Survivalists Mean Fewer Refugees and Faster Recovery from Disasters

After a local, regional, or national disaster, the number of refugees will be inversely proportionate to the number of survivalists in the area. In other words, the more preppers you have in an area, the less strain the hospitals, volunteer organizations, and government-run refugee centers will have.

Preppers are More Able to Help Their Fellow Man

After a disaster, you're not going to see very many refugees donating their food, supplies, or time. It's not that they don't want to, but rather, it's because they are in a fight for their lives and may be dehydrated, hungry, and tired.

Survivalists who have food storage, water, water-treatment devices, and who have prepared themselves psychologically for disasters, will be able to help in several ways.

First, they are less likely to become refugees or use the time and resources of first responders. Second, since they are prepared for disasters, they can help the people in their immediate area, which will lessen the load on first responders and reduce the number of refugees. Third, by helping themselves and their neighbors, survivalists will increase the quality of care for people who do need first-responder care or who need to relocate to a refugee center. In short, the more survivalists we have, the more stable our families, cities, and country are as a whole.

Being Ready
In the military, soldiers are conditioned and trained beforehand and made to be as prepared as possible for the real hardships on and off the battlefield. The survivalist can be more mentally and physically prepared for the unraveling of civilization that so many feel is inevitable.

Self-reliance also has to do with being ready for the sudden loss of everything we all have become way too accustomed to. Experiencing a type of mock realism can make you more mentally prepared. The following tips should help you cope better when things do start to fall apart.

1. See what it is like to go without the utilities, such as electricity, by turning them off for at least a couple of hours.
2. Go at least 24 hours without electronic conveniences: no computer, no television, no cell phone, etc. This will be a wakeup call for many.
3. The internet will not be there after many catastrophes, so become accustomed to receiving information from other sources, such as books.
4. Spend some nights using only candles and/or battery-operated lights to illuminate the darkness.
5. Start storing rainwater, and then water your plants and garden with it.
6. Try cooking some of your meals using a solar oven, barbecue, fire-pit, or something not dependent on the grid.
7. Flush the toilet for one day or more using only water you have previously stored, or use a portable toilet.
8. Instead of throwing away a piece of damaged clothing, try to repair it, sew it, then re-wear it.
9. Take any household item and write down every creative way you can use it.

10. Find an alternative for your trash disposal, something besides the city trash collection.
11. Have a simulated illness and fictionally treat it with what you have on hand to see what you are missing.
12. Gather your family and friends together and see what it's like for all of you to be confined to a smaller space.
13. Use other means of cooling or heating your home for a few days—remember to do so safely.
14. Try walking or bicycling, rather than using a motor vehicle, to run errands.
15. Start spending some very quiet time alone. You may have to be alone after TSHTF.
16. Try using alternative means of bathing, like using one of those solar showers or heating water over a fire to be used to bathe with.
17. Look at "junk" in a different manner. Instead, see it as "obtainium," the term coined by Chris Hackett to mean recycling scrap for useful purposes.
18. Try washing dishes and clothes without using the dishwasher or washing machine, and dry clothes on a clothes line.
19. Purify polluted water using various methods (don't drink unless you are sure it is clean).
20. Take along a pad of paper and write down everything you see at a park or recreation area. Observation skills will help you stay alive better after chaos breaks loose.
21. Try to locate someplace off the beaten path using only a paper map, compass, or landmarks.
22. Spend some days outdoors when the weather is miserable (not dangerous), since you may have to live this way in the future.
23. See how fast you can get your essentials together and how quickly you can get ready to leave.
24. Use alternative means to forecast the weather, such as an altimeter, barometer, and thermometer.

25. If you plan to stay where you are, thoroughly become familiar with every street, landmark, tree, house, etc., within two miles of your home, and walk the area often.
26. See what it's like to ration food and water for a day or two.
27. Safely test your physical limits by seeing how far you can walk with a backpack of supplies.
28. Start saving spare parts—screws, springs, nails, etc.— and fix something only using what you have stored.
29. Take classes on identifying safe plants to eat, and then practice in your area.
30. Go to garage sales and flea markets, and trade rather than use cash to sharpen your bartering skills. Start a trading system with other like-minded people. These are wonderful ways to practice post-apocalyptic commerce.
31. Without endangering your safety, learn the ways that local homeless people get by with what they have and can find.
32. Go to your local supermarket and make a mental map of the store and where you can go as quickly as possible to get what you need when panic buying starts.
33. Find places to rapidly hide your food and supplies that are not already hidden.
34. Put together a safe room, and spend some serious time there, only coming out to go to the bathroom.
35. Travel to all your predetermined escape routes, and calculate the time it takes to reach each destination.
36. Have supplies ready, such as plywood, to board up windows to secure your home from intruders.
37. Establish a list of "human leeches," and regard them as threats to your survival supplies.
38. Train small children and pets to go to a safe area by command.
39. Federal, state, and local disaster drills are way too infrequent for your mind to take hold of. Strive for weekly drills of your own.

40. Depending on your location, write down in great detail what you can expect in various disastrous situations. This will help you prepare for worst case scenarios.
41. Practice staying calm and thinking straight; use breathing exercises and anything to keep you as collected during emergency situations as possible.
42. Spend some nights sleeping outside in your backyard, or go camping.
43. Instead of completely relying on electronic devices for storing important information, make a habit of writing things down or printing them out so that you have a hardcopy.
44. Learn to play various card and classic board games or anything that can entertain you and your family that does not require electricity or batteries.
45. Become a master of learning human idiosyncrasies, mannerisms, facial expressions, and movements. This is invaluable when dealing with irrational and/or probably unsafe people after a calamity occurs.

The truly "ready" survivalist should be training to be prepared to undergo things that are going to be vastly different and very difficult to adjust to. By using some or all of these preparation tips now and before the aftermath of "the nightmare" that is coming, you will be more able to adapt. Add your personal-preparation exercises to this list to make you even more "mega disaster" ready.

Courage for the Crisis

No one needs to be told that the world is moving into ever-deepening crisis. The tragic fact is obvious to us all. Recently the pace of analysis has quickened. Scarcely a day goes by before a new story emerges that not only warns, but shows us the imminent peril of our civilization.

A recent survey conducted by National Geographic asked Americans the following question:

"Which of the following, if any, do you think might happen in the United States in the next 25 years? Please choose all that apply."

These were the results:

Significant Earthquake 64%
Significant Hurricane 63%
Terrorist Attack 55%
Financial Collapse 51%
Significant Blackout 37%
Pandemic, Such as From a Super-Virus 29%
Nuclear Fallout 14%
None of These 13%

People are genuinely afraid of the future. They are convinced that mankind is moving toward some major catastrophe. They may differ as to its nature, but not about its certainty. The depression, frustration, and despair that will envelop the hearts of millions in a cloud of gloom is almost upon us.

What we all need in this "time of trouble" is not merely knowledge of the crisis, but courage to meet it. We need to build up reserves of mental and spiritual strength sufficient to face any calamity victoriously. We need to develop an inner calm that will remain unruffled no matter what may happen. We must learn how to greet the future with optimism and stand unmoved in the evil day.

Where shall peace of mind and tranquility of spirit be found? It is my conviction that sources of spiritual strength exist which may be tapped by all who sense their need of it, and from that flows courage sufficient to meet every emergency.

Courage may flow into our hearts from the knowledge that God is Creator and Sustainer of the universe. The many Bible promises of His care and protection will also give strength to the weak. The cross itself, with its dramatic assurances of God's concern for the human race, lends compassion to the broken-hearted. From those essentials of Christian living, such as Bible study, prayer, worship, and ministry to others, comes true purpose and meaning of life.

Such are some of the sources of true courage, courage sufficient for every trial, courage that will endure undiminished until the worst is over and darkness yields to the light.

Spiritual Considerations

- Collect your thoughts and emotions.
- Identify your personal beliefs.
- Use self-control.
- Recall past interventions by God, both small and great, that helped you overcome adversity. This will strengthen and encourage you, giving you hope to endure to the end.
- Talk to God.
- Give thanks that God is with you.
- Pray for protection and a positive outcome.
- Recite Scripture or hymns, repeating them to yourself and to God.
- God is bigger than your circumstances.
- Never lose hope.
- Never give up.
- With other survivors, identify or appoint a religious leader.
- Share Scriptures and songs.
- Pray for each other.
- Have worship services.
- Remember, God loves you!

Scriptures in Support of Survivalism

Proverbs 6:6–11 (NLT)
6Take a lesson from the ants, you lazybones. Learn from their ways and become wise! 7Though they have no prince or governor or ruler to make them work, 8they labor hard all summer, gathering food for the winter. 9But you, lazybones, how long will you sleep? When will you wake up? 10A little extra sleep, a little more slumber, a little folding of the hands to rest—11then poverty will pounce on you like a bandit; scarcity will attack you like an armed robber.

Proverbs 27:12 (NLT)
A prudent person foresees danger and takes precautions. The simpleton goes blindly on and suffers the consequences.

1 Timothy 5:8 (NIV)
If anyone does not provide for his relatives, and especially for his immediate family, he has denied the faith and is worse than an unbeliever.

Psalm 144:1 (NLT)
A psalm of David. Praise the LORD, who is my rock. He trains my hands for war and gives my fingers skill for battle.

Luke 22:36 (NIV)
He said to them, "But now if you have a purse, take it, and also a bag; and if you don't have a sword, sell your cloak and buy one.

Hebrews 11:7 (NIV)
By faith Noah, when warned about things not yet seen, in holy fear built an ark to save his family. By his faith he condemned the world and became heir of the righteousness that comes by faith.

Genesis 6:21 (NIV)
You are to take every kind of food that is to be eaten and store it away as food for you and for them."

Genesis 41:33–36 (NLT)
"Therefore, Pharaoh should find an intelligent and wise man and put him in charge of the entire land of Egypt. 34Then Pharaoh should appoint supervisors over the land and let them collect one-fifth of all the crops during the seven good years. 35Have them gather all the food produced in the good years that are just ahead and bring it to Pharaoh's storehouses. Store it away, and guard it so there will be food in the cities. 36That way there will be enough to eat when the seven years of famine come to the land of Egypt. Otherwise this famine will destroy the land."

Genesis 41:48–49 (NIV)
48Joseph collected all the food produced in those seven years of abundance in Egypt and stored it in the cities. In each city he put the food grown in the fields surrounding it. 49Joseph stored up huge quantities of grain, like the sand of the sea; it was so much that he stopped keeping records because it was beyond measure.

Genesis 19:16–17 (NLT)
16When Lot still hesitated, the angels seized his hand and the hands of his wife and two daughters and rushed them to safety outside the city, for the Lord was merciful. 17When they were safely out of the city, one of the angels ordered, "Run for your lives! And don't look back or stop anywhere in the valley! Escape to the mountains, or you will be swept away!"

Genesis 19:30 (NIV)
Lot and his two daughters left Zoar and settled in the mountains, for he was afraid to stay in Zoar. He and his two daughters lived in a cave.

Mark 13:14 (NIV)
"When you see 'the abomination that causes desolation' standing where it does not belong—let the reader understand—then let those who are in Judea flee to the mountains.

Scriptures for Troubled Times

Psalm 4:8 (NIV)
I will lie down and sleep in peace, for you alone, O LORD, make me dwell in safety.

Isaiah 26:3 (NIV)
You will keep in perfect peace those whose minds are steadfast, because they trust in you.

Matthew 6:27 (NIV)
Who of you by worrying can add a single hour to his life?

John 14:1 (NIV)
"Do not let your hearts be troubled. Trust in God; trust also in me.

John 14:27 (NLT)
I am leaving you with a gift—peace of mind and heart. And the peace I give is a gift the world cannot give. So don't be troubled or afraid.

Philippians 4:7 (NIV)
And the peace of God, which transcends all understanding, will guard your hearts and your minds in Christ Jesus.

Philippians 4:19 (NLT)
And this same God who takes care of me will supply all your needs from his glorious riches, which have been given to us in Christ Jesus.

2 Timothy 1:7 (KJV)
For God hath not given us the spirit of fear; but of power, and of love, and of a sound mind.

Joshua 1:9 (NIV)
Have I not commanded you? Be strong and courageous. Do not be terrified; do not be discouraged, for the LORD your God will be with you wherever you go."

Psalm 112:7 (NIV)
They will have no fear of bad news; their hearts are steadfast, trusting in the Lord.

Isaiah 41:10 (NIV)
So do not fear, for I am with you; do not be dismayed, for I am your God. I will strengthen you and help you; I will uphold you with my righteous right hand.

Isaiah 43:1–3 (NIV)
"Do not fear, for I have redeemed you; I have summoned you by name; you are mine. 2 When you pass through the waters, I will be with you; and when you pass through the rivers, they will not sweep over you. When you walk through the fire, you will not be burned; the flames will not set you ablaze. 3 For I am the Lord your God, the Holy One of Israel, your Savior;

Nahum 1:7 (NLT)
The LORD is good, a strong refuge when trouble comes. He is close to those who trust in him.

Romans 8:31 (NLT)
If God is for us, who can ever be against us?

1 Peter 5:7 (KJV)
Casting all your care upon him; for he careth for you.

Luke 21:28 (NIV)
When these things begin to take place, stand up and lift up your heads, because your redemption is drawing near."

Hebrews 13:5, 6 (NIV)
"Never will I leave you; never will I forsake you." 6 So we say with confidence, "The Lord is my helper; I will not be afraid. What can mere mortals do to me?"

Matthew 28:20 (KJV)
And, lo, I am with you alway, even unto the end of the world. Amen.

Family-Communication Card (FCC)

The FCC card provides a simple way for you to reunite with lost family members and/or friends during a disaster when communications are down.

- Choose predetermined meeting locations or areas.
- Each person will need a FCC card with matching information.
- Start with the first evacuation point and end with the last.
- Include specific details about the chosen locations.
- If the locations have phone numbers, include them.
- After the word "Start," fill in the time you will begin checking the location for your family and/or friends, then circle "AM" or "PM." In the blank space next to it, fill in when you will end checking for the day, and circle the "AM" or "PM." For "Frequency," fill in how frequently you will return to the site during the specified time span.
- The "Notes" box is for drawing small maps or adding additional important information, like nearest hospital or police station in proximity to the meeting point. Even nearest water source, shelter, known gang areas, etc., can be added.
- You can also write on the opposite, blank side of the card.

Choose multiple evacuation locations. Your first selected area may become compromised by hazardous conditions or civil unrest, or you may be unable to reach the location due to travel restrictions, so have options for bypassing a compromised or unsafe location.

To prepare your FCC card, make a photocopy of the next page, cut it out, fill in your information, and then laminate it to keep if from falling apart. Remember to carry it with you wherever you go, and have your family and friends do so as well.

Address 1 _____

Start _____ AM / PM

Frequency _____

Days _____

Address 2 _____

Start _____ AM / PM

Frequency _____

Days _____

Alternate Locations _____

_____

_____

Emergency Telephone Numbers

_____

_____

Notes

Glossary

AO: Area of operations is an overarching term, encompassing more descriptive terms for geographic areas in which military operations are conducted.

AK-47: Selective-fire, gas-operated, 7.62×39mm assault rifle first developed in the USSR by Mikhail Kalashnikov.

AR-15: Semi-automatic civilian variant of the U. S. Army M16 rifle.

BMI: Body mass index is a simple index of weight-for-height that is commonly used to classify being underweight, being overweight, or being obese.

BOB: A bug-out bag is some kind of duffle bag or back pack equipped with emergency supplies. It is also known as a "go bag."

BOL: Bug-out location is a place in which you plan to evacuate to during a disaster, usually a remote location that has varying degrees of provisions.

BOV: A bug-out vehicle is anything from your everyday car to some seriously expensive, purpose-built vehicles that are able to withstand small-arms fire. Its purpose is to get you out of town and to safety in the event of a disaster.

Bug In: Just the opposite of bug out. To bug in means to shelter in place. This is where some type of event is on the way and it is impossible to leave your home or whatever shelter you are currently in.

Bug Out: A term meaning to get out of town. Some type of event is on the way and you need to get out of its path as quickly as humanly possible.

Cache: This is a stash of supplies hidden for later use.

DHTRO: Defecation hits the rotating oscillator (in other words, when the "$#;+ hits the fan")

E-Tool: An entrenching tool is a small, collapsible shovel that can fit into a bug-out bag.

EDC: Every-day carry refers to a small collection of tools, equipment, and supplies that are carried on a daily basis to assist in tackling situations ranging from the mundane to the disastrous.

EMP: An electromagnetic pulse is a burst of electromagnetic radiation.

FCC: A family-communication card is a contact card that every family member should carry in case of separation during disaster, so that loved ones may be easily located.

FEMA: Federal Emergency Management Agency is more accurately termed, "Foolishly Expecting Meaningful Aide."

FIFO: This refers to first in, first out canned food storage rotation.

Ghetto Bird: Police aircraft that patrol low income and minority neighborhoods in urban regions. Ghetto birds may be used in active policing to track suspects and assist officers on the ground, or they may be used as a form of deterrent, to remind citizens on the ground that they're being watched. Watch out for falling donuts!

GOOD: Get out of Dodge is a generic term for leaving the big city in a big hurry.

GHB: A get-home bag should contain the minimal amount of items to support you in getting home within a 24-hour period.

Hordes: People leaving the big cities looking for supplies. Hordes often refer to the biblical term, "hordes of locust." Just as with locust, the people from the large cities will remove all supplies from the smaller surrounding areas.

INCH: I'm never coming home. A bag with supplies needed to sustain oneself indefinitely, in case returning home becomes impossible.

IOTF: International Obesity Task Force was originally convened in 1995 by Professor Philip James to prepare the first scientific research report on the global epidemic of obesity. Its mission is to inform the world about the urgency of the problem and to persuade governments that the time to act is now. Thought of as an independent think tank, its ties to pharmaceutical giants has raised concerns regarding conflict of interest.

K.I.S.S.: Keep it simple stupid is a general term for not over complicating things.

Molotov cocktail: A breakable glass bottle containing a flammable substance, such as gasoline with some motor oil added, and usually a source of ignition, such as a burning cloth, held in place by the bottle's stopper, then lit and thrown to create a type of fire bomb.

MPL: A master-preparedness list is a suggestion of supplies and items to have on hand before disaster strikes.

MRE: Meal ready to eat is a military ration. Its normal shelf life is several years. The contents are sealed in a tough plastic coating.

Multi-tool: This is built around a pair of pliers with up to 21 additional tools stored in the handles, including knives (straight and serrated blades), screwdrivers (flat, Phillips), saws, wire cutters and strippers, an electrical crimper, and a bottle opener and can opener. It can be used daily for an unlimited amount of tasks.

PAW scenario: This refers to a post-apocalyptic world situation.

Posse Comitatus Act: This was passed in 1878 to prevent U.S. military personnel from acting as law enforcement agents on U.S. soil and is even in effect today.

Prepper: A prepper is someone who is uncomfortable relying on others for the basics of survival and protection and therefore prepares for uncertain times ahead.

REK: Roadside-emergency kit includes basic items to help you get back onto the road quickly and safely.

Shemagh: A traditional desert headwear designed to protect the head and neck from sun and sand. It is currently in use with US and Coalition forces in Iraq and Afghanistan.

SHTF: $#;+ hits the fan is some kind of disastrous event. A term used in relation to your location, normally a local, regional, or national event, not a world-wide one.

TEOTWAWKI: The end of the world as we know is some kind of cataclysmic worldwide event, so kiss your old life goodbye.

WHO: World Health Organization is a specialized agency of the United Nations (UN) that is "concerned" with international public health. It was established on April 7, 1948, with headquarters in Geneva, Switzerland and is a member of the United Nations Development Group. The WHO gets more money from private pharma and related industry sources than from world governments—does conflict of interest come to mind?

WTSHTF: When the $#;+ hits the fan. I'm sure you know what this means by now.

WROL: Without rule of law is a term that describes the total breakdown of society.

YOYO: You're on your own. When the government ceases to provide essential services, such as fire and police-department protection and when utilities no longer provide water, sanitation, electricity, and phone service.

3532139R00247

Printed in Great Britain
by Amazon.co.uk, Ltd.,
Marston Gate.